Dominik Nösner
Sponsorship Culture in the German University Popular Music Festival Market

D1619818

Editorial

The book series "Transdisciplinary Studies in Popular Culture" focuses on the critical study of popular culture in the media and the arts, in society, politics, and the economy. It presents a broad spectrum of research on popular culture from theoretical and methodological as well as empirical, historical, and systematic perspectives. A pluralism of topics, theories, methods, and disciplines is essential to the series in order to capture and understand the diversity, openness, and dynamics of this highly relevant field of study adequately in a multiperspectival and transdisciplinary way.

The series is edited by Beate Flath, Charis Goer, Christoph Jacke and Martin Zierold.

Dominik Nösner, born in 1987, works as a research associate at the Faculty of Arts and Humanities at Universität Paderborn, Germany. Additionally to his research interest in the field of event studies, he is an entrepreneur in the event industry.

Dominik Nösner

Sponsorship Culture in the German University Popular Music Festival Market

[transcript]

Thesis, University of Paderborn, 2022

Bibliographic information published by the Deutsche Nationalbibliothek
The Deutsche Nationalbibliothek lists this publication in the Deutsche Nationalbib-liografie; detailed bibliographic data are available in the Internet at http://dnb.d-nb.de

Cover layout: Maria Arndt, Bielefeld
Printed by: Majuskel Medienproduktion GmbH, Wetzlar
https://doi.org/10.14361/9783839465783
Print-ISBN 978-3-8376-6578-9
PDF-ISBN 978-3-8394-6578-3
ISSN of series: 2702-4342
eISSN of series: 2747-3554

Printed on permanent acid-free text paper.

Contents

Introduction

Many young people attend popular music festivals on a regular basis to experience live music, partying and socializing with friends. The festival phenomenon has become a way of life, where a day, weekend or a whole week
is experienced in a non-ordinary environment. Visitors take a short break of
regular life and dive into a world full of music, friendship, celebration as well
as escapism.

Sponsorship of these events enjoys great popularity among many companies, both nationally and internationally. In sponsorship, companies provide
resources to support an event that is staged by a third party in order to realize
their own (marketing) objectives being linked and publicly entangled with the
event. Companies that support events enable experience-oriented encounters
between people and brands that often have a more profound effect than classic advertising measures. The use of sponsorship messages at events makes it
feasible to address target groups (which are usually more difficult to reach) in
an environment that is perceived as pleasant and amiable by the consumer.
Sponsoring brands are integrated into the context of the event attended and
can be experienced in the same multi-sensory way the event itself is experienced.[1]

The desired result is a positive attitude transfer from the event to the
sponsoring brand. In addition, event sponsorship generates a goodwill effect among event attendees, since companies that engage in sponsorship of
the respective events are often identified as having altruistic motives, even

---

1   Chris Anderton, "Branding, Sponsorship and the Music Festival," in *The Pop Festival: His-
     tory, Music, Media, Culture*, ed. George McKay (New York: Bloomsbury Academic, 2015),
     199–212; Jan Drengner and Steffen Jahn, "Erlebniswelten im Sponsoring," *Marketing Re-
     view St. Gallen* 30, no. 2 (February 2013): 60–67, https://doi.org/10.1365/s11621-013-0212-
     3.

though there is a fundamental awareness that the main triggers for sponsorship activities are usually economic in nature.[2] Nevertheless, with the help of their support, companies contribute to the feasibility of events that are of interest to consumers and thus trigger positive effects for both sides. Since in modern markets constantly growing supply is not matched by adequate demand, competition in such saturated markets is intensifying. The resulting interchangeability now applies not only to the objective quality of goods and services, but also to their marketing.

From a socio-economic perspective, the mentioned trends regarding (popular) music festivals and their sponsorship are supported by a change in social values that are significantly characterized by an increasing orientation toward experience(s) within society which has been shown for the 'post war generation' in Germany.[3] This is symbolized by an orientation of the individual toward one's own subject, whereby one attempts to trigger desired subjective experiences by purposefully influencing external circumstances. Empirical evidence shows that experience-related values such as personal happiness, enjoyment of life and self-realization are gaining in importance.

A further socio-economic framing for this dissertation is an inner-German competition between cities predicted by internal migration and demographic change. Cities and municipalities are competing for school and university graduates as well as skilled workforce in order not to lose touch with a shrinking population and to remain well-positioned for the future. Medium-sized German cities in particular are under special pressure to act here in order to be able to keep up with major German cities such as Berlin, Hamburg, Munich or Cologne in terms of city image as well as associated expectations regarding a certain quality of life in these cities.[4] These considerations further include challenges for the German higher educational

---

2   Manfred Bruhn, *Sponsoring* (Wiesbaden: Springer Fachmedien Wiesbaden, 2018), http s://doi.org/10.1007/978-3-658-13313-9.

3   Gerhard Schulze, *Die Erlebnisgesellschaft: Kultursoziologie der Gegenwart*, 8. Aufl., Studienausgabe (Frankfurt am Main: Campus-Verl., 2000).

4   Bernhard Frevel, ed., *Herausforderung demografischer Wandel*, 1. Auflage, Perspektiven der Gesellschaft (Wiesbaden: VS Verlag für Sozialwissenschaften, 2004); Nicola Hülskamp, "Der IW-Demografieindikator—Wie gut ist Deutschland auf den demografischen Wandel vorbereitet?," *IW-Trends*, no. 3 (2008), https://doi.org/10.2373/1864-810X .08-03-07; "Bevölkerungs- und Haushaltsentwicklung im Bund und in den Ländern," Demografischer Wandel in Deutschland (Wiesbaden: Statistisches Bundesamt, 2011), www.statistikportal.de.

system. Universities of the aforementioned medium-sized cities, which are generally intertwined with their hometowns in a variety of ways, share these challenges.

Events like a university popular music festival tie in with all the mentioned points and this is mainly due to its specificity when compared to events outside the university campus. On the one hand they function as multisensory event-marketing tools, which are of great importance for university image building. On the other hand, they represent a flagship within city or municipal marketing. And furthermore, they serve as an important channel of communication for sponsors to the German student body at a time when more and more enterprises are having to compete in an increasingly competitive communications environment. Corporate marketing has recognized this relevance of university events when it comes to generating awareness and getting important 'messages' by the valuable student community.[5]

Against the background of the mentioned considerations as well as the fact that research within this music festival niche market and its sponsorship is virtually unresearched, this dissertation aims at exploring an underlying sponsorship culture within the university popular music festival market in Germany. In this context, a suitable multidimensional concept of culture will be discussed and implemented to describe the interplay between event organizer, sponsors and the attending audience in an adequate manner as well as link sponsorship culture to the aforementioned socio-economic considerations.

Motivation and Goals of the Thesis

This dissertation's research topic is embedded in various socio-economic, cultural, and partially psychological perspectives. This becomes clear at several points, beginning in the structure of the theoretical framework of the thesis, but even more how the individual studies deal with the subject matter. The author, as a graduate economist doing his doctorate at an arts and humanities faculty, was himself caught between these different disciplines, views and

---

5   Sven Jöckel, Nico Hesser, and Andreas Will, eds., *Trendsetter, Innovatoren, Studentenbudget? Eine Mehr-Methoden-Studie zu Werbung und Produktpräferenzen bei Studierenden*, vol. 4, Menschen—Märkte—Medien—Management: Schriftenreihe (Ilmenau: Universitätsverlag Ilmenau, 2009), http://uri.gbv.de/document/gvk:ppn:621462640.

approaches when writing the dissertation. However, the motivation for the dissertation project lies precisely in the complexity of this interdisciplinarity. Certainly, this topic could have been treated or pursued purely from an economics or a purely arts and humanities standpoint, but the result would most likely have been a different formulation of results, which would probably have been more distant from reality.

The market for university popular music festivals is becoming an important part of the German event industry. In contrast, it has generated little academic research, beyond this dissertation. A university popular music festival is one example of an event, and this thesis is situated in the growing field of event studies as an event's or university popular music festival's sponsorship is enshrined within this interdisciplinary field of study.[6]

University popular music festivals, as a niche form of popular music festivals, are integrated in an exceptional manner into regional relationships between universities, cities, municipalities, and organizers. They not only (re)shape the image of the university itself, but also the image of the city and its region, which is becoming increasingly relevant against the backdrop of a proclaimed socio-demographic change in Germany and a resulting (increasing) competition between German cities and universities. Furthermore, university popular music festivals are of great interest to participating companies and sponsors, as their unique audience consists of well-educated future academics with an expected high future income. For this reason, sponsorship within context of university popular music festivals in particular, but especially its transformation, has become an increasingly important field of research in event studies.[7]

With a current volume of around 5.5 billion euros, sponsorship in Germany has developed into a significant and above-average growth segment in the communications sector in recent years.[8] While arguments based on prod-

---

6   Donald Getz and Stephen J. Page, *Event Studies: Theory, Research and Policy for Planned Events*, 4th ed. (Fourth Edition. | New York: Routledge, 2020. | Series: Events management series | "First edition published by Butterworth-Heinemann 2007. Third edition published by Routledge 2016"—T.p. verso.: Routledge, 2019), https://doi.org/10.4324/97 80429023002; Rodoula Tsiotsou * and Dionysis Lalountas, "Applying Event Study Analysis to Assess the Impact of Marketing Communication Strategies: The Case of Sponsorship," *Applied Financial Economics Letters* 1, no. 4 (July 2005): 259–62, https://doi.org/1 0.1080/17446540500143764.

7   Bruhn, *Sponsoring*.

8   Bruhn.

uct benefits and additional services often no longer offer sufficient differentiation from the competition, companies are increasingly looking for communication instruments that enable experiential benefits and a special target group approach. Both can be found in sponsorship of an on-campus student event, which is now frequently established as a fixed component within the communication-mix. Possible activities are diverse and range from commitments in the sports, cultural, social, and environmental sectors to media sponsoring.

Exploring sponsorship culture within the German popular music festival market with emphasis on the aforementioned subbranch of university popular music festivals can be formulated as the main goal of this interdisciplinary dissertation. Incorporating all stakeholder groups, meaning (1) event organizers, (2) event sponsors and (3) event audience with their different views and assessments on knowledge, behavior is as important for tackling this challenge, than exploring norms, power structures and interactions between the stakeholders in the sphere of sponsorship.

Research Objectives

This doctoral thesis investigates sponsorship culture in the German popular music festival market with emphasis on university popular music festivals. As will be seen, this is an undertaking which, due to the (cultural) terminology alone, requires a not only multidimensional concept and understanding of the word "culture" but thus further examines the existing different stakeholder groups within sponsorship culture. Therefore, the thesis comprises three different empirical studies that use an exploratory approach.

The exploratory qualitative study (Study One) is guided by the following fundamental research objectives:

a) How do professional stakeholders assess the market for university popular music festivals in Germany?
b) Which patterns about the procedural elements of sponsorship culture(s) exist?
c) What factors determine the existing company's communication and decision-making culture?

In particular,

- How does (financial) support for an event come about?
- What does the decision-making process look like?
- What are the first steps after a sponsoring partner is accepted?
- What are the interactions before, during and after the event?

d) What interrelations between sponsor and audience arise from the sponsorship engagement?

In particular,

- How good is brand recall after the event?
- How much has the perception of the sponsor's image changed?
- How does the audience feel about sponsorship engagement?

e) How 'ticks' the audience of a university popular music festival?

In particular,

- Does the audience identify with its university?
- How can motivational constructs for festival attendance be described?
- What role plays social media regarding the festival experience?

The focus group study (Study Two) represents the second empirical study of the thesis and is guided by the following research objectives:

f) Specifically explore and understand underlying motivational constructs for attending a popular music festival in Germany.
g) Identify key themes in order to describe and define motivations for attending a popular music festival in Germany.

The quantitative surveys (Study Three) form the third component of the empirics and are guided by amending the existing research results from exploratory qualitative study (Study One) and focus group study (Study Two) as well as existing research literature on the topic. In order to achieve this, this study pursues two objectives:

h) Explore sponsorship culture of the two biggest university popular music festivals 2019 in Germany with emphasis on audience to provide descriptive knowledge and outline audience profile(s).

i) Understanding motivational constructs for university popular music festival attendance by building upon results from focus group interviews and identifying a factor structure which stimulates members of an audience to visit these events.

The results regarding the above-mentioned research objects are discussed within the individual studies in an exploratory manner. In a final overall discussion step, sponsorship culture is filtered from the results of all three studies combined.

Structure of the Thesis

This doctoral thesis employs a multi-methodological approach: it links conceptual, qualitative, and quantitative research studies and aims at getting profound and explorative insights through triangulation[9]. Therefore, the structure of this thesis follows the analytic procedure of the studies as shown in one, twelve chapters comprise the dissertation.

Chapter two, three and four are dedicated to theoretically frame and conceptualize the topic of the dissertation.

Extant literature on current socio-economic developments is reviewed and set into context to the interdisciplinary field of study. The four theoretical foundations of this thesis are drawn from different fields. The first perspective deals with population demographics in Germany, especially studies with emphasis on inner-German city/municipal competition and the medium-term challenges of the German university system are taken into account. Furthermore, events within existing city and municipal marketing mix are discussed.

In the ongoing second theoretical perspective, literature regarding *eventization* and associated inner orientation of society is presented and shall lead

---

9   Using a combination of research is also known as triangulation, this involves using both qualitative research methods as well as quantitative in order to use the strengths of each approach to compensate for the weaknesses of the other. Based on: Udo Kuckartz, *Mixed Methods* (Wiesbaden: Springer Fachmedien Wiesbaden, 2014), https://doi.org/10.1007/978-3-531-93267-5.

to a carved out *eventization* of the university campus. These insights are linked to literature regarding motivational research for event attendance as well as an outline of the modern digitalized music industry with high incorporation of liveness within Pine and Gilmore's concept of an *experience economy*.

The third theoretical perspective continues with literature review on popular music, popular music festivals and their event sponsorship. It serves to define these concepts for the dissertation. Furthermore, the functionality of sponsorship within corporate communication as well as corporate culture is laid out in accordance with literature.

Furthermore, the fourth theoretical perspective chapter contains extensive literature review on different angles of culture terminologies and incorporates a certain more dimensional culture term for this work, aiming to demarcate the doctoral thesis from mere economic or mere arts and humanities investigations. Chapter six summarizes the theoretical perspectives.

In chapter seven the methodological research structure and the triangulation through qualitative and quantitative studies are outlined.

These are the building blocks of the analytical framework and guide the proceedings of this thesis. The rationale for choosing the empirical setting, which is the two biggest university popular music festivals in Germany, is explained and background information on structure of these two events is given.

The exploratory qualitative interview study (Study One) is described in chapter eight explaining the motivation, study design, and method in detail. The results of the qualitative study identify professional stakeholder's (e.g. festival organizer and festival sponsors) assessments of the market, patterns of existing procedural elements of sponsorship culture, factors determining existing communication and decision-making culture, interrelations between sponsors and audience and how this (student) audience "ticks".

Chapter nine comprises the focus group study (Study Two) which explores motivational constructs for popular music festival attendance in a ground-laying step. In contrast to the qualitative exploratory interview study from the previews chapter that focus on professional stakeholders within sponsorship culture in the popular music festival market, the focus groups examine the third entity of the research object: the audience and its motivational constructs for attending popular music festivals.

Figure 1: Structure of the Thesis: Contents of the Chapters 1-11

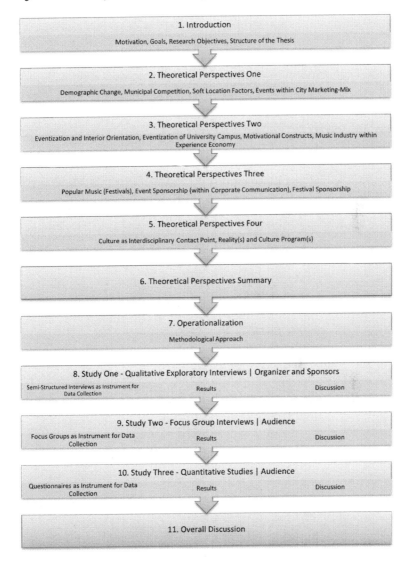

The quantitative surveys (Study Three) are described in chapter ten. Results of both studies aim at amending the existing research results from exploratory qualitative study and focus group study. Both studies explore sponsorship culture with emphasis on generation y visitors and outline audience profile(s) to provide descriptive knowledge of the two biggest university popular music festivals held in 2019 in Germany. Additionally, motivational constructs for university popular music festival attendance are measured via questionnaire and a factor structure which stimulates an audience to visit these events is built by synthesis of the quantitative results and upon results from focus group interviews.

Chapter eleven combines all individual results from the empirical studies and are abstracted one step further from individual studies' discussions. It connects the insights gained and presents a comprehensive summary and managerial and socio-economic implications for sponsorship culture within the university popular music festival market are derived. However, since a holistic view is now taken on to all acting stakeholder groups within sponsorship culture, the discussion is structured according to the three groups and substructered into Siegfried Schmidt's multi-dimensional concept of culture incorporating a reality model and practical culture program.

Theoretical Perspective One: Sociodemographic Induced Challenges

To theoretically frame this dissertation in an adequate manner, one must start looking at certain socio-economic phenomena and developments that have directly affected the research project's issue and indirectly affected the field of study through its intimately associated areas.

In this first part of the theoretical groundwork, a phenomenon is dealt with, which is typical for developed economies and their societies and that can be observed in several parts of the world. A demographic change in the population due to consequence of an average increase in life expectancy, a falling birth rate and a resulting older society. The demographic change in Germany is set to be the "starting point" of this dissertation due to its partly foreseeable changing and transformational processes it brings to many aspects of the socio-economic entity of the country. One of many processes initiated by this development is the challenge of a cut-throat competition between medium-sized German cities and municipalities. This then leads in a further step to considerations of the extent to which the German university system is affected by demographic change, since on the one hand there is a strong interconnection with the corresponding cities and on the other hand every university would be deprived of its basis and existence by declining student numbers.

Demographic Change in the Federal Republic of Germany

The long predicted demographic change has started to become slowly recognizable in statistical data on population development in Germany for a while now.[1] The declining number of people of younger age and the simultaneously increasing number of older people are shifting the demographic framework in a way never seen before in the republic's young history after the second world war.[2]

Every second person in Germany is older than 45 and every fifth person is older than 66 years. On the other hand, Germany has seen unusually high levels of immigration, especially among young people in recent years. After a long-term decline, birth rates have been minimal increasing since 2012.[3]

A comparison of the country's age structure from 2018 with the year of the German Unification in 1990, displays the recent progress of the demographic change very clearly: The most sizeable age-range from 1955 to 1970, which belongs to the so-called 'baby boomers', formed the largest age group in 1990 when they were 20 to 35 years old. Today, still representing the largest part of the population, the baby boomers have reached their higher working age and will retire within the next two decades. The number of people aged 70 and older, thus, rose from eight to 13 million between the years 1990 and 2018. Furthermore, data regarding the oldest groups in society make it clear that not only women but also men are now reaching an older age. This ongoing process will continuously lead to various socio-economic challenges for the state, the economy and society. Especially the current systems of state pension insurance, state health insurance and long-term care insurance, as well as changes in the country wide settlement structure are to be mentioned here. This change in settlement structure leads to small, but also medium-sized German cities and municipalities facing the phenomenon of a certain rural exodus in the last decade while cities with more than half a million habitants seem to profit from this development.

Existing literature shows, the majority of German cities with more than half a million inhabitants have had increasing populations again in the past ten years, as a report by the *German Institute for Economic Research* (DIW) shows.[4] At the same time, the number of employees in the bigger cities rose

1   Frevel, *Herausforderung demografischer Wandel*.

2   Hülskamp, "Der IW-Demografieindikator—Wie gut ist Deutschland auf den demografischen Wandel vorbereitet?"

3   Destatis, "Bevölkerung im Wandel—Annahmen und Ergebnisse der 14. koordinierten Bevölkerungsvorausberechnung" (Wiesbaden, 2019).

4   Deutsches Institut für Wirtschaftsforschung, "Bevölkerungsentwicklung in Deutschland bis 2050: Nur leichter Rückgang der Einwohnerzahl?" (Berlin, 2017).

Figure 2: Age Groups in Germany 2018/1990

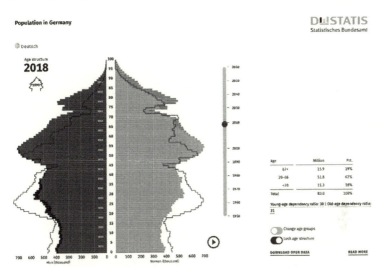

Statistisches Bundesamt, "Bevölkerungsvorausberechnung," n.d., https://service.destati
s.de/bevoelkerungspyramide/.

by almost four percent, while the Country as a whole, stagnated on average overall. According to the DIW, it is especially the young, well-educated part of the population with higher incomes who feel attracted by the metropolises with their attractive employment opportunities, cultural offerings and the cities' image.[5]

The winners could include the cities in which, in addition to headquarters of global corporations, the new service functions of finance, insurance and real estate industries, research centers and the media industry have settled, and which also have achieved to develop a rich cultural offer for its citizens.[6]

---

5   Deutsches Institut für Wirtschaftsforschung.

6   Dirk Schubert, "Ausgleich oder Spaltung? | bpb," bpb.de, 2018, https://www.bpb.de/pol
itik/innenpolitik/stadt-und-gesellschaft/216868/aufrechterhaltung-gleichwertiger-lebe
nsverhaeltnisse.

It's the service sector, the *knowledge economy*[7] as well as the *creative economy*[8] that are now seen as the engines for growth with regard to this changing municipal environment.[9] The urban economy is no longer shaped by large enterprises, but by smaller companies, manual work has given way to mental work. The threat posed by the demographic drifting apart between the regions and municipalities is often underestimated. Thus, the consequence that the requirement anchored in the German Basic Constitutional Law to create 'equivalent' (non-identical) living conditions in all parts of the country might not be met in the near future.

Despite the population decline throughout Germany, there are municipalities and regions whose population remains stable or even grows for another one to two decades due to their birth deficit being positively balanced out by inner-German migration. The relocation movements within Germany result into 'demographic winner- and loser-' municipalities, with the population gain of each target community being offset by an equal loss of population in the municipality of origin. The former GDR states are without exception among the disadvantaged in internal migration, but there are also areas in the northern Ruhr area, in southern Lower Saxony, northern Hesse, in the Saarland and in northern Bavaria with constant internal migration losses. The selection effect of the migration is decisive: If it is predominantly the younger

---

7   For the purpose of theoretical framing this work, the author understands *knowledge economy* as a system of consumption and production that is based on intellectual capital and knowledge-intensive activities that contribute to an accelerated pace of technical and scientific advance. This has come to represent a large component of all economic activity in most developed countries. This understanding is based on: Walter W. Powell and Kaisa Snellman, "The Knowledge Economy," *Annual Review of Sociology* 30, no. 1 (August 2004): 199–220, https://doi.org/10.1146/annurev.soc.29.010202.100037.

8   For the purpose of theoretical framing this work, the author understands *creative economy as the broadest reference to the phenomenon of creativity influencing the size, growth rate, and general dynamics of an economy and that creativity itself should now be viewed as a defining commercial factor.* This understanding is based on: John Howkins, *The Creative Economy, or, How Some People Profit from Ideas, Some Don't, and the Effect on All of Us* (London: Allen Lane, 2001).

9   Trevor J Barnes, Jamie Peck, and Eric Sheppard, *The Wiley-Blackwell Companion to Economic Geography.* (Hoboken: Wiley-Blackwell [Imprint] John Wiley & Sons, Incorporated, 2016), http://onlinelibrary.wiley.com/book/10.1002/9781118384497.

and well-educated who migrate, this weakens the economic development potential and further increases the migration.[10]

The increased location independence of companies, but also the increasing mobility of citizens regarding their choice of their place of residence, shopping and leisure locations have sparked this intense competition between municipalities in Germany. Administrations, universities, cities and entire regions compete for company settlements, qualified employees, for residents, tourists, students, for the organization of trade fairs and major events, for the establishment of well-respected administrative and scientific institutions, not least for subsidies.[11]

Some regions are also subject to an extensive structural change, which requires them to find a new identity in the shortest possible time and to anchor it internally and externally (e.g. Ruhr Area). If this does not succeed, a negative image quickly emerges, which can lead to a dangerous downward spiral. Companies that are independent of their location are leaving, as are socially stable and high-income households. The associated decrease in purchasing power leads to the migration of retail and leisure businesses, to the decrease of public and social infrastructure, which then leads to a loss of attractiveness for potential visitors.

In order to stop such processes, alongside economic and social policy measures, a way must be found to bind the local players and strengthen their commitment to the location.

The (perceived) quality of life in cities is a key decision-making factor for young specialists and skilled employees when choosing a job or a new home. In many cases, this decision is not being made based on knowledge of the real conditions in the city, but based on a selective, complexity-reduced image.[12] These (city) images, which can vary greatly depending on the specific point of view, have direct economic effects due to their behavioral relevance. For this reason, companies, but also universities and research institutions,

---

10   "Bevölkerungs- und Haushaltsentwicklung im Bund und in den Ländern"; Schubert, "Ausgleich oder Spaltung?"

11   Stefan Hochstadt, ed., *Stadtentwicklung mit Stadtmanagement?*, 1. Aufl. (Wiesbaden: Verlag für Sozialwissenschaften, 2005); Raimund Bellinghausen, *Das Musikfestival: Wirtschaftliche und touristische Aspekte* (Hamburg: disserta Verlag, 2014).

12   Jürgen Friedrichs, "Ist die Besonderheit des Städtischen auch die Besonderheit der Stadtsoziologie?," in *Die Besonderheit des Städtischen*, ed. Heike Herrmann et al. (Wiesbaden: VS Verlag für Sozialwissenschaften, 2011), 33–47, https://doi.org/10.1007/978-3-531-93338-2_2.

are increasingly approaching municipalities demanding to get involved in a proper city marketing which specifically addresses the so-called soft location factors.[13]

Inner-German Municipality Competition

The development of social structures in the highly industrialized countries is currently characterized by an accentuated socio-economic polarization of cities and regions, whereby the problems and conflicts of social restructuring are more and more concentrated on individual level(s)—especially in bigger cities.[14] German cities are subject to increased pressure to act due to a growing 'inner-German competition' and as a result must actively strengthen the economic development potential at their location.[15] Bathelt and Glückler[16], however, take the position that in the context of regional and urban development, there is no competition between the regions in a true sense. In contrast to companies, cities and regions have no profit-motive and do not produce any goods. In addition, they cannot go bankrupt and dissolve as a result. Nevertheless, they have an interest in increasing the welfare of their inhabitants and keeping companies and the associated jobs at the location or in attracting them to the location. In order to achieve this, cities and regions consider it sensible to create an attractive environment for companies and the population. In addition, the 'human capital' (diverse qualified labor supply), the 'social' and 'institutional capital' (network promotion), the 'knowledge and creative capital' (promotion of innovative activities), the 'cultural capital' (quality of life through [public] cultural offerings for highly qualified work-

---

13   Stefanie Wesselmann and Bettina Hohn, *Public Marketing: Marketing-Management für den öffentlichen Sektor*, 4., vollständig überarbeitete Auflage, Lehrbuch (Wiesbaden: Springer Gabler, 2017).

14   Stefan Krätke, *Stadt/Einführung in aktuelle Problemfelder der Stadtökonomie und Wirtschaftsgeographie/von Stefan Krätke*. (Wiesbaden: VS Verlag für Sozialwissenschaften, 1995).

15   Wesselmann and Hohn, *Public Marketing*.

16   Harald Bathelt and Johannes Glückler, *Wirtschaftsgeographie: ökonomische Beziehungen in räumlicher Perspektive; 22 Tabellen*, 3., vollst. überarb. und erw. Aufl., UTB Geowissenschaften, Soziologie, Wirtschaftswissenschaften, Politikwissenschaften 8217 (Stuttgart: Ulmer, 2012), 144.

ers) or the 'infrastructure capital' should be taking into account. Spieß[17] also attests a shift in values within the population in the course of the location competition within Germany, to which the cities and regions must react. An increased focus on leisure time and activities and the obviousness of an experience society (which will be discussed in more detail in the following theoretical perspective) as well as greater environmental awareness are generating additional location demands. These are articulated in expectations regarding the leisure, educational and cultural offerings of a municipality or city area as well as in a preference for an attractive and ecologically unpolluted landscape. Such location demands gain particular importance insofar as classic location qualities such as good transport connections are widespread throughout the Federal Republic of Germany. Furthermore, such location requirements become especially important when companies have a need for highly qualified workers. The choice of locations that meet such location requirements is then associated with possible competitive advantages on the labor market. A reaction to this development of an inner-German municipality competition can be seen in the significant increase in the number of initiatives that pursue city or regional marketing according to their own understanding. At the same time, there are great differences in the understanding of marketing and of its design and its execution. The spectrum of what is referred to as city or regional marketing ranges from the advertising activities of individual administrations to the cooperative development of sophisticated projects that also include event marketing as well as specifically developed marketing events.[18]

The German University-System facing Demographic Change

The demographic change described above, is expected to result in a significant decrease in the number of young people within Germany's society. Among many other socio-economic consequences, this process represents a significant challenge for the educational system. The question arises as to what demand, which educational service will continue to exist in the future? On the other hand, how can the educational offer be adapted to this development? Since the demographic change is spatially very different in its peculiarity, lo-

---

17   Steffen Spieß, *Marketing für Regionen: Anwendungsmöglichkeiten im Standortwettbewerb* (Berlin, 1998), http://link.springer.com/openurl?genre=book&isbn=978-3-8244-0395-0.

18   Spieß.

cation questions also arise: Which facilities, in which locations should change their offerings and how? Are facilities expected to be closed?

According to the population forecast by the Federal Institute for Research on Building, Urban Affairs and Spatial Development, the number of people of typical student age between 19 and 25 will decline by 20.2 % from 2013 to 2030.[19] The number of students is falling at many university locations in eastern Germany as well as in several regions of western Germany outside the metropolitan areas. This finding may come as a surprise because the numbers at Germany's universities with 2.9 million enrolled students are currently still at a record level. The student body is, however, unevenly distributed: the universities and technical colleges located in the new German states are already shrinking at 41 institutions, primarily in Saxony, Thuringia and Saxony-Anhalt. The phenomenon can also be observed in western Germany, outside the metropolitan areas, and will exacerbate the skills shortage in the republic.[20]

Furthermore, universities are important engines of economic and social development in their regions. That is why a close cooperation with companies, business development agencies and municipalities is important in order to ensure a successful transition for graduates to regional jobs.

Soft Location Factors' Change in Significance

The perceptible structure of an economic area or venue is in general the result of various decisions made by various contributors. Companies, households, and the state as the public sector are among the most important stakeholders who interact with one another in various areas. Thus, not only companies make decisions regarding their venue, but also private households, which becomes clear when taking their personal choice of workplace or choice of place of residence into account. Various decisions with big impact regarding a venue are obviously also made by the public sector. For instance, by influencing the quality of the venue itself or determining 'the political and social

---

19   Bundesinstitut für Bau-, Stadt- und Raumforschung im Bundesamt für Bauwesen und Raumordnung, "Beiträge zum Siedlungsflächenmonitoring im Bundesgebiet—Flächenverbrauch, Flächenpotenziale und Trends 2030," 07 (Berlin, 2014).

20   Studie des SVR-Forschungsbereichs 2015-2, "Zugangstor Hochschule Internationale Studierende als Fachkräfte von morgen gewinnen," Study (Berlin, 2016).

conditions' for the people or companies living there.[21] These processes and interrelationships are also dependent on social and socio-economic developments. The former industrial society has evolved into a knowledge (driven) society in the last few decades, in which the older approaches (such reduction of transportation costs) of location theories have mainly lost their relevance.[22] In today's knowledge society, decisions for or against a venue, city or region are controlled by the requirements of a specific activity, the location conditions and the required degree of 'networking' of involved stakeholders in the process of 'producing'. This results in a spiral of increasing complexity.[23]

The tertiarization[24] as well as the growing qualification of involved employees bring another aspect into the equation: the transitioned relation between work and leisure. Thus, soft location factors like the city- and landscape, the general living and quality of life as well as cultural life for the further urbanistic development of regions and cities will gain in importance. Moreover does the cultivation of a certain regional image and with it, its accompanying and with the subject matter associated marketing activities in the municipality and regional area gain in importance.[25] The exact (numeric) economic relevance of soft location conditions is yet unclear, while general statements on the importance of soft location factors are not considered to be reasonable due to their importance depending on various issues such as the industry, the type and size of company, the type of location decision or the share of high qualified labor.[26] According to Grabow, the most important location factors continue to comprise hard factors such as taxes, supply of qualified labor, transportation infrastructure, proximity to universities, etc.[27] Nevertheless,

---

21 Gunther Maier, Franz Tödtling, and Gunther Maier, *Standorttheorie und Raumstruktur*, 5. Aufl., Regional- und Stadtökonomik, Gunther Maier; Franz Tödtling ; 1 (Wien: Springer, 2012), 9f.

22 Ingo Liefner and Ludwig Schätzl, *Theorien der Wirtschaftsgeographie*, 10., [neu bearb. und umfassend erw.] Aufl., UTB Wirtschaftswissenschaften, Geographie 782 (Paderborn: Schöningh, 2012), 14f.

23 Liefner and Schätzl, 131f.

24 A shift from the primary and secondary economic sectors to the tertiary sector.

25 Verena Mayer, Mark Schlick, and Martin Groeger, "Landschaft als weicher Standortfaktor," *Raumforschung und Raumordnung* 59, no. 2–3 (March 31, 2001): 131–41, https://doi.o rg/10.1007/BF03184348.

26 Busso Grabow, Dietrich Henckel, and Beate Hollbach-Grömig, *Weiche Standortfaktoren*, Schriften des Deutschen Instituts für Urbanistik, Bd. 89 (Stuttgart: W. Kohlhammer: Deutscher Gemeindeverlag, 1995), 45f.

27 Grabow, Henckel, and Hollbach-Grömig, *Weiche Standortfaktoren*.

employees' 'soft' preferences (i.e. their place of residence, regional image, cultural offerings) have an immediate impact on labor markets and therefore, are directly linked to an important hard location factor. Hence, there are mechanisms in place by which employees can effectively express their location preferences. A latent demand for work within attractive locations increases the existing labor market. In addition, employers fear their skilled workers being demotivated or even decide to leave the company if they are transferred to a location that is not considered to be 'attractive'.[28]

A fitting and (at the time of completion of this work) up to date example of this issue can be observed in Gruenheide, Germany while the American electric car manufacturer Tesla decided to build its 2nd car plant outside the U.S., 30 mins outside the German Capital of Berlin, instead of the well-established and for a factory of this type expected location, known car industry regions such as Bavaria or Baden-Wuertemberg. Tesla's C.E.O. explicitly commented on this fact in an interview, where he addressed the importance of soft location factors for attracting skilled workers.[29][30] The decision in favor of the Berlin area underlines once more, that the soft location factors that have fueled the Berlin economic comeback of recent years are now also becoming more important outside branches like 'tech' and 'media' and even in the automotive industry.

This example stands in line with the findings of Richards and Wilson pointing out the positive linkage between cross-regional events and city image to tackle the mentioned phenomena of increased competition between cities for the attention of stakeholders (e.g. investors, residents).[31]

---

28   Friedrich Thiessen, ed., *Weiche Standortfaktoren: Erfolgsfaktoren regionaler Wirtschaftsentwicklung: interdisziplinäre Beiträge zur regionalen Wirtschaftsforschung*, Volkswirtschaftliche Schriften, Heft 541 (Berlin: Duncker & Humblot, 2005), 30f.

29   The Local de, "'Germany rocks': Elon Musk makes first visit to Berlin Tesla construction site," April 9, 2020, https://www.thelocal.de/20200904/germany-rocks-elon-musk-makes-first-visit-to-berlin-tesla-construction-site/.

30   Jens Blankennagel, "Um gute Mitarbeiter zu bekommen, kann Tesla mit dem guten Ruf Berlins werben," May 20, 2021, https://www.berliner-zeitung.de/mensch-metropole/um-gute-mitarbeiter-zu-bekommen-kann-tesla-mit-dem-guten-ruf-berlins-werben-li.159923.

31   Greg Richards and Julie Wilson, "The Impact of Cultural Events on City Image: Rotterdam, Cultural Capital of Europe 2001," *Urban Studies* 41, no. 10 (September 2004): 1931–51, https://doi.org/10.1080/0042098042000256323.

Events within the City and Municipality Marketing Mix

As stated, cities, their municipalities and local universities are in an intense locational competition and against this background have intensified their marketing activities in recent years.[32] From a marketing point of view, the main 'dilemma' of cities lies in the social, cultural, and economic differences, because under the conditions of the enormous competition for attention, a focus on a few topics and target groups is essential for building a unique profile. At the same time, however, urban diversity can be described as a primary factor in attractiveness.

Table 1: Target Groups in City Marketing (Own representation)

'Internal Target Groups'	'External Target Groups'
Inhabitant (Residents)	Potential investors
Local Businesses	Tourists
Local Retailer	Potential inhabitants
Hotels/Restaurants	Professional labor
Cultural Facilities	Potential students
Social Organisations	Commuters
Universities/Research Facilities/Students	People interested in shopping
Local Media	Organizer of Events

Wesselmann and Hohn, *Public Marketing*.

One attempt to solve this dilemma is to agree on a city identity, which its citizens perceive as coherent, and outsiders perceive as attractive and distinctive.

---

32   Hochstadt, *Stadtentwicklung mit Stadtmanagement?*

Because, each city incorporates and displays a certain image, evokes certain images, depending on the radius of its popularity and its diversity. The question is whether it is feasible and whether it is desirable to influence these images. If it is intended to influence this construct, it is necessary to find out which image the city currently has among different stakeholders and which images it would like to be associated with in the future.[33]

At this point, city marketing operates: It is primarily about making the specific interests of the mentioned target groups transparent and then, committing to a common overall concept that pursues the following main goals:

- improve satisfaction and identification of different stakeholders with the city and improve the quality of life for everyone
- permanently secure economic power, employment and population potential and thus promote competitiveness
- improve the city's attractiveness and image[34]

Marketing activities in German cities and municipalities are diverse and not easily put together. The spectrum ranges from simple advertising for a (sub-)community to presenting complex urban development concepts and future visions. The content of such an undertaking can also be described as heterodox. On the one hand, it is about developing the current city center with regard to its shopping experience for instance. On the other hand, in line with economic development it is about setting new accents in the area of cultural and experience development in order to attract people from other regions.[35]

The organization of events, fairs and (music-) festivals is thus becoming increasingly essential. Today's experience society has created new forms of communication not only for companies but also for municipalities. Events have become increasingly important within the marketing mix of companies and institutions in recent years. In particular, when the possibilities of classic

---

33   Bundesvereinigung City- und Stadtmarketing e.V. et al., eds., *Praxishandbuch City- und Stadtmarketing* (Wiesbaden: Springer Fachmedien Wiesbaden, 2018), https://doi.org /10.1007/978-3-658-19642-4; Thomas Breyer-Mayländer and Christopher Zerres, eds., *Stadtmarketing: Grundlagen, Analysen, Praxis* (Wiesbaden: Springer Fachmedien Wiesbaden, 2019), https://doi.org/10.1007/978-3-658-26254-9.

34   Wesselmann and Hohn, *Public Marketing*; Hochstadt, *Stadtentwicklung mit Stadtmanagement?*

35   Bundesvereinigung City- und Stadtmarketing e.V. et al., *Praxishandbuch City- und Stadtmarketing*.

advertising media are exhausted, attention can further be achieved with the *special and uniqueness* of events. The *eventization*[36] of marketing is nowadays by no means limited to companies. Politics and public institutions are now equally following the rules of the attention economy. Today's society is heavily influenced by the media, thus, companies as well as products and people are exposed to similar public expectations. In all social spheres a competition for attention is existing, whereas the methods for image building and profiling are becoming more and more the same.[37]

This goes 'hand in hand' with Schulze's considerations[38] (which will be discussed in more detail in chapter 3.1.) regarding the concept of his 'experience society' (*Erlebnisgesellschaft*) that assumes the everyday actions and behavior of people in Germany are increasingly characterized by experience oriented emotionalization. Schulze sees a change in conventional rationality patterns and builds upon this with his understanding of the experience society. His considerations are closely connected with the growing leisure time of western societies since the 1990s and a development towards an inner orientation of societies. More in-depth considerations regarding these topics follow in the following theoretical perspective and chapter 3.1.

One of the most important, but also most difficult tasks is to set themes for events. During the event's conception within the city marketing, the storytelling for the city or the integration of the city image is considered and thought through. In addition to the city marketing concept, fixed annual days or anniversaries offer good starting points for city marketing events. Many city productions only work with strong citizen participation. Serious participation, however, presupposes that there is real room for maneuver. For the participation of the population, associations and cultural institutions to be successful, the framework conditions are mostly clearly defined and communicated beforehand.[39]

---

36 Eventization at this point refers to the increased emergence of eventized formats within marketing. The term eventization in the following course of the work refers to the term eventization that was coined by Hitzler, which contests a fundamental trend toward the eventization of life in contemporary society. (See chapter 3.1)

37 Bundesvereinigung City- und Stadtmarketing e.V. et al., *Praxishandbuch City- und Stadtmarketing*.

38 Schulze, *Die Erlebnisgesellschaft*.

39 Eva Gancarz, "Events als Instrument des Stadtmarketing," April 2, 2019, https://zukunftdeseinkaufens.de/stadtmarketing/.

Furthermore, successful projects distinguish between core programs, supporting programs and frequency drivers. The core program mainly determines the quality of the urban staging and thus of the event. With the supporting programs, a large number of participants can be integrated into the program and niche formats for narrower target groups can be included. Already established, uncomplicated frequency generators such as fair festival elements are less costly to organize and can be calculated in terms of impact and visitor numbers.[40]

The conception and implementation of city events is one of the challenging tasks of city marketing. Even though many general conditions have changed significantly in recent years, it is precisely the emotional impact of events that offers the opportunity to influence the identity of a city. It is important to find the defining identity characteristics of a city, to develop them further and, if necessary, to use them to develop a story and a program for the event, to set this up as a participatory project and to endure the resulting unpredictability.[41]

40   Breyer-Mayländer and Zerres, *Stadtmarketing*.
41   Bundesvereinigung City- und Stadtmarketing e.V. et al., *Praxishandbuch City- und Stadtmarketing*.

Theoretical Perspective Two: Eventization

After describing the upcoming challenges of demographic change in Germany and its impact on (especially mid-sized) cities, municipalities and their im-age-marketing, the next section shall shine a light on the fundamental eventi-zation of society and economy which is also recognizable within the German university landscape. Furthermore, the related interior orientation is laid out and ties in with motives and motivational constructs for cultural consump-tion. The chapter is concluded by the disruption of the music industry with emphasis on the German market as well as underlying socio-economic de-velopments and their distortions which are also linked to eventization and festivalization of the industry.

Eventization and Interior Orientation

Trying to comprehend the underlying sponsorship culture within the market for university popular music festivals in Germany roots in several socio-eco-nomic developments that have occurred in parallel. In order to introduce the topic, a study by Hafen[1] conducted in 1992 is to be mentioned. "Hedonism and Rock music" investigated the live experience of teenagers attending rock con-certs and can be seen as an early pioneer regarding motivational research for consuming and experiencing live popular music in Germany. Furthermore, the view of this study was directed to what in sociological studies has been described as a hedonistic component of activities, attitudes, and behavior. At the same time, the beginning of the nineties, the German sociologist Gerhard Schulze coined the term of an experience society (*Erlebnisgesellschaft*) which

---

1   Roland Hafen, *Hedonismus Und Rockmusik: Eine Empirische Studie Zum Live-Erlebnis Ju-gendlicher* (Paderborn, 1992).

every individual is very (selfishly) focused on achieving as much (individual) pleasure as possible. His considerations are characterized by the importance of the interior orientation of life for the construction of the social world. Anesthetizing and psychologizing the everyday world is therefore the hallmark of a society whose existential core problems no longer exist to survive physically or socially, but to live and experience a beautiful life.[2]

Schulze assumes that the differentiation of society into socioeconomic segments, has become increasingly blurred in the course of the development from the scarcity society of the postwar years to today's abundance society. Socioeconomic differences are being replaced by individual differences in the way people experience their own lives. According to Schulze, society differentiates into five experience milieus. People within an experience milieu have homogeneous ideas about when they experience pleasure or when their own life is beautiful.[3]

For one of this study's purposes, the concept of Schulze can very well be linked with the theories of human motivation by Maslow.[4] Motivational constructs for visiting a popular music festival to that effect are hold by both theories, since the satisfaction of the need to participate in such an event can on the one hand be described as intrinsically motivated and in additionally positioned in the fourth or fifth level of Maslow's pyramid of desires. As stated by Schulze, the consumption of *experience(d) goods and services* is not sufficient to satisfy the consumers urge for excitement. Experiences are processes and psychophysical states, and responsible for reaching them is the subject itself (change from exterior to interior orientation). This goes hand in hand with the uncertainty and fear of disappointment as to whether the consumed experience good (or service) really leads to the expected excitement. This uncertainty increases the willingness to adopt manners and actions, which form the basis for experience orientated similarities between people. Thus, this behavior can be revealed by consumption in general as well as the motivation to attend a (popular [music]) festival.

Two decades later, Hitzler introduces the concept of eventization, which he describes as a social development that is driven by the supply of cultural experience offers. His event concept is formulated in a very broad sense and

---

2   Schulze, *Die Erlebnisgesellschaft*.

3   Schulze, 169–213.

4   A. H. Maslow, "A Theory of Human Motivation.," *Psychological Review* 50, no. 4 (1943): 370–96, https://doi.org/10.1037/h0054346.

includes happenings that are excluded from everyday life, are temporally and spatially compressed, performative-interactively and offering a high attractiveness for a relatively large number of people. Especially in western societies, however, these culturally appropriate opportunities are available in day-to-day life,[5] which serve to transport us into 'extraordinary worlds of experience'. Events are often described as planned occasions or happenings of a very special, spectacular nature. Also, the characteristics exclusiveness, uniqueness, limited in time and/or artificially created are mentioned.[6] These characteristics, however, meet far more events than a festival of popular music (sports events, political events, religious events etc.).

All event characteristics listed according to Hitzler are fulfilled by a festival of popular music and therefore reflect the development that prevails according to his words. Bennett et al.[7] go one step further and refer to the *Festivalization of Culture*, which explores the links between various local and global cultures, communities, identities, and lifestyle narratives as they are both constructed and experienced in the festival context. Therefore, festivals in general can be seen no longer merely periodic, cultural, religious, or historical events within communities, but rather as a popular means through which citizens consume and experience culture.

Eventization of the University Campus

Taking the described challenges from the first theoretical perspective above into account, a more professional marketing is becoming more and more important for German cities, municipalities as well as for their local universities. The central goal to increase the attractiveness and/or the transmitted image of a city and/or municipality for its own population, foreign and local companies, potential migrates and future academics. Logically, the intentions of

---

5   Legalized and non-legalized drugs; e.g. Technical media such as books, videofilms, television, radio, recordings or CDs, compu- ter games, etc.; But also social events such as cinemas, play halls, nightclubs, worship services, art exhibitions, sports competitions, fashion shows, folk festivals.

6   Winfried Gebhardt, Ronald Hitzler, and Michaela Pfadenhauer, eds., *Events: Soziologie des Aussergewöhnlichen*, Erlebniswelten, Bd. 2 (Opladen: Leske + Budrich, 2000).

7   Andy Bennett, Jodie Taylor, and Ian Woodward, *The Festivalization of Culture* (London; New York: Routledge, 2016), http://www.tandfebooks.com/isbn/9781315558189.

city, municipality and university are clearly overlapping, due to the interwovenness of a modern university with its hometown. In addition to structural, spatial, and social concepts, cultural projects play an increasing constructive role here.

German state universities are in direct competition with one another in terms of research as well as their individual teaching offers. In contrast to the higher educational system in the United States for instance, German universities can be described as much more homogeneous to one another from a 'qualitative' point of view. This is mainly due to the equal public mandate, every institution must follow. This makes them not only very alike to each other in terms of structure but also lets them operate in a very similar manner.[8] Furthermore, due to the digitalization of teaching and the growing number of private teaching and research institutions, the competition for new students has intensified.[9] Since the (federal) funding of the university landscape in Germany depends on the university's state, in the future more of a predatory competition between German universities within the individual federal states is to be expected. The University Framework Act (*Hochschulrahmengesetz*) has already created rivalry and sanctioning mechanisms that universities cannot oppose.[10]

As already addressed in the first theoretical perspective, German cities and municipalities have already integrated (marketing) events of various types and sizes into their city-marketing-mix. Accordingly, this idea is attracting increasing attention in the executive boards of German universities as well. In addition to the obvious fun for attendees and the resulting economic and tourist potential, the establishment of (marketing) events would—especially for universities in medium-sized German cities—promote the external image and awareness of the institution(s) across the country.[11] In a survey investigating the staff situation within German university's own event marketing

---

8   Michael Dobbins and Tonia Bieber, "Bildungspolitik in den USA," in *Handbuch Politik USA*, ed. Christian Lammert, Markus B. Siewert, and Boris Vormann (Wiesbaden: Springer Fachmedien Wiesbaden, 2016), 381–401, https://doi.org/10.1007/978-3-658-02 642-4_24; Jeffrey Hamburger, "Vergleich deutscher und amerikanischer Universitäten," *Die Zeit—Forschung und Lehre*, 2008, https://www.academics.de/ratgeber/usa-deutschla nd-vergleich-wissenschaft-bildung.

9   Ulrike Wefers, *Hochschulmarketing in Deutschland: Chancen und Herausforderungen* (Saarbrücken: VDM Verl. Dr. Müller, 2007).

10   Wefers.

11   Bellinghausen, *Das Musikfestival*.

department, two to three employees are already available across more than half of examined German universities. Only one employee can be provided for event marketing in 39 % of the universities surveyed. 6 % have four to five employees. Around 1 % of the universities have more than five employees.[12]

In this context, it is the universities' effort to address and approach as many potential students as possible to link greater attention and emotionalization to the institutions. Furthermore, coinciding, (advertising) enterprises increasingly rely on the same communication tool(s) within the German university landscape as part of their marketing and PR activities.

In any case, the attendees of student events are interesting for marketing and advertising activities, simply due to the fact that today's students are most likely the higher-income earners of tomorrow. Thus, companies as well as organizers design events more and more exclusively for this special location called *campus*.[13]

For instance, *Deutsche Telekom* has been organizing the week-long on campus cooking event *Telekom Campus Cooking* for several years. Besides mediaeffective collaborative cooking with the university's canteen personnel, it utilizes the happening together with star/TV chefs as a subliminal communication tool for its brand and products. *Campus Cooking* has been held very successfully in cooperation with the respective student unions since 2008, who also see it as an opportunity to strengthen their image(s). The company *CAMPUSdirekt*, which specializes in university marketing, university advertising and university publicity, handles the ticketing and is responsible for on-site bookings. In addition, both companies use the advertising networks to run accompanying ambient campaigns.[14]

12   Cornelia Zanger and Wissenschaftliche Konferenz Eventforschung, eds., *Erfolg mit nachhaltigen Eventkonzepten: Tagungsband zur 2. Konferenz für Eventforschung an der TU Chemnitz*, 1. Aufl., Gabler Research Markenkommunikation und Beziehungsmarketing (Wissenschaftliche Konferenz Eventforschung, Wiesbaden: Gabler, 2012).

13   Jöckel, Hesser, and Will, *Trendsetter, Innovatoren, Studentenbudget? Eine Mehr-Methoden-Studie zu Werbung und Produktpräferenzen bei Studierenden*.

14   "Pasta e Basta: Telekom Campus Cooking serviert die Nudel in all ihren Facetten," Kruger Media PR Agentur Berlin | Musik, Lifestyle, Entertainment, May 13, 2019, https://www.kruger-media.de/2019/05/13/pasta-e-basta-telekom-campus-cooking-serviert-die-nudel-in-all-ihren-facetten/.

Companies such as *Unicum Marketing*[15] pass on brand communication from a wide range of companies via their (university) network, including through the famous *Uni-Starter-Bags* for first semester students who just got enrolled at their institution. In addition, sponsorships, and fully organized university events and especially parties are sometimes sold directly to student bodies, student initiatives and student committees. A further step is taken with students, who are directly employed to sponsoring companies as so-called brand ambassadors on a working student basis and are eager to represent the company or brand image through direct contact with the student body.[16]

In Dortmund, the Technical University (TU) collectively invites its freshmen to the Westfalenstadion every year together with the BVB soccer club, the city, the opera, the theater, and the concert hall. Many of the approximately annual 6.000 new students start their winter semester with waves of la-ola: On the north stand of the stadium, the students experience a varied program with corresponding event character every year and a university wide raffle links sponsored vouchers for the university canteen.[17]

After also having carried out a welcome event in the home stadium for several years in Paderborn, the university board decided to switch back to the campus and gave a considerable part of the university building core for regional organizers to carry out the first *College Kickoff* in 2019. Spread across campus, twelve DJs spun everything from trash, electronica, and hip hop to electronic dance music on four stages within the building. New enrolled students were given 1,250 free admission wristbands, sponsored by the President's Office.

Building on this willingness and affinity for the use of events as an enhancement of the external image within university administration, the nowadays large-scale music festivals of German universities are well developed

---

15   Unicum Marketing is a below-the-line agency, based in Bochum, Germany and specializing in young target groups and part of the UNICUM group (of companies). Core competence is the conception and implementation of promotions, events, samplings and guerrilla marketing.

16   "UNICUM—Kommunikation mit jungen, intelligenten Zielgruppen," UNICUM Media, 2020, https://unicum-media.com/.

17   "Erstsemester: Traditionelle Begrüßung im Stadion | pflichtlektüre," accessed August 26, 2020, http://www.pflichtlektuere.com/18/10/2016/erstsemester-traditionelle-begru essung-im-stadion/.

events that have gained notoriety beyond the student body. Thus, the market for university popular music festivals is becoming an important part of the German event industry. These events, as a form of popular music festival with a mainly student audience structure and corresponding complexity in connection with music consumption, are specially integrated into regional conjunctions between universities, cities and organizers. They not only shape the public image of the university itself, but also have an impact on the university's home city or municipality's image; which is becoming increasingly relevant against the backdrop of the mentioned socio-demographic change in Germany and the increasing inner-German competition between cities and universities. The largest and best-known university popular music festivals include *Hum festival (Köln)*, *Red Bull Campus Touchdown (Mainz)*, *Unifest Karlsruhe*, *Campus Festival Mittweida*, *Campus Festival Aachen*, *AStA Sommerfestival (Paderborn)* as well as the *Campus Festival Bielefeld*. The events in Paderborn und Bielefeld, which serve as the events for the surveys within Study Three of this work, embody university popular music festivals with a long tradition (Paderborn) or represent the biggest event of its kind (in 2019) within Germany.

Motivational Constructs for Event Attendance

When undertaking theoretical research on cultural consumption, events and ultimately their sponsorship as well as event attendance, one might get the feeling that the terms *motive* and *motivation* are being mixed up or used as a synonym. However, this does not necessarily mean, that the simultaneously use of the two terms is being interpreted wrong by the reader, because what's being analyzed in these corresponding papers, is a general sense of 'why someone is doing what' or the underlying driving force for an individuals' action. And in that sense, using both terms for the sake of the same issue is reasonable. Additionally, the question of how motives can be exactly measured is no less difficult than its definition.[18]

A motive is a disposition to strive for a certain valued target state, meaning a long-term tendency to align one's activities to reach a specific goal. This disposition-aspect makes it very clear that in motivational psychology, the

---

18   Joachim Funke, "Allgemeine & Theoretische Psychologie" (Heidelberg, 2003), https://www.psychologie.uni-heidelberg.de/ae/allg/lehre/wct/index.htm.

term *motive* is understood a bit more abstract than it is being used in everyday life (or some previous motivational research regarding event attendance).[19]

However, as motives, motivations are a key factor when dealing with event marketing and sponsorship, in this dissertation the difference between motive and motivation shall be pointed out. Furthermore, in the ongoing text both terms will be used and amended by the overlying term *motivational construct(s)*.

Motives are the driving force behind all human behaviors[20], whether someone decides to buy a red instead of a blue car or whether he decides to buy a ticket of a certain music festival. According to the theory of human motivation introduced by Maslow in 1943, humans are motivated by a hierarchy (often displayed as a pyramid) of needs in which a person must meet one need before moving to the next. Maslow's theory argues, humans are motivated in achieving certain needs, thus as soon as one of these is fulfilled the person will seek to fulfill the next higher one. Maslow proposed a hierarchy of human needs that individuals challenge to, at some point reach individual fulfillment. The most basic and therefore also physiological need is the need to maintain homeostasis. Once these basic needs are met, humans can progress to the next, known as the security need. In this stage, humans seek a sense of certain security and safety, necessary for survival.[21] As soon as the basic needs are met, motives evolve and can be described as an internal factor that arouses, directs and integrates a person's behavior and action.[22] Correspondingly, the decision to attend a popular music festival will be determined by an individual's motive to fulfill a desired need within Maslow's third, fourth or fifth[23] stage embedded in his *hierarchy of needs*.

Motivation contrarily is a current process that is triggered by the stimulation of a motive. While a motive has been defined as an enduring quality of a person, motivation is a person's state at a particular point in time, i.e. in a certain situation. It can be described as an interaction between moti-

---

19   Funke.

20   Maria Manolika, Alexandros Baltzis, and Nikolaos Tsigilis, "Measuring Motives for Cultural Consumption: A Review of the Literature," *American Journal of Applied Psychology* 3, no. 1 (2015): 1–5.

21   Maslow, "A Theory of Human Motivation."

22   Manolika, Baltzis, and Tsigilis, "Measuring Motives for Cultural Consumption."

23   Maslows' Hirachy of needs: 1st & 2nd level: Basic needs. 3rd & 4th level: Psychological needs. 5th level: Self-fulfillment needs.

vated subject and motivating situation[24] or a momentary focus on a goal of action, a motivation tendency, which for explanation, one needs to take both sides of the situation into account.[25] A distinction is made between two forms of motivation. On the one hand, intrinsic motivation refers to behavior that is driven by internal rewards. In other words, the motivation to engage in a behavior arises from within the individual because it is naturally satisfying to the individual. This contrasts with extrinsic motivation, which involves engaging in a behavior in order to earn external rewards or avoid negative conclusions.[26]

In 2015 Manolika et al. reviewed various quantitative research findings identifying the main motives for cultural consumption. Overall, 13 factors seem to capture participants' motives when attending cultural events. Their categorization and frequency of appearance is presented in *Table 2*. Results shall provide a first idea of how motives for cultural consumption are linked; based on the findings of the analyzed studies, it is obvious that the most important and probably core motives are: socialization, family togetherness, escape and novelty.

---

24   Carl F. Graumann and Carl Friedrich Graumann, *Motivation*, 6. Aufl., unveränd. Nachdr. d. 5. Aufl., Einführung in die Psychologie, hrsg. von C. F. Graumann; 1 (Wiesbaden: Akad. Verl.-Ges. [u.a.], 1981).

25   Heinz Heckhausen, *Motivation und Handeln: mit 52 Tabellen*, 2., völlig überarb. u. erg. Aufl., Springer-Lehrbuch (Berlin: Springer, 1989).

26   Bernard Weiner et al., *Motivationspsychologie*, 3. Aufl., unveränd. Nachdr. d. 3. Aufl. 1994 (Weinheim: Beltz, Psychologie-Verl.-Union, 2009); Jutta Heckhausen and Heinz Heckhausen, eds., *Motivation und Handeln*, 5., überarbeitete und erweiterte Auflage, Springer-Lehrbuch (Berlin [Heidelberg]: Springer, 2018), https://doi.org/10.1007/978-3-662-53927-9.

Table 2: *Motives for Cultural Consumption*

Motives for Cultural Consumption	Frequency	Percentage
Socialization	35	58,4 %
Family togetherness	22	53,7 %
Escape	20	48,8 %
Novelty	18	43,9 %
Learning	12	29,3 %
Relaxation	12	29,3 %
Excitement	9	22 %
Entertainment	8	19,5 %
Festival attributes	8	19,5 %
Cultural exploration	7	17,1 %
Self-esteem enhancement	6	14,6 %
Aestethic	3	7,3 %
Curiosity	2	4,9 %

Manolika, Baltzis, and Tsigilis, "Measuring Motives for Cultural Consumption."

Attending a (university) popular music festival is consumption of a cultural offering. Concerning cultural consumption, three major reasons for identifying and understanding the cultural consumer motivation exist. First, motives play a key role to design and offer suitable products for consumers, who seek to satisfy a variety of divergent needs. Second, motives are a way to monitor satisfaction and finally, identifying, and prioritizing motives are a major element in understanding the consumer's decision process.[27] Motives with regard to a (multi-day) visit of a music-framed event are additionally influenced by individual music preferences and the role, music plays for each visitor.

This was already investigated by Dollase et al.[28] in 1986. The authors explored how opera visitors differ from concert visitors of different genres. The idea was to explain how musical preferences are formed and how political,

---

27   John L. Crompton and Stacey L. McKay, "Motives of Visitors Attending Festival Events," *Annals of Tourism Research* 24, no. 2 (1997): 425–39.

28   Rainer Dollase, Michael Rüsenberg, and Hans J. Stollenwerk, *Demoskopie im Konzertsaal* (Mainz; New York: Schott, 1986).

cultural, and social attitudes arise. It was observed that the symbolic function of music 'is most pronounced where the intellectual engagement with music in the sense of a culture of discussion is greatest.

Bowen & Daniels[29] investigated to what extent music was a motivational aspect for people to attend the *Celebrate Fairfax!*, an annual music festival in Virginia, USA. Their findings suggest that four different clusters of visitors are existent: *Just Being Social, Enrichment Over Music, The Music Matters and Love It All*. The authors point out that the first two clusters, which represent approximately half of the sample, evidenced a relative disinterest in the music. This reinforces the importance for festival planners to provide non-musical entertainment and attractions and for marketers to emphasize them in their marketing and sponsorship communications.

In 2009, Gelder & Robinson[30] did a study of visitor motivations for attending *Glastonbury* and *V Festival* in the UK. Results display different motivations between the two events: for V Festival the overall dominant reason for attendance was 'to watch or see the music/artists playing', with the second highest ranked reason named 'the festival being located close to home'. For Glastonbury, however, the dominant motivation for attending the event was named 'atmosphere and socializing'. The authors highlight the importance of including a qualitative approach into the research, which will be taken into consideration for this research project. Results show further that there are differences regarding motivations for visiting a festival depending on the actual festival, as well as the importance of highlighting multiple activities including non-musical experiences and creating a special festival atmosphere when it comes to sponsorship.

Kulczynski et al.[31] took a quantitative approach in order to investigate concert motivations and particular combinations of motivations unique to popular music concert attendance. Based on their analysis they developed the

---

29   Heather E. Bowen and Margaret J. Daniels, "Does the Music Matter? Motivations for Attending a Music Festival," *Event Management* 9, no. 3 (January 1, 2005): 155–64, https://doi.org/10.3727/152599505774791149.

30   Gemma Gelder and Peter Robinson, "A Critical Comparative Study of Visitor Motivations for Attending Music Festivals: A Case Study of Glastonbury and V Festival," *Event Management* 13, no. 3 (November 1, 2009): 181–96, https://doi.org/10.3727/152599509790029792.

31   Alicia Kulczynski, Stacey Baxter, and Tamara Young, "Measuring Motivations for Popular Music Concert Attendance," *Event Management* 20, no. 2 (July 25, 2016): 239–54, https://doi.org/10.3727/152599516X14643674421816.

Concert Attendance Motivation Scale (CAMS), a tool consisting of ten factors for measuring motivations for popular music concert attendance: nostalgia, aesthetics, escape, physical attraction, status enhancement, physical skills, social interaction, concert-specific music, hero worship and uninhibited behavior. The presented overview of existing research in the field of motivation and cultural consumption and especially festival and (popular) music attendance show that there is a gap in research, especially in the German-speaking literature. Furthermore, the complexity of motivations to attend different events becomes obvious and shall be narrowed down for this research project. Hence, the concept of *Popular Music and Popular Culture* will also be taken into account. The strict definition of the object under research is still considered a challenge and will be taken up for the sake of this endeavor in chapter 4.1.[32]

Today's digitalized Music Industry within the Experience Economy

The media economy has always dealt with data. Even in the early days of newspapers or the invention of the first sound medium, the actual product was the content that was archived, reproduced, and delivered to the customer.[33] This is one reason, why the digitalization made its first stop at this business area. According to the theory of media morphoses by Blaukopf[34], communication technologies represent productive forces of culture which reflect the 'state of the technological development of a society'. Smudits developed this theory further regarding the digital morphosis, in which we are currently located and which follows the first and second graphic, mechanic as well as the electronic morphosis. All five stages represent a change from vivid and pres-

32   Peter Wicke, " 'Populäre Musik' Als Theoretisches Konzept" (Humboldt-Universität zu Berlin, 1992), http://dx.doi.org/10.18452/20156.

33   Jürgen Wilke, "Die Digitalisierung und der Strukturwandel des Mediensystems," in *Medienwandel durch Digitalisierung und Krise: Eine vergleichende Analyse zwischen Russland und Deutschland*, ed. Mike Friedrichsen, Jens Wendland, and Galina Woronenkowa, 1st ed. (Baden-Baden: Nomos Verlagsgesellschaft mbH & Co. KG, 2010), 27–33, https://doi.org/10.5771/9783845227085-27.

34   Kurt Blaukopf, *Musik im Wandel der Gesellschaft: Grundzüge der Musiksoziologie*, 2., erw. Aufl. (Darmstadt: Wissenschaftl. Buchges, 1996).

ence-intensive to graphical-symbolic and more competence-technical based encoding[35].[36]

At the same time, the boundaries of these differences are blurred in digital media morphosis, resulting in 'hybrid forms of communication', meaning a coevolution and coexistence of communication technologies which in case for the music business, influence all forms of musical expression (e.g. Vinyl/CD/mp3).

The recent technological innovations have changed the way how people access music from the ground up. The first step towards a digitalized music market was the possibility to rip a music CD and save the created file on everyone's own home computer. Thus, the consumer had two new ways to share his purchased music. In addition to burn the file onto a new empty CD and the creation of a new physical sound medium, the file could also simply be sent electronically to other people. The in 1992 introduced method for compressing digital audio signals (mp3) elevated this process. The established corporations of the music industry had to acknowledge that use for records dwindled, and that (their) copyrights could be undermined, which doubly endangered the recording industry's business foundation.[37] P2P sharing apps such as Napster supported this illegal method of sharing mp3s by globally connecting music consumers with each other. The of information created technological innovations, which transformed the music business from a product to a service business where it, according to Tschmuck no longer corresponds to its old paradigm's logic.[38]

The digital music revolution has been established in the music industry and alters its entire system of production, distribution, and reception.

---

35   Codes in this case are defined by verbal language, images (including photography, film and video), music and body language, as well as other forms of expression, such as design, architecture and fashion, which must first be realized in media in order to become perceptible.

36   Alfred. Smudits, *Mediamorphosen des Kulturschaffens: Kunst und Kommunikationstechnologien im Wandel*, Musik und Gesellschaft 27 (Wien: Braumüller, 2002).

37   Peter Tschmuck, *Creativity and Innovation in the Music Industry* (Berlin: Springer Berlin Heidelberg, 2012), http://link.springer.com/10.1007/978-3-642-28430-4.

38   Company-owned music publishers had control of creative inputs. Record contracts ensured that successful musicians were bound to the company. Company-owned labels produced music when it seemed commercially successful. Yet, the majors left musical experimentation to independent producers and record labels.

Thus, the stagnation of global music sales in the 2000s made it unlikely that the industry could achieve future growth through the existing business models which rely on the distribution of physical music products and the associated reception of it. Apple took advantage of this development and managed to get all important music licensees, especially the major record companies, on board for their iTunes launch in 2003 in order to provide an extensive catalog of music titles. It was the starting point for the development of (legal) business models for the now more feasible distribution of music via the Internet.[39] Due to its dynamic and disruptive nature, the digitalization, the future evolution of the music industry, its value creation and the handling of its product *music* is and will be subject to constant organic change.[40]

While sales of recorded music continue to diminish due to a combination of the mentioned illegal music consumption, music streaming[41] and only a partial compensation by legal digital sales and streaming[42], the popularity of popular music festivals appears to be enjoying an unprecedented boom. In particular, music festival popularity has been boosted by more available information regarding the music branch, provided by the Internet,[43] the same technology that (grotesquely) initially allowed illegal downloading of recorded music. Live performances as well as popular music festivals play an important role in exposing artists and their music to prospective fans, facilitating purchases, assisting with commercial breakthrough and image building.[44] The music event sub-sector comprises all companies that organize live concerts and events or provide specialized services to these organizers. In 2017, private households spent around 3.1 billion Euros on concerts and music per-

---

39   Mark Fox, "E-Commerce Business Models for the Music Industry," *Popular Music and Society* 27, no. 2 (March 2004): 201–20, https://doi.org/10.1080/03007760410001685831.

40   Gerhard Gensch, Eva Maria Stöckler, and Peter Tschmuck, eds., *Musikrezeption, Musikdistribution und Musikproduktion: der Wandel des Wertschöpfungsnetzwerks in der Musikwirtschaft*, 1. Aufl., Gabler Edition Wissenschaft (Wiesbaden: Gabler, 2008).

41   IFPI, "Musikindustrie-Umsatz weltweit 2016 | Statistik," Statista, 2017, https://de.statista.com/statistik/daten/studie/182361/umfrage/weltweiter-umsatz-der-musikindustrie-seit-1997/.

42   IFPI, "IFPI Digital Music Report 2015," January 2015.

43   Jane Ali-Knight, ed., *International Perspectives of festivals and Events: Paradigms of Analysis*, Advances in Tourism Research Series (Amsterdam: Academic Press, Elsevier, 2009).

44   Kulczynski, Baxter, and Young, "Measuring Motivations for Popular Music Concert Attendance," July 25, 2016.

formances in Germany, which makes this sector to a thriving business field within the industry.[45]

Moreover, a continuing positive development is also expected in the future. In the context of the "Music Economics Study" from 2020, nearly 60 % of the entrepreneurs interviewed (before the Covid 19 outbreak), expected a further positive development of revenue for the coming year(s).[46]

The decreased willingness to pay for music when consumed privately on the one hand and the increased popularity of popular music festivals on the other also reveal a shift in consumer's expenditure behavior. The growth and establishment of popular music festivals in Germany can be viewed as a reaction to market incentives induced by demand. In order to be consistent with the empirical observation of a strongly rising number of festivals over the last decades, it is necessary to identify those factors affecting demand, which have as well increased over this period.

Furthermore, scholar interest from economics and arts and humanities as well as from the (marketing-)industry regarding customer experience has increased within the last two decades. Pine II and Gilmore's often cited article which was published in 1998 in the Harvard Business Review ("Welcome to the Experience Economy") is seen by many as a pioneer work in this area of research. However, the first idea of an experience economy appeared in *Future Shock*[47], where futurist Alvin Toffler wrote of an 'experiential industry', in which people would be willing to allocate high percentages of their income to exceptional experiences.

Indeed, Pine II and Gilmore's article has been cited by authors from a wide range of scientific areas, not only in business and management but also tourism, sport, leisure, hospitality and others within the sciences of arts and humanities.

At the end of the 20th century, Pine II and Gilmore concluded how economies are subject to constant change: They contended that the experience economy would follow (and expand) the already completed economic cycles of agrarian, industrial and service. The authors state that experiences are personal and unique as well as determined by an individual's interpretation of events. Emotional responses are stimulated and judged during service delivery and are dependent on many contextual factors, which challenge

45   Bundesverband Musikindustrie e. V., "Musikwirtschaftsstudie 2020," 2020.
46   Bundesverband Musikindustrie e. V.
47   Alvin Toffler, *Future Shock*, Bantam Books (New York: Bantam Books, 1990).

organizations to monitor and deal with customer experience and their linked emotions.[48] With regard to enjoying music, the hedonistic component of consumption especially needs to be taken into account as well because it can be an explanation for the consumer behaviors that deal with the multi-sensory, fantasy and emotive phases of product usage experience.[49] It offers a complimenting paradigm to the traditional information processing, focusing on the *experiential* aspects of the consumption experience which are subjectively based, such as sensation seeking, emotional arousal and fantasizing. Hence, many companies use this fact and are able to sell their products better and worthier when they are embedded in an additional experience.[50] However, the question with regard to this consideration concerns, what if the actual offering is an experience itself?

It seems rather unlikely to wrap an additional experience around a popular music festival with the intention to sell more tickets. Nevertheless, the concept by Pine II and Gilmore applies, because products or other kinds of offerings still are embedded into the festival experience. But the parties who do so, are usually not the organizers of the festival, but mainly companies that pay the organizers a (sponsorship) fee for using the event as a communication tool. Research on event sponsorship has taken this into account for years. Nevertheless, some questions remain open. This applies, for instance, to the question of the effectiveness of hints on the event sponsors, if at the same time many information and stimuli flow into the visitors and thus not the desired attention can be given to all messages.[51] This subsidiary development also reveals the significance of the research object from an additional perspective and a better understanding of an event of such kind and its visitor's underlying motivational constructs to attend it may help to adapt existing approaches to sponsor and place brands, products or services at the event.

---

48   B. Joseph Pine, James H. Gilmore, and others, "Welcome to the Experience Economy," *Harvard Business Review* 76 (1998): 97–105.

49   Kathleen T. Lacher, "Hedonic Consumption: Music As a Product," *ACR North American Advances* NA-16 (1989), https://www.acrwebsite.org/volumes/6932/volumes/v16/NA-16.

50   Pine, Gilmore, and others, "Welcome to the Experience Economy."

51   Yvonne Siebert, *Einstellungs- und Verhaltenswirkungen im Event-Sponsoring* (Wiesbaden: Springer Fachmedien Wiesbaden, 2013), http://link.springer.com/10.1007/978-3-658-0 2938-8.

Theoretical Perspective Three: (Live) Popular Music (Cultures)

This dissertation's third theoretical framework perspective deals with the subject matter of popular music and popular music festivals, which shall form a foundation of theoretical insight regarding the issue in order to understand the matter of sponsorship in the event branch as well as the stand of sponsorship within context of corporate communication and culture in a further step. Ultimately, this leads to expanding the corresponding theoretical knowledge for the investigation of sponsorship culture in the empirical part of this work.

Popular Music

While in economics literature dealing with the subject of *popular music*, it is often referred to as all types of music that are mass-produced, mass-marketed, and is generally treated as a commodity. Since the concept of *pop* is to be expanded for this interdisciplinary dissertation's purposes, in addition to purely economic characteristics of certain music genres, a preferred definition needs to be further observed from an arts and humanities viewpoint which offers a variety of definitory considerations regarding the subject matter.

In literature a vast number of different definitions for popular music are existent. For some authors, it is simply a mass distributed and mass-consumed style of music[1] or a light (entertaining) music with excessive instru-

---

1   Jürgen Wölfer, *Die Rock- und Popmusik: Eine umfassende Darstellung ihrer Geschichte und Funktion*, Orig.-Ausg, Heyne-Bücher; Nr. 7108 (München: Heyne, 1980).

mentation and simple melodic twists.[2] For others it represents music in an entertainment sense which has been specifically industrialized since 1900, is mass produced and owes its creation to the invention of phonograms. Within context of these three different definitions alone, it becomes apparent that many approaches and attempts within musicology alone are existent to grasp the specifics of popular music.

However, the general idea for this dissertation is to use a wider popular music concept which is not based solely on the musicological considerations mentioned above. According to Geisthövel and Mrozek, a gradual realization evolved (in recent years), that *popular culture* is rather a space of communication in which large sections of society negotiate their needs and in which politics therefore may be made. They even go a step further stating that the mass democracies of the second half of the 20th century could no longer (historically) be adequately described without pop.[3] Due to this intellectualization, pop has become academically native to old and new disciplines over the past 25 years as it has evolved through the various disciplines.[4]

According to Frith, popular music is defined by a stylistic variety, by a wide distribution and by a versatile use.[5] Furthermore, Frith explicitly does not describe popular music as an artform, but as a craft, and justifies this by stating that artists do not strive for the realization of individual visions through their doing but to assume profit and commercial success as ambition of the players in the music industry. However, *for Frith*, popular music also includes music that is meant to be shared as well as collectively enjoyed and explicitly consumed socially at events such as a popular music festival for instance.[6]

---

2   Peter Urban, *Rollende Worte, die Poesie des Rock: von d. Strassenballade zum Pop-Song: e. wissenschaftl. Analyse d. Pop-Song-Texte*, Orig.-Ausg (Frankfurt am Main: Fischer-Taschenbuch-Verlag, 1979).

3   Alexa Geisthövel and Bodo Mrozek, eds., *Popgeschichte Band 1: Konzepte und Methoden* (Berlin: transcript Verlag, 2014), https://doi.org/10.14361/transcript.9783839425282.

4   Bodo Mrozek and Zentrum für zeithistorische Forschung Potsdam, "Popgeschichte," *Docupedia-Zeitgeschichte*, 2010, https://doi.org/10.14765/ZZF.DOK.2.321.V1.

5   Simon Frith, ed., *Popular Music*, Critical Concepts in Media and Cultural Studies (London; New York: Routledge, 2004).

6   Lee Marshall, Dave Laing, and Simon Frith, eds., *Popular Music Matters: Essays in Honour of Simon Frith*, Ashgate Popular and Folk Music Series (Farnham, Surrey, UK, England; Burlington, VT, USA: Ashgate, 2014); Frith, *Popular Music*.

Anderton proposes an understanding of popular music within the afore-mentioned sphere of collectively enjoyed events in form of popular music fes-tivals by theorizing the cultural, social, and geographic importance of outdoor music festivals. He argues that professionalization, corporatization, mediati-zation, regulatory control, and sponsorship/branding should not necessarily be regarded as a process of transgressive alternative culture being co-opted by commercial concerns; but instead, such changes represent a reconfiguration of the (live music) sector in line with changes in society, and a broadening of forms and meanings that may be associated with forms of outdoor music events.[7]

For comparison, a partly similar, German definitional approach is pre-sented by Jacke, who stressed his considerations by a complementary ap-proach and describes popular music and popular culture as

> "in contrast to other concepts synonymous with the popular and popular cul-ture to emphasize their belonging to a commercial social sector. This sector industrially produces and mediates topics that are then adopted by large groups of people and processed further into new products."[8]

Following this line of thought further, means understanding (mass-)mediat-ing and marketing themes as what happens conjointly by various actants in the live popular music festival market as will be shown in the following chap-ter, and this decisively leads to incorporating the sponsorship of these events within Jacke's consideration regarding popular culture. The dialectics of pop represents a clear significance for the economy and various markets due to this certain ability to attract attention[9] and have effect across society but ob-viously across the younger (student) generation.

Furthermore, Jacke characterizes the embedded actants of popular cul-ture being under very special innovation- and thus time pressure. This shall also be seen as an appropriate link of Jacke's definitional considerations re-garding pop and the following empirical investigations of this work since it shares the similar characteristics particularly within the event marketing and

7   Chris Anderton, *Music Festivals in the UK: Beyond the Carnivalesque*, Ashgate Popular and Folk Music Series (London; New York: Routledge, Taylor & Francis Group, 2019).

8   Christoph Jacke, "Pop," in *The Creativity Complex: A Companion to Contemporary Culture*, ed. Timon Beyes, Cultures of Society, volume 36 (Bielefeld: transcript Verlag, 2018), 202.

9   Jacke, 202–5.

event management industry which thus shall also be understood as a certain subfield of live popular music.

Additionally, he sees the stakeholder of popular culture as particularly resourceful in terms of the attention economy due to this innovation and time pressure. The obvious relationship between sponsorship culture and the attention economy hits the same nerve likewise here. Hence, Jacke's considerations and definition regarding popular culture and thus incorporating popular music as part of popular culture seem suitable for this work.

Popular Music Festivals

The phenomenon of interest in this dissertation shall explore sponsorship culture within the German university popular music festival market. To establish the context within which the event's sponsorship and its stakeholders are situated, this chapter provides an outline of origins, academic literature, and research on music festivals in general as well as popular music festivals in particular. Furthermore, the preceding considerations from this work's second theoretical perspective regarding *eventization* and *interior orientation* as well as the definitional considerations on popular culture and popular music find their common overlap in the following section.

Music festivals are a global phenomenon. The largest, ticketed, music festival is *Mawazine* in Rabat Morocco, with over 2.5 million festivalgoers; the largest free music festival is the *Donauinselfest* in Vienna, Austria had 2.7 million attendees (both in 2019).[10] It seems obvious that events of this size, are managed and executed by highly professional profit oriented companies.

The majority of organized popular music festivals in Germany, however, seem to be—according to market data from 2015[11] and ticketing data from 2019[12]—smaller, boutique festivals and are operated independently or by

---

10   Felix Richter, "The Largest Music Festivals in the World" (Statista, 2019), https://www.s tatista.com/chart/17757/total-attendance-of-music-festivals/.

11   Hessisches Statistisches Landesamt, "Verteilung Der Musikfestivals Und -Festspiele in Deutschland Im Jahr 2015 Nach Besuchergrößenklassen" (Statistische Ämter des Bundes und der Länder, 2017).

12   Festivalalarm, "Alle Festivals Deutschland 2019," n.d., https://www.festival-alarm.com/festival/region/Deutschland/2019/DE.

smaller organizations.[13] This goes especially for the popular music festivals that are staged on German university campuses where the biggest events range between an audience of 10,000 to 20,000 visitors as will be shown in chapter 10.1.2.

For categorization purposes, music festivals are positioned within the live music sector, which itself is part of the music industry. As discussed in Chapter 3.4, the recording sector of the music business had hegemonic status in the last century but due to disruptive developments provoked by digitalization, the exploitation of other forms than the actual sound recording increased and this goes eminently for the festivals of popular music.[14] Music festivals are evolving to the primary form for the staging of live (popular) music, whereas live music has emerged to the core of the current music industries.[15]

With respect to the industrializing aspect and the liveness of performed music, a popular music festival can furthermore be interpreted as a cultural happening that combines several aspects such as obvious characteristics of a (big) event as well as Jacke's considerations[16] regarding commercialized (pop cultural) (third) places.[17] Consumption and entertainment are constantly being mixed with each other, the (only) difference is that this (third) place exists only a few (or one) day(s) each year and therefore further represents a certain exclusivity to the consumer/audience. Due to the fact that the festival is staged anew every year, it may always adapt to the changing needs of the visitors, a characteristic that is of particular importance with regard to the event's sponsorship. In that sense, popular music festivals are cultural events that attract audiences for a variety of reasons. But in contrast to other entertainment events, they not only provide unique opportunities for social

13   Bundesverband der Veranstaltungswirtschaft, "Live Entertainment in Deutschland" (Hamburg, 2017).

14   Fabian Holt, *Everyone Loves Live Music: A Theory of Performance Institutions*, Big Issues in Music (Chicago: The University of Chicago Press, 2020), 157–60.

15   Erik Hitters and Carsten Winter, "The Festivalization of Live Music: Introduction," 2020.

16   Jacke describes a commercialization of third places, such as small shopping stores, which also have a social function, to large shopping centers, which only serve the fastest and largest possible consumption.

17   Christoph Jacke, *Einführung in populäre Musik und Medien*, 2. Aufl., Populäre Kultur und Medien 1 (Berlin: LIT-Verl, 2013), 203.

and cultural enrichment, but also economic development, place branding and marketing purposes.[18]

With regard to this work, it shall be noted at this point that university popular music festivals (still) occupy a special and, above all, as yet insufficiently researched niche within the broader German market for music festivals in general.

Building on the willingness and affinity for the utilization of events by universities and municipalities as an enhancement of the external image within university administration, the nowadays large-scale music festivals of German universities (nevertheless) are well developed events that have gained notoriety beyond the student body. Thus, the market for university popular music festivals is becoming an important part of the German event industry. These events, as a form of popular music festival with a mainly student audience structure and corresponding complexity in connection with music consumption, are specially integrated into regional conjunctions between universities, cities, and organizers. They not only shape the public image of the university itself, but also have an impact on the university's home city or municipality's image; which is becoming increasingly relevant against the backdrop of the mentioned socio-demographic change in Germany and the increasing inner-German competition between cities and universities.

Early (Mass-)Popular Music Festivals

There is some debate about when popular music festivals originated but this tends to be whether jazz, which at the time was a 'popular' genre of music, even qualifies as the origin of the current popular music festival.[19] Media documentaries have promoted the notion that the music festival began with festivals in the USA: Monterey in 1967, Newport in 1968, Woodstock in 1969; and in the UK: Isle of Wight Festival in 1969 and Glastonbury that originally began as the Pilton Pop, Blues and Folk Festival in 1970.[20]

---

18   Margarida Abreu-Novais and Charles Arcodia, "Music Festival Motivators for Attendance: Developing an Agenda for Research," *International Journal of Event Management Research* 8, no. 1 (2013): 34–48; Anderton, *Music Festivals in the UK*.

19   George McKay, *Glastonbury: A Very English Fair* (London: V. Gollancz, 2000); Simon Frith, ed., *The History of Live Music in Britain*, Ashgate Popular and Folk Music Series (London: Routledge, Taylor and Francis Group, 2019).

20   Sam Bridger, *Festivals Britannia*, Documentary, 2010, https://www.imdb.com/title/tt2190265/; Julien Temple, *Glastonbury*, 2006.

However, McKay's "The Pop Festival: History, Music, Media, Culture" renews the authors claim that music festivals originated in the 1950s with jazz music and not through the late 1960s festivals.[21] McKay has already made this argument for the roots of the music festival one decade earlier.[22]

In Germany, starting in the 1980s, festivals such as *Rock am Ring* with more than 60,000 visitors on the Nürburgring were held annually. Ten years later, the founding of new festivals increased, and open-air festivals of popular music have been booming since the 1990s.[23] This was supported by a differentiation of popular music genres, such as indie rock, metal, gothic, hip hop, reggae, and electronic music. Furthermore, additional growth was possible due to the German reunification, which led to a sudden increasing number in potential customers, coming (and being characterized) from a former communist, real socialist dictatorship. Hence, a whole post-war generation with the need to catch up on cultural, joyful experiences. Furthermore, the partly sparsely populated territory of the former German Democratic Republic has offered event organizers additional (secluded) event locations combined with fewer bureaucratic effort regarding organizing events as in the west.[24]

University popular music festivals have been a relatively new phenomenon in Germany. There is a small number of events such as the *AStA Sommerfestival*, which is hosted at Paderborn University, and which has a two decade long history. Events with such a long history are nonetheless the exception.[25]

Academic Research

Specific research on music festivals is to be found either in the longer existing event studies as well as in the independent festival studies that developed

---

21 George McKay, ed., *The Pop Festival: History, Music, Media, Culture* (New York: Bloomsbury Academic, 2015).

22 McKay, *Glastonbury*.

23 Folkert Koopmans, ed., *Von Musikern, Machern & Mobiltoiletten: 40 Jahre Open Air Geschichte*, Orig.-Ausg., 1. Aufl. (Hamburg: FKP SORPIO, Konzertproduktionen GmbH, 2007).

24 Gunnar Otte, "Die Publikumsstrukturierung eines Open-Air-Festivals für elektronische Musik," in *Empirische Kultursoziologie*, ed. Jörg Rössel and Jochen Roose (Wiesbaden: Springer Fachmedien Wiesbaden, 2015), 27–64, http://link.springer.com/10.1007/978-3 -658-08733-3_2.

25 This statement is substantiated by the author's research and by conversations he has had with organizers and sponsors of university events in Germany.

from them. A number of existing reviews regarding event topics were covered and have been undertaken by Getz[26]; Harris et al.[27]; Hede at al.[28]; Bowdin[29]; Page and Connell[30]; Mair and Laing[31] and have identified that a number of economic and social science theories have been utilized. However, the claim has been that most studies dealt with economic impact and thus have dominated event research.[32]

Notwithstanding the supposed dominance of the economic impact focus within event research, there are, in fact, more studies on the socio-cultural[33] and environmental impacts of events, in addition to interests in other areas of events and their management, than have been recognized. Many of the studies have been undertaken by tourism literature, where events and festivals are seen as part of the tourism product offer.

Festival studies as an independent research category seem to have emerged into an established academic field in English speaking countries

---

26   Donald Getz, "Event Tourism: Definition, Evolution, and Research," *Tourism Management* 29, no. 3 (June 2008): 403–28, https://doi.org/10.1016/j.tourman.2007.07.017; D. Getz, "The Nature and Scope of Festival Studies," 2010.

27   R. Harris et al., "Towards an Australian Event Research Agenda: First Steps," *Event Management* 6, no. 4 (April 1, 2000): 213–21, https://doi.org/10.3727/152599500108751372.

28   Anne-Marie Hede, Leo Jago, and Margaret Deery, "An Agenda for Special Event Research: Lessons from the Past and Directions for the Future," *Journal of Hospitality and Tourism Management* 10 (January 2003): 1–14.

29   Michael Williams and Glenn A J Bowdin, "Festival Evaluation: An Exploration of Seven UK Arts Festivals," *Managing Leisure* 12, no. 2–3 (July 2007): 187–203, https://doi.org/10.1 080/13606710701339520.

30   Stephen Page and Joanne Connell, eds., *The Routledge Handbook of Events* (London; New York: Routledge, 2015).

31   Judith Mair and Jennifer Laing, "The Greening of Music Festivals: Motivations, Barriers and Outcomes. Applying the Mair and Jago Model," *Journal of Sustainable Tourism* 20, no. 5 (June 2012): 683–700, https://doi.org/10.1080/09669582.2011.636819.

32   Bernadette Quinn, "Arts Festivals and the City," *Urban Studies* 42 (May 2005): 927–43, https://doi.org/10.1080/00420980500107250; Charles Arcodia and Michelle Whitford, "Festival Attendance and the Development of Social Capital," *Journal of Convention and Event Tourism* 8 (January 2007), https://doi.org/10.1300/J452v08n02_01; Linda Wilks, "Social Capital in the Music Festival Experience," in *The Routledge Handbook of Events* (Routledge, 2008), https://doi.org/10.4324/9780203803936.ch17.

33   Getz, "The Nature and Scope of Festival Studies."

for some time now[34], in which festivals are usually analyzed with regard to place-making and place marketing strategies[35] or in terms of geopolitical cultural positioning[36]. In 2010 a review by Getz of over 400 festival studies in 2010 identified a set of under-explored discourses concerning festivals' social and cultural impacts and roles in establishing place or group identity[37] and set the course for further research in the field.

In more current academic research, Anderton[38] analyzes the (UK) land-scape of festivals and undertakes an extended investigation into the commer-cialized popular music festival sector (in the UK) and examines events of all sizes. Moreover, he argues that changes in the sector since the mid-1990s, such as professionalization, corporatization, mediatization, regulatory con-trol, and sponsorship/branding, should not necessarily be regarded as a pro-cess of transgressive 'alternative culture' being co-opted by commercial con-cerns; instead, such changes represent a reconfiguration of the sector in line with changes in society, and a broadening of the forms and meanings that may be associated with outdoor music events.

The aforementioned book "The Pop Festival: History, Music, Media, Cul-ture" by Mc Kay[39] combines scholarship in cultural studies, media studies, musicology, sociology, and history to explore the music festival as a key event within the cultural landscape and aims to explain the general underlying na-ture of music festivals.

Anderton[40] adds to a growing subfield of music festival studies by exam-ining the business practices and cultures of the commercial outdoor sector,

---

34   Bennett, Taylor, and Woodward, *The Festivalization of Culture*; Chris Newbold et al., *Focus on Festivals: Contemporary European Case Studies and Perspectives*, 2015; McKay, *The pop festival*.

35   Richard Prentice and Vivien Andersen, "Festival as Creative Destination," *Annals of Tourism Research* 30, no. 1 (January 2003): 7–30, https://doi.org/10.1016/S0160-7383 (02)00034-8.

36   Marijke Valck, de, *Film Festivals: From European Geopolitics to Global Cinephilia* (Amster-dam: Amsterdam University Press, 2007), https://doi.org/10.5117/9789053561928.

37   Getz, "The Nature and Scope of Festival Studies."

38   Anderton, *Music Festivals in the UK*.

39   McKay, *The pop festival*.

40   Chris Anderton, "Music Festival Capitalism," in *The Oxford Handbook of Global Popular Music*, by Chris Anderton, ed. Simone Krüger Bridge (Oxford University Press, 2021), https://doi.org/10.1093/oxfordhb/9780190081379.013.4.

with a particular focus on rock, pop and dance music events. Anderton considers the events of this sector require substantial financial and other capital in order to be staged and achieve success, yet the market is highly volatile, with relatively few festivals managing to attain longevity. It is argued that these events must balance their commercial needs with the socio-cultural expectations of their audiences for hedonistic, carnivalesque experiences that draw on countercultural understanding of festival culture (the countercultural carnivalesque).

Holt[41] shows how (big) festivals such as *Lollapalooza, Coachella,* and *Glastonbury* and other institutions of musical performance have evolved in recent decades. He further questions how these 'glamorous pop culture events' are changing the visitors' relationship to music, leisure, and public culture as the hosted sites that were once meaningful sources of community and culture are increasingly subsumed by corporate stakeholders.

Research specifically dealing with (university) popular music festivals in Germany is not existent. However, there are some studies that also deal with the interaction and/or interdependency of music festivals and their hosting cities or regions.

Köhler did a comprehensive impact assessment of the non-monetary effects of events, using the 2011 *Melt!*[42] festival as an example. In order to analyze different effects of the festival, surveys and interviews were conducted with different stakeholders, such as with the festival audience, the local population (of the neighbored villages), the festival organizer and the regional tourism organization.

Bellinghausen[43] examines the economic and tourist effects of music festivals. This is done using the example of the festival *Bochum Total*, which takes place in Bochum, Germany and is one of the largest German open-air events with a long tradition. Furthermore, the possibilities of city marketing to use the festival for municipal purposes are considered.

---

41   Holt, *Everyone Loves Live Music*, 157–239.

42   Melt! is a music festival with 20,000 visitors annually, which was first held in 1997. Since 1999, the festival has been held near Gräfenhainichen, Germany in the 'city of iron' (Ferropolis) as part of the Saxony-Anhalt Music Festivals. It sees itself as a music festival without genre boundaries.

43   Bellinghausen, *Das Musikfestival*.

Flath[44] undertook an empirical study on value creation processes between May 2016 and June 2017 by the example of the *Orange Blossom Special Festival*. The goal was to evaluate the multiple values and value creation processes of the annually hold event, a small indie pop festival organized in the city of Beverungen, Germany.

The interest in this work's context, however, is predominantly focused on sponsorship culture with emphasis on university popular music festivals (in Germany) that are enclosed and ticketed festivals. Research, linking the areas of popular music festivals in Germany and incorporating an underlying sponsorship culture that also addresses the specifics of a student (popular music) festival audience does not exist and represents a research gap that this work shall close. For the purpose of this paper, the author adopts the following understanding of a university popular music festival:

A one-day commercial mass music event that is integrated into city- and university-marketing aspects, is largely designed for the student-body of a German university and is held on the same campus.

Event Sponsorship

This section is dedicated to the communication tool of event-sponsorship. Before going into the specific characteristics and its relevance within corporate communications, applicable definitions are shown to illustrate the concept and nature of event-sponsorship.

Sponsorship (in general) has become a common and everyday occurrence. With a current volume of around 5.5 billion euros[45], sponsorship in Germany has developed into a significant segment in the communications sector above-average growth rate in recent years. Due to the fact, that more additional product benefits and additional services often no longer offer a sufficient and needed demarcation from their competitor's goods and services, companies are more and more looking for communication tools that enable experience-based benefits and a special way for approaching their target group. Both of these aspects can be found in sponsorship activities, which is now often

---

44   Beate Flath, "'Wert-e-schöpfung-en' des Orange Blossom Special Festival (OBS)" (Beverungen, 2017), https://www.orangeblossomspecial.de/wp-content/uploads/2018/01/Festivals_in_rural-regions_OBS_Beate-Flath_proposal_VMBRDays_2017.pdf.
45   Bruhn, *Sponsoring*.

established as an integral part of a company's communication mix. Possible activities are diverse and range from involvement in sports, culture, social and environmental areas to media sponsoring and aims to include events that are in the focus of public interest and consequently resonate in the mass media in the communication work of companies, in order to achieve long term communicative effects.[46]

Although numerous authors have developed approaches to define the term of sponsorship, no universally and internationally accepted definition of the term has prevailed to this day.[47]

In order to clarify the development of the concept of sponsorship and its understanding, the first definition of the term, which originated in Great Britain, is cited in the following. The Sports Council of the United Kingdom defined it in 1971:

> "Sponsorship is a gift or payment in return for some facility of privilege which aims to provide publicity for the donor".[48]

Although this citation highlights the central feature of sponsorship, namely the exchange relationship between sponsoring and sponsored party, this definition has been criticized several times over the course of time and is considered obsolete from today's perspective. The literature provides several reasons regarding the criticism of the definition. First, due to the contradictory nature of the terms *gift* and *return*, it does not become clear enough whether the sponsor's performance is a gift or financial support in expectation of a return. In addition, the objective addressed is being formulated very imprecisely.[49]

---

46   Arnold Hermanns and Florian Riedmüller, eds., "Entwicklung und Perspektiven des Sportsponsoring," in *Management-Handbuch Sport-Marketing*, 2., vollst. überarb. Aufl. (München: Vahlen, 2008), 389–407; Arnold Hermanns, "Charakterisierung und Arten des Sponsoring," in *Handbuch Marketing-Kommunikation*, ed. Ralph Berndt and Arnold Hermanns (Wiesbaden: Gabler Verlag, 1993), 627–48, https://doi.org/10.1007/978-3-32 2-82539-1_32.

47   Tripodi John A., "Sponsorship—A Confirmed Weapon in the Promotional Armoury," *International Journal of Sports Marketing and Sponsorship* 3, no. 1 (January 1, 2001): 82–103, h ttps://doi.org/10.1108/IJSMS-03-01-2001-B007; Björn Walliser, "An International Review of Sponsorship Research: Extension and Update," *International Journal of Advertising* 22, no. 1 (January 2003): 5–40, https://doi.org/10.1080/02650487.2003.11072838.

48   John A. Meenaghan, "Commercial Sponsorship," *European Journal of Marketing* 17, no. 7 (July 1983): 3, https://doi.org/10.1108/EUM0000000004825.

49   Walliser, "An International Review of Sponsorship Research."

In the relevant German literature, Bruhn's definition is considered one of the most known. His interpretation is based on three basic requirements which, according to his conception, must be fulfilled within the context of sponsorship:

(1) Sponsorship is based on the principle of providing a service and returning it. The sponsor provides a service in order to receive a service in return from the sponsored party.
(2) Sponsorship is associated with the promotion of sports, cultural, social, or other causes. The sponsors' idea of promotion varies, depending on the field of application.
(3) Sponsorship fulfills communicative functions for enterprises. These functions may be performed directly by the sponsored party, transported by the media, or created by the sponsor itself.[50]

Taking these premises into account, Bruhn finally concludes his definition of sponsorship, which is discourse-determining cited in the German-speaking (marketing) literature:

> "Sponsorship is planning, organizing, implementing, and controlling all activities that involve the provision of money, material resources, services or know-how by companies and institutions to promote people and/or organizations in sports, culture, social affairs, the environment and/or are well connected to the media in order to achieve corporate communication goals simultaneously."[51]

In his definition, Bruhn points out that the use of the communication tool, like the use of other corporate communication instruments, must be carefully planned, organized, implemented, and controlled. Bruhn's phase-oriented approach, which emphasizes the activities from sponsorship planning to sponsorship control, competes with those that attempt to capture the characteristic components of this communication construct in an enumerative-explicative manner.[52]

---

50   Manfred Bruhn and Rudolf Mehlinger, *Rechtliche Gestaltung des Sponsoring: Vertragsrecht, Steuerrecht, Medienrecht, Wettbewerbsrecht*, 2., überarbeitete und aktualisierte Aufl. (München: C.H. Beck, 1995), 4.
51   Bruhn, *Sponsoring*, 5.
52   Bruhn, *Sponsoring*.

When moving from sponsorship in general to a characterization of the somewhat narrower concept of event sponsoring, literature suggests sponsors are increasingly realizing that classic sponsorship of (single) individuals or teams can be very risky, since in the event of a collapse in the image of the sponsored party (caused, for example, by scandals or series of defeats), the sponsor's reputation may also be at stake. For this reason, international companies in particular are increasingly acting as sponsors of attractive major events that have an enormous appeal to the public and where they do not have to fear the mentioned risk(s) as much.[53] In this context, one speaks of event sponsorship:

"Event sponsorship has moved from primarily philanthropic activities to mutually advantageous business arrangements between sponsors and the sponsored. The objectives being sought by sponsoring organizations are focusing more and more on exploitable commercial potential and bottom-line results, and less on altruism or a sense of social responsibility without expectation of return".[54]

In the context of event marketing, a basic distinction can be made between the two perspectives of *marketing at events* and *marketing with events*.[55] In the first case, existing events are being utilized by companies as advertising medium for messages in order to pursue their individual communication policy. The term event sponsorship has become established for this. The latter, on the other hand, is event marketing. Special events are explicitly initiated and staged for certain products, brands, or enterprises. The most important advantages of event sponsorship are: The communicative address takes place in

---

53   Gerd Nufer, *Wirkungen von Event-Marketing Theoretische Fundierung und empirische Analyse* (Berlin, 2002).

54   Kevin P. Gwinner, Brian V. Larson, and Scott R. Swanson, "Image Transfer in Corporate Event Sponsorship: Assessing the Impact of Team Identification and Event-Sponsor Fit," 2009, International Journal of Management and Marketing Research, 2, no. 1 (2010): 10.

55   It must be noted that although this dissertation is written in English, the differentiation between the terms event sponsorship and event marketing in the aforementioned forms is not being made in (English) scientific literature. In both cases, most authors use the term of event marketing and do not distinguish whether the sponsor is also the organizer of the event, focus lies on the analysis of the event sponsorship. For this work, a focus on popular music festivals is given. Marketing events do exist in this market but will not be subject to the examination(s) made here.

an attractive, memorable environment. High coverage and thus comparatively low cost per thousand contacts can be achieved. Additionally, the multiplier effect of partaking mass media can be fully exploited. The fundamental aim is to achieve a positive image transfer from the positively perceived event to the sponsoring brand or company. The disadvantages are high costs and a limited number of events that fulfill these goals.[56]

Since this work focuses on the explorative research of sponsorship culture of university popular music festivals, the form of event-sponsorship is explained in more detail below and then minimally adapted to the peculiarities of popular music festival sponsorship.

Event-sponsorship is defined as:

> "(...) the provision of resources (e. g. money, people, equipment) by an organization directly to an event or activity in exchange for a direct association to the event or activity. The providing organization can then use this direct association to achieve either their corporate, marketing, or media objectives".[57]

Thus, the essential criterion of event sponsorship is the mentioned provision of resources to support an event staged or organized by a third party, in order to utilize the created link to the event for meeting own goals by communicating with relevant target groups attending the event. What's characteristic for event sponsorship is that the sponsored event would usually (theoretically) take place without the sponsor. Planning and implementation are not the responsibilities of the sponsor but is normally fully handled by the sponsored party.[58]

An event representing a separate element of corporate communication is defined as marketing event meaning a special event (organized by the corpo-

---

56 Gwinner, Larson, and Swanson, "Image Transfer in Corporate Event Sponsorship: Assessing the Impact of Team Identification and Event-Sponsor Fit."

57 D.M. Sandler et al., *Olympic Sponsorship Vs. "Ambush" Marketing: Who Gets the Gold?*, Working Papers Series (New York: School of Business and Public Administration, Bernard M. Baruch College of the City University of New York, 1988), 10, https://books.google.de/books?id=tox5GwAACAAJ].

58 Jan Drengner, *Imagewirkungen von Eventmarketing: Entwicklung eines ganzheitlichen Messansatzes*, 3., aktualisierte Aufl., Gabler Edition Wissenschaft (Wiesbaden: Gabler, 2008).

ration itself) that is multi-sensory experienced by selected recipients and is mainly used as a platform for corporate communication.[59]

In the literature, a distinction is made between event sponsorship and event marketing as a form of communication. In comparison to event sponsorship, event marketing describes:

> "An innovative communication tool that serves the experience-oriented implementation of marketing goals of a company through the planning, preparation, realization and post wrap-up of marketing events".[60]

The main distinguishing feature is that in event marketing, the event is organized by the company itself. While in event sponsorship, the sponsor participates in an event staged by a third party, which would also take place without his participation. In the context of event marketing the implementation of the event is only made feasible by the sponsor. In addition to the organizational form, a further differentiation criterion is the type and scale of the communicative appearance. An event is usually organized by a single company, while many different brands act as sponsors. The organizer has a different status, which is not limited regarding a communicative appearance. Whereas the communicative possibilities of the sponsors are regulated by contract.[61] An example for a marketing event where this difference can be seen very clearly according to mentioned definitions, is the internationally known Red Bull Flugtag invented, created, organized (and nowadays even been sold) in several countries by the Austrian energy drink company. However, there are many similarities between the two instruments: It is crucial that both utilize the event as communication platform to get in touch with the same target group(s), while similar objectives are being pursued. If both

---

59   Bruhn, *Sponsoring*; Jan Drengner and Julia Köhler, "Stand und Perspektiven der Event-forschung aus Sicht des Marketing," in *Events und Sport*, ed. Cornelia Zanger (Wiesbaden: Springer Fachmedien Wiesbaden, 2013), 89–132, https://doi.org/10.1007/978-3-658-03681-2_5; Drengner, *Imagewirkungen von Eventmarketing*.

60   Frank Sistenich, *Eventmarketing Ein innovatives Instrument zur Metakommunikation in Unternehmen* (Berlin, 1999), 61, https://doi.org/10.1007/978-3-663-08486-0.

61   Nufer, *Wirkungen von Event-Marketing Theoretische Fundierung und empirische Analyse*, 28f.

approaches are being looked at differently, it is important considering that both communication tools may be used at the same event.[62]

Sponsorship within Corporate Communication

In today's well saturated markets which are characterized by purchasing restraint, any forms of marketing communication play an important role by distinguishing a company's product or service from those of its competitors, arousing the interest of target groups in these services, persuading consumers to make a purchase and, building on this, developing long-term relationships with customers. Event Sponsorship is an established communication instrument that providers use to achieve these communication goals.[63]

The sponsorship commitment of companies has changed fundamentally in the past. While for a long time it was mainly the negative attitude towards sporting, cultural and social organizations, associations, and individuals as well as restrictive legal frameworks that stood in the way of a positive development of sponsorship, since the mid-1980s sponsorship has developed into a central communication instrument.

Analyses of 2010 sponsorship expenditure show that even in times of financial crises and tight budgets many companies continue to rely on communication instruments such as sponsorship.[64] Comparing the data of IEG Sponsorship Reports between 2010 and 2019, two aspects become apparent: First, spending on sponsorship measures across various forms of event sponsorship is steadily increasing worldwide. Second, music sponsorship in general as well as music festival sponsorship numbers have a similar development.[65] While $ 46.3 billion was spent on corresponding activities worldwide in 2010 for instance, the 2011 number already grew to $ 48.6 billion. A steady

---

62   Kerstin Weihe, *Erlebens- und Einstellungswirkungen von Marketing-Events: eine Analyse unter Berücksichtigung der Besonderheiten des Event-Marketing und Event-Sponsoring*, 1. Aufl. (Göttingen: Cuvillier, 2008).

63   Drengner and Jahn, "Erlebniswelten im Sponsoring."

64   Arnold Hermanns, "Corporate Social Responsibility Und Sponsoring Im Fokus Sponsoring Trends 2010" (München, 2011), https://www.vibss.de/fileadmin/Medienablage/Mar keting/Sponsoring/Studie_Sponsoring-Trends-2010.pdf.

65   IEG, "Music Sponsorship 2018," Annual Report (IEG, 2019), https://www.sponsorsh ip.com/Latest-Thinking/Sponsorship-Infographics/Music-Sponsorship-2018--$1-61- Billion.aspx; IEG, "Fair And Festival Sponsorship Spending," 2017, https://www.sponsor

average growth rate of around 4-5 % p.a. between 2010 and 2019 can be stated as accurate.

In Germany, more than two thirds of the companies in 2010 also state that they use (event) sponsorship as part of their communication policy with the use of sponsorship activities in the area of sports is dominating nationally and internationally.[66]

The starting point for today's known event sponsorship was made the 1960s with a phase of *surreptitious advertising*. This form of the transmission of advertising messages under exclusion of an appropriate permission, which is to be found in particular at sporting events and broadcasts as well as feature films, is characterized by the fact that the actual advertising is not really immediately recognized as the purpose of achieving a communicative effect.[67]

The subsequent 1970s were marked by the emergence of a phase of sports advertising. During this period, sports were initially only tentatively included in corporate advertising and promotion measures, for instance in the form of panel and jersey advertising. However, pure panel-board advertising should not be confused with sponsorship, since booking a panelboard at an event is identical with renting an advertising medium and the underlying idea of support is missing.[68]

Professional sponsorship as a separate term has only been used since the 1980s. During this time, companies, especially in the sports sector, began to plan their involvement systematically and integrated selected sponsorships into their marketing and corporate communications, which means that this period is considered a phase of sports sponsorship.[69]

At the beginning of the 1990s, companies also began to develop new areas of advertising and promotion outside sports as well. Companies were increasingly aiming to convey a sense of social responsibility through their social and ecological commitment and thus generate image benefits. Especially areas of culture, social and environmental affairs gained in importance, so that this

ship.com/Latest-Thinking/Sponsorship-Infographics/Fair-And-Festival-Sponsorship-Sp ending-To-Tota--1-.aspx.

66   Hermanns, "Corporate Social Responsibility Und Sponsoring Im Fokus Sponsoring Trends 2010."

67   Sandler et al., *Olympic Sponsorship Vs. "Ambush" Marketing: Who Gets the Gold?*

68   Philip Gross, *Growing Brands Through Sponsorship* (Wiesbaden: Springer Fachmedien Wiesbaden, 2015), https://doi.org/10.1007/978-3-658-07250-6.

69   Carmen Hafner, "Sozialsponsoring als Benefit für beide Seiten?," 2009, https://doi.org/ 10.25365/THESIS.3751; Bruhn, *Sponsoring*.

time span was thus characterized by a phase of cultural, social, and environmental sponsorship.[70] During the beginning of the support in these three areas, however, companies understood sponsorship more as a sort of patronage, i.e., it was carried out primarily for altruistic or selfless motives and was rarely associated with a specific consideration from the sponsored.

Since the mid-1990s, companies have been increasingly active in the presentation of television and radio programs, so that this period has long been referred to as a phase of program sponsorship. The basis for this were expanded legal options to act as a sponsor in the context of audiovisual programs. In the meantime, however, sponsorship has also become widespread in other media, such as print and the Internet, so that the term media sponsorship better describes the form from the mid-1990s onwards.[71] Digital/Internet sponsorship is often also presented as an independent form. Whereas in the 2000s, companies and the *Interactive Advertising Bureau (IAB)* still predicted the greatest growth potential for this new form of sponsorship. However, this euphoria had subsided a year later, and the growth forecasts have been relativized over time.[72]

The phase of integrative event sponsorship developed in the 2000s as well and will continue to gain in importance in the future.[73] The increasing volume of sponsorship, coupled with stagnating investments in other tools of communication, means that the budget for sponsorship is covering an ever-greater proportion of the total corporate communications budget. Accordingly, 18.3 % of the communications budget of German companies was spent on sponsorship in 2016, whereas it was 12.4 % in 2013.[74] Reasons for the increasing use of sponsorship activities in recent years are changed social framework conditions, new value trends such as an increasing focus on leisure, experience and enjoyment or striving for individuality and self-ful-

70   Bruhn, *Sponsoring*; Helmut Zollinger, "Thesen und Trends im Sponsoring" (St. Gallen: Tomczak, T./Miiller, F./ Miiller, R., 1995), 118–24.

71   Gross, *Growing Brands Through Sponsorship.*

72   Pilot Checkpoint, "SPONSORS: Sponsor Visions 2010" (Hamburg, 2010).

73   Gross, *Growing Brands Through Sponsorship*; Gwinner, Larson, and Swanson, "Image Transfer in Corporate Event Sponsorship: Assessing the Impact of Team Identification and Event-Sponsor Fit."

74   Ostfalia, "Sponsoring Trends 2016," 2017, https://de.statista.com/statistik/daten/studie /302340/umfrage/anteil-des-kommunikationsbudget-von-unternehmen/.

fillment.[75] Leisure time is becoming increasingly important in people's lives[76] and thus opens up interesting potential for addressing target groups in appropriate environments, e.g. through event sponsorship.[77] In addition, changing markets have influenced the development of sponsorship. In many cases, the constantly growing supply of goods contrasts with insufficient demand development, especially in developed countries. The consequence are saturated markets and increasing competitive pressure. Nowadays it seems rather difficult to differentiate products from their competition, based on product-related quality advantages in many industries,[78] thus the importance of well thought and successful market communication is increasing.[79] The intention is to provide consumers with worlds of experience in order to gain brand advantages. The triggering of perceptions and impressions perceived as special, intensive, and pleasant is the main goal of experience-oriented marketing such as modern sponsorship. For this purpose, instruments are particularly suitable that are able to establish direct contact with customers and have great potential to offer consumers extraordinary experiences.[80]

A further advantage of sponsorship within corporate communication is that, compared to typical advertising, it generally enjoys greater acceptance among the population.[81] Sponsorship is predominantly seen as positive and sensible, as the sponsorship commitment is assessed to generate benefits for society. Event visitors are aware that the organization of an event is only made possible by the participation of sponsors.[82] Nevertheless, consumers know that companies do not pursue altruistic motives alone, but that economic objectives are behind the sponsorship decision. It can be assumed that event

---

75   Nufer, *Wirkungen von Event-Marketing Theoretische Fundierung und empirische Analyse.*

76   Drengner and Köhler, "Stand und Perspektiven der Eventforschung aus Sicht des Marketing."

77   Meenaghan, "Commercial Sponsorship."

78   Kirsten Marei Fehring, *Kultursponsoring—Bindeglied zwischen Kunst und Wirtschaft? eine interdisziplinäre und praxisorientierte Analyse*, 1. Aufl., Rombach Wissenschaften Reihe Cultura 3 (Freiburg im Breisgau: Rombach, 1998).

79   Drengner and Jahn, "Erlebniswelten im Sponsoring."

80   Gwinner, Larson, and Swanson, "Image Transfer in Corporate Event Sponsorship: Assessing the Impact of Team Identification and Event-Sponsor Fit."

81   Meenaghan, "Commercial Sponsorship."

82   Hermanns, "Corporate Social Responsibility Und Sponsoring Im Fokus Sponsoring Trends 2010."

participants can realistically judge that companies pursue both general interest and selfish motives. Nevertheless, sponsorship measures are perceived as necessary and not very disturbing.[83]

Music Festival Sponsorship

When dealing with sponsorship in the music business, the music activities of artist(s) as well as the festival experience represent the means for the sponsor's communication message. The sponsor wants to use the popularity of the artist(s) or the respective event to transfer or link the (positive) image of the artist or event to his brand or his company.[84] According to Anderton, this special relationship between the two stakeholder groups have played a significant role in making the astonishing growth of the music festival sector in the UK possible over the past 20 years.[85] Sponsorship of a music festival provides the organizers with a degree of financial security in a high-risk and highly volatile market and, for example, secures the appearance of expensive headlining acts so that tickets for the event can go on sale. McKay also agrees with these considerations and illustrates this by (UK) negative examples of sponsors bailing out and thus burying the individual festivals.[86]

Music festival sponsorship is part of arts and culture sponsorship and has in contrast to English speaking (research) literature rarely been of specific interest in German research literature. This stands well in contrast to the general popularity of music festivals among the German society. According to Tschmuck, sponsorship is contextualized in the so-called secondary music market within his definition regarding the economics of music. In addition to the music publishing market, the phonographic market, and the music event business, music also plays an essential role in these mentioned secondary markets. Music is an integral part of radio and television programs,

83   Bruhn, *Sponsoring*.
84   Detlef Heinrich, "Musik-Sponsoring als Wettbewerbsinstrument," *der markt* 29, no. 2 (June 1, 1990): 59–61, https://doi.org/10.1007/BF03031807.
85   Anderton, "Branding, Sponsorship and the Music Festival."
86   McKay, *The pop festival*.

TV and feature films, e-gaming, and advertising. The primary music markets are linked to these secondary markets via license agreements.[87]

The economy has recognized the high purchasing power of younger people who build the *big chunk* of today's music festival audience and that it is an advantage to attract (and link) young buyers to a brand at an early stage in life. The target group of young adults can be reached very well through music sponsorship and an unusually high spread factor can be achieved through media coverage of these events according to Bruhn.[88] Thus, music sponsorship has become the normality within today's music event business, funded by many brands. There is no major concert tour or festival that is not financially supported by a potent sponsor.[89]

To understand the music and festival sponsorship business and its underlying characteristics, one must look at the biggest player in the live event business: the American corporation *Live Nation* which is based in Beverly Hill, California.

In 2016 *Live Nation* stated in their annual report to develop additional ancillary revenue streams by acquisitions and other activities around the ticket purchase. This reveals the structural change within the music event business very clearly. Focusing less on the obvious way how money has been made to other revenue sources such as catering, merchandising and sponsorship.

Sponsorship being the smallest business unit in terms of sales, but the most powerful in profit due to very high margins made sure *Live Nation* stayed profitable in 2016[90] *Live Nation* is only able to afford organizing concerts, festivals, and non-music events because this business segment is being cross subsidized by ticketing, sponsorship, and advertising income.

CTS Eventim, the second biggest company in this branch and the major player in Europe, is acting in a similar way and clustered its sponsorship offerings that were previously managed decentral in a new founded business unit.[91]

---

87   Peter Tschmuck, *Ökonomie der Musikwirtschaft*, Musikwirtschafts- und Musikkultur-forschung (Wiesbaden: Springer Fachmedien Wiesbaden, 2020), https://doi.org/10.1 007/978-3-658-29295-9.

88   Bruhn, *Sponsoring*.

89   Anderton, *Music Festivals in the UK*.

90   Live Nation, "Annual Report 2016," 2017, https://investors.livenationentertainment.com /sec-filings/annual-reports.

91   CTS Eventim, "Geschäftsbericht 2018," Geschäftsbericht, 2019.

This is the core of the event giants' business model. Artists are offered very generous conditions for organizing and handling concert tours and festivals which then create market barriers for smaller music organizers and seal off their own market. The losses accepted are then more than compensated by sponsorship and advertising income. In addition to the aforementioned benefits for the organizing institutions behind the events, music festival sponsorship also offers many advantages for the sponsoring brands or companies.

A sponsorship package usually includes a marketing campaign, online presence, on-site as well as off-site sponsorship rights, post-event coverage, hospitality, and additional options, such as use of video walls, depending on on-site availability or options for guerilla marketing. Not only is the target group reached, but at the same time an ideal environment for product or brand presentation is created. The attendee, on the other hand, perceives the communication mix as part of the festival and is much more open to new impressions during this time, as he is in an exceptional situation. At a festival, everyday life is completely forgotten, and the focus is on friends, leisure, and fun.[92]

---

92   Jennifer Rowley and Catrin Williams, "The Impact of Brand Sponsorship of Music Festivals," *Marketing Intelligence & Planning* 26, no. 7 (October 24, 2008): 781–92, https://doi.org/10.1108/02634500810916717.

Theoretical Perspective Four: Reality Model(s) and Cultural Program(s)

In this chapter, the dissertation's fourth theoretical perspective is outlined. It explores literature surrounding different concepts, perceptions, and definitions of the term *culture* within interdisciplinary boundaries to build a theoretical foundation for the research project. Due to this interdisciplinary theme of this work, this is being done from both, an economic as well as from an arts and humanities standpoint. The goal should be, to equip the theoretical structure of this work with one fitting concept of the term *culture* which is applicable for the dissertation's intent. The reason for this lies in the junction of results as this dissertation encloses three separate studies investigating sponsorship culture within the German university popular music festival market and incorporating three stakeholder groups of sponsors, organizer, and audience.

As this work has been written in the English language by an author whose native language is German, before diving into this chapter dealing with different (broad) culture definitions, this is the point where the differences between the English term cultural studies and the German term *Kulturwissenschaften* needs to be pointed out to avoid linguistic complications in the ongoing text.

The German term *Kulturwissenschaften* denotes two things: On the one hand, it holds a material purpose and stands for the exploration of social meaning, how it is produced, passed on and transformed through interactions—especially in media-mediated form. Understood in this way, *Kulturwissenschaften* are the sciences of individual cultural phenomena and areas (image, literature, media, art, memory, gender studies, the history and theory of science, etc.). Thus, the material definition (translated from the German language by the author) states:

"'Kulturwissenschaften' researches the institutions created by man-kind and in particular the interpersonal, medially conveyed forms of action and conflict as well as their value and norm horizons. It develops theories of culture(s) and material fields of work that are *systematically and historically examined*."[1]

On the other hand, the term *Kulturwissenschaften* is reflexively determined and describes a transdisciplinary project that consists in using both humanities and social science disciplines to work on common and socially relevant questions at the same time. Thus, the reflective determination (translated from the German language by the author) states:

"'Kulturwissenschaften' form the meta-level of reflection(s), a control level for the modernization of the humanities and functions like a kind of moderation of the multi-perspective networking of individual results from disciplines that would normally not fit together easily."[2]

Cultural studies, however, are not to be equated with the above circumscribed (German) definition(s) of the (German) term Kulturwissenschaften. Cultural studies have been examining culture(s) as practice(s) since its inception. As the most influential figure in cultural studies, Stuart Hall does not limit cultural theory to analyze the role and function of culture, but rather how power relations are created in the cultural sphere and dominance is maintained as well as challenged.[3] They do not only neglect to equate culture with high culture, but also their declared goal is to research all cultural practices in their relation to social and historical structures. Unlike ethnology, they emerged in the context of modern industrial societies. Therefore, they have also developed their own concept of ethnography. Under changed social conditions, cultural studies rearticulate methods and theories in order to gain new perspectives in

---

1   Hartmut Böhme, Peter Matussek, and Lothar Müller, *Orientierung Kulturwissenschaft: was sie kann, was sie will*, Orig.-Ausg., 3. Aufl., Rororo Rowohlts Enzyklopädie 55608 (Reinbek bei Hamburg: Rowohlt-Taschenbuch-Verl, 2007), 104.

2   Markus Fauser, *Einführung in die Kulturwissenschaft*, 4., durchges. und aktualisierte Aufl., Einführungen Germanistik (Darmstadt: Wiss. Buchges., 2008), 9; Siegfried J. Schmidt, *Unternehmenskultur: Die Grundlage für den wirtschaftlichen Erfolg von Unternehmen*, 6. Aufl. (Weilerswist: Velbrück Wiss, 2014).

3   Rainer Winter, "Stuart Hall: Die Erfindung Der Cultural Studies," in *Kultur. Theorien Der Gegenwart*, ed. Stephan Moebius and Dirk Quadflieg (Wiesbaden: VS Verlag für Sozialwissenschaften, 2006), 381–93, https://doi.org/10.1007/978-3-531-90017-9_30.

the analysis of social problems.[4] This section aims at finding an appropriate more dimensional concept of culture for the following scientific investigation, cultural studies will be named as such whereas Kulturwissenschaften will be translated as arts and humanities.

Culture as Interdisciplinary Contact Point

As well as the term *communication*, the term *culture* is a particularly treacherous term, because it is used both in the everyday language of the bourgeoisie, in politics and beyond in a variety of scientific disciplines.[5]

During the 19th and the 20th century a still obvious gap between two *research cultures* developed: the *sciences* and the *humanities*. This constellation of disciplines regarding scientific organization is more and more being challenged and questioned. This results in a variety of complications that are being discussed within the research community under the keyword of inter- and transdisciplinarity. For a long time, economists—among them the followers of New Economic History—could hardly deal with representatives of the cultural studies (as well as the arts and humanities) and vice versa. However, this rejection on both sides has been slowly changing since the 1970s.[6]

In his works published during the 1970s and 1980s, North combined, in the spirit of New Institutional Economics, the theory of relative pricing of neoclassic with the assumption that exchanging economies do not automatically tend to welfare-optimal states with regard to transaction costs, considering institutions as *filters* between economic subjects and the stock of capital on the one hand and the stock of capital and the performance of the economy on the other.[7] In this context, North shared Marx's view that, given the tendency toward stable institutional arrangements, developmental dynamic

---

4   Christoph Jacke, *Medien(sub)kultur: Geschichten, Diskurse, Entwürfe*, Cultural studies, Bd. 9 (Bielefeld: transcript Verlag, 2004), (Foreword by Rainer Winter).

5   Schmidt, *Unternehmenskultur*.

6   Friedrich Jaeger and Burkhard Liebsch, eds., *Handbuch der Kulturwissenschaften: Grundlagen und Schlüsselbegriffe* (Stuttgart: J.B. Metzler, 2011), https://doi.org/10.1007/978-3-4 76-00468-0.

7   Douglass C. North, *Institutions, Institutional Change, and Economic Performance*, The Political Economy of Institutions and Decisions (Cambridge; New York: Cambridge University Press, 1990).

mostly evolves primarily within the production sphere, with the accumulation of knowledge and skills function as a dynamizing factor.[8]

Legal norms, customary law, rules of conduct, culture-specific attitudes, signals and codes, cultural and social capital, all of this can now be examined to determine whether and to what extent it determines people's social relationships. Comparative studies are popular, in which a large number of cases are examined as to whether and to what extent certain rules and sets of rules influence the economic performance of a society. Systematic contexts of meaning are made up of rules that can basically be analyzed from a microeconomic perspective, but at least in parts, rules are mostly of an implicit nature so that neither the stakeholders themselves nor their observers are able to overlook them in their entirety. The analysis of phenomena in one's own culture is mainly unproblematic because the researcher can naturally interpret his observations in the same context as the stakeholders he is observing. Misinterpretations occur as soon as the stakeholders take a different context for their actions into account than the researcher.[9]

In contrast to other research projects which exist in the thematic spheres of event management, event studies or event marketing, this approach tries to take an interdisciplinary look at things. The culture of sponsorship with all its actants and all their different perspectives on the matter, with all they do and how they act, know, and deduce from gained knowledge and experiences can be understood as located at this intersection of the scientific disciplines and needs to be comprehended as such.

Culture from the Perspective of Economics

In most economic literature that deals with a certain concept or insertion of culture as a term in some sense, one finds mostly an incorporation of culture, that is embedded in either corporate- or organizational-culture. In this context, the utilized term *culture* originally is evolved from the social anthropology sciences:

---

8   Gertraude Mikl-Horke, Reinhard Pirker, and Andreas Resch, *Theorie der Firma: Interdisziplinär* (Wiesbaden: VS Verlag für Sozialwissenschaften, 2011), https://doi.org/10.1007/978-3-531-93257-6.

9   Gerold Blümle, ed., *Perspektiven einer kulturellen Ökonomik*, Kulturelle Ökonomik, Bd. 1 (Münster: Lit, 2004); Siegfried J. Schmidt, *Kulturbeschreibung—Beschreibungskultur: Umrisse einer Prozess-orientierten Kulturtheorie*, 1. Auflage (Weilerswist: Velbrück Wissenschaft, 2014).

After early studies of primitive societies in the south sea, Africa, native America revealed vastly different ways of life when comparing them to the technological influenced European or partly American societies. These societies also were different among themselves. Thus, the concept of culture was here first utilized to broadly describe the package of qualities of any specific human group passed on from generation to generation.[10]

The catalyst for this research was U.S. companies studying Japanese companies who were prosperous and successful.[11][12][13] Scholars began to examine organizational culture to help leaders and managers better make sense of organizational characteristics in order to manage both orderliness and chaos, and to improve organizational effectiveness, performance, and change within the workplace.[14] Yet with this extensive research, debate was stimulated as to how defining culture best as well as organizational culture, its dimensions, and origin.

According to Roland, economists define culture in their research as

"The set of values and beliefs—people in a given community—have about how the world (both nature and society) works as well as the norms of behavior derived from that set of values. Beliefs relate to expectations about natural phenomena and people's behavior or reactions to other peoples' behavior. Values are about what gives meaning to someone's life and about what is considered important in (their) life."[15]

Roland's definitional summary of culture may be seen as quite understandable because it comprises the advantage of culture to be consistent with empirical measures of culture that are now increasingly available at the international or regional level.

---

10   John P Kotter, *Corporate Culture and Performance* (New York: Free Press, 2014), http://www.myilibrary.com?id=899109.

11   William G. Ouchi, *Theory Z: How American Business Can Meet the Japanese Challenge*, Avon Business (New York: Avon Books, 1993).

12   Richard Tanner Pascale and Anthony G. Athos, *The Art of Japanese Management: Applications for American Executives* (New York: Warner, 1982).

13   Thomas J. Peters and Robert H. Waterman, *In Search of Excellence: Lessons from America's Best-Run Companies* (London: HarperCollinsBusiness, 1995).

14   Harrison Miller Trice and Janice M. Beyer, *The Cultures of Work Organizations* (Englewood Cliffs, N.J: Prentice Hall, 1993).

15   Gérard Roland, "Economics and Culture," in *Emerging Trends in the Social and Behavioral Sciences* (New York, 2015), 1, https://doi.org/10.1002/9781118900772.etrds0091.

How the influence of culture on the economy is conceptualized is closely related to the understanding of the relationship between the economy and society. The economy can be seen as an integral part of society, which can hardly be separated from it analytically. This view is often taken especially for premodern societies.[16] However, many authors assume that during modernization there has been a functional differentiation of the economy from society.[17] Furthermore, the economy can be viewed as an independent sub-area of society.[18] This leads to the question of how strongly and in what way this sub-area is differentiated as a subsystem. Because with the analytical separation nothing more is said about the relationship between economics and society. The (empirical) question(s) therefore arise(s) as to how strong the society's influence or the other social sub-areas is on this differentiated economic area.

Corporate Culture

"An organization is a machine consisting of two major parts: culture and people. Each influences the other, because the people who make up an organization, determine the kind of culture it has, and the culture of the organization determines the kinds of people that fit in."[19]

Processes regulate the *what* in a company. What should be done, who is involved, what different stages exist within a process? All these questions are good and correct, but completely useless for cultivating or improving corporate culture. For this, companies need the *how* questions. Questions regarding the *how*, are the main drivers of cultural development within the enterprise. How does a company want to lead? How does cooperation look like? How

16   Pierre Bourdieu, *Forms of Capital*, General Sociology, Volume 3 (Cambridge: Polity Press, 2021).

17   Michael Hölscher, *Wirtschaftskulturen in der erweiterten EU: die Einstellungen der Bürgerinnen und Bürger im europäischen Vergleich*, 1. Aufl. (Wiesbaden: VS Verlag für Sozialwissenschaften, 2006).

18   Niklas Luhmann, *Die Wirtschaft der Gesellschaft*, 1. Aufl. [Nachdr.], Theorie der Gesellschaft, Niklas Luhmann[...] (Frankfurt am Main: Suhrkamp, 2008).

19   Ray Dalio, *Principles* (New York: Simon & Schuster, 2017), 64.

should a company look like in five years? If a process is the path that should lead to a destination, culture is the means of transport to choose from.[20]

Until the 1980s, the phenomenon of corporate culture had been more or less ignored by the sciences of business and economics.[21] Culture has been considered at the level of society[22], but hardly looked at in relation to an enterprise. Instead, one has searched for culture-free models.[23] Culture was merely a contextual factor influencing the company from the outside.[24]

It was not until the early 1980s that the subject reached a certain popularity within the scientific debate after the term *corporate culture* had briefly been mentioned in the 1950s.[25] Starting with Pondy and Mitroff[26], numerous scientists in the 70s dealt conceptually with the topic and transferred the concept of culture from society to business.[27]

The popularity of corporate culture in research literature has mainly been triggered by publications of popular American management books.[28] Two of them received particular attention: Peters and Waterman[29], for the first time, identified *soft factors* as the source for achieving a high level of excellence. Deal and Kennedy went even further placing corporate culture as the key factor for success at the heart of strategic business management.[30] However, popular science contributions have largely ignored differences in corporate culture.[31]

---

20   Schmidt, *Unternehmenskultur*; Peter Dill, *Unternehmenskultur: Grundlagen und Anknüpfungspunkte für ein Kulturmanagement*, Schriften zur Kommunikationsarbeit (Bonn: BDW-Service-u.-Verl.-Ges. Kommunikation, 1987).

21   Michael Kutschker and Stefan Schmid, *Internationales Management: mit 100 Textboxen*, 7., überarb. und aktualisierte Aufl. (München: Oldenbourg, 2011).

22   Dill, *Unternehmenskultur*.

23   Kutschker and Schmid, *Internationales Management*.

24   Dill, *Unternehmenskultur*.

25   J. F. Clark and A. Clark, "The Changing Culture of a Factory," *Mental Health* 11 (1951): 39–40.

26   Pondy, L.R and Mitroff, J.J., "Beyond Open System Models of Organization," *Research in Organizational Behavior* 1 (1979): 3–39.

27   Dill, *Unternehmenskultur*.

28   Maximilian Gontard, *Unternehmenskultur und Organisationsklima: Eine empirische Untersuchung*, Profession 36 (München: Hampp, 2002).

29   Peters and Waterman, *In Search of Excellence*.

30   Terrence E. Deal and Allan A. Kennedy, *Corporate Cultures: The Rites and Rituals of Corporate Life*, reissued (Cambridge: Perseus Publ, 2000).

31   C Ochsenbauer and B Klofat, "Überlegungen zur paradigmatischen Dimension der Unternehmenskulturdiskussion in der Betriebswirtschaftslehre," in *Unternehmenskul-*

In particular in Germany, Bleicher[32], Matenaar[33], Ebers[34] and Heinen[35] were the pioneers of the scientific debate. Following from this, since the 1980s, a new paradigm in management research is being discussed.[36] It should be noted that the need for complementing the fact-rational aspects of corporate governance with socio-emotional factors has been recognized. In addition to the explanations that conceptually deal with corporate culture and its significance, the success of corporate culture has also been empirically proven in numerous studies.[37] Pümpin summarizes:

"The corporate culture influences the productivity of the company and thus the company's success in the most decisive way".[38]

To this day, corporate culture is receiving a great deal of attention, not only in business administration sciences but also within other disciplines.[39] This is mainly the case for cultural anthropology, psychology, and sociology.[40] There

tur—Perspektiven für Wissenschaft und Praxis (München: Heinen, E./Fank, M., 1997), 76–106.

32   Konrad Bleicher, "Organisationskulturen Und Führungsphilosophien Im Wettbewerb," Zfbf, no. 35 (1983): 135–46.

33   Dieter Matenaar, Organisationskultur und organisatorische Gestaltung: die Gestaltungsrelevanz der Kultur des Organisationssystems der Unternehmung, Betriebswirtschaftliche Forschungsergebnisse, Bd. 85 (Berlin: Duncker & Humblot, 1983).

34   Mark Ebers, Organisationskultur: Ein neues Forschungsprogramm?, 1985, http://link.spring er.com/openurl?genre=book&isbn=978-3-409-13105-6.

35   Edmund Heinen, "Entscheidungsorientierte Betriebswirtschaftslehre und Unternehmenskultur," ZfB, no. 55 (1985): 980–91.

36   Charles Lattmann, Die Unternehmenskultur: Ihre Grundlagen und ihre Bedeutung für die Führung der Unternehmung (Berlin, 1990), http://link.springer.com/openurl?genre=book &isbn=978-3-7908-0465-2.

37   Edmund Heinen, "Unternehmenskultur als Gegenstand der Betriebswirtschaftslehre," in Unternehmenskultur—Perspektiven für Wissenschaft und Praxis, 2nd ed. (München: Heinen, E./Fank, M., 1997), 1–48.

38   C Pümpin, "Unternehmenskultur, Unternehmensstrategie und Unternehmenserfolg," GDI Impuls, 2, 1984, 2.

39   Schmidt, Unternehmenskultur.

40   Reiner Franzpötter, Organisationskultur: Begriffsverständnis und Analyse aus interpretativsoziologischer Sicht, 1. Aufl., Nomos Universitätsschriften, Bd. 4 (Baden-Baden: Nomos, 1997); Gontard, Unternehmenskultur und Organisationsklima; Bettina Beer and Hans Fischer, eds., Ethnologie: Einführung und Überblick, 6., überarb. Aufl., Ethnologische Paperbacks (Berlin: Reimer, 2006).

are numerous reasons for the strong consideration of the corporate culture issue: Flexibility within organizations and thus weakening the necessity to a specific workplace should be compensated by corporate culture.

Instead of materialistic motivation for workers, more and more motivation occurs through corresponding culture within the enterprise. In the sociological branch of organizational theory, it is stated that quantitative investigation methods and functionalistic mindsets cannot sufficiently explain the complex organizational processes. Furthermore, the surprising success of Japanese management methods in the 1980s underlined the cultural governance of companies.

The intensive discussion of corporate culture has not led to a consistent result yet: For instance, there is no consensus on the definition of corporate culture[41] and there are hardly any systematic, scientifically precise derivations of the term.[42] Rather, numerous schools have formed that take on different perspectives[43], which then, in every case depends on what is enfolded by corporate culture.

Culture from the Perspective of Arts and Humanities

In arts and humanities literature, a great variety of terms, their definitions and boundaries exist. To begin carving out a fitting culture definition for this dissertation, a glimpse on Reckwitz[44] is made, who discusses the cultural-scientific interpretation of culture based on various cultural terms and theories and the concept of a *cultural-scientific research program*.

The *normative* (i.e., evaluative, and prescriptive) concept of culture is based on an evaluative juxtaposition or distinction of certain aesthetic phenomena, objects and practices that are highly valued within a society and preserved throughout the forming of tradition. This also means that a discussion about what constitutes culture is only recognized if it moves on the terrain of this

---

41   Ebers, *Organisationskultur*; G. Hofstede et al., "Measuring Organizational Cultures: A Qualitative and Quantitative Study across Twenty Cases.," *Administrative Science Quarterly* 35 (1990): 286–316.

42   U Brinkmann, "'Shared values' oder 'shareholder value'?—Die Untauglichkeit der 'Unternehmenskultur' als Integrationstechnik," *sofid Industrie- und Betriebssoziologie*, no. 2 (2006): 11–34.

43   Heinen, "Unternehmenskultur als Gegenstand der Betriebswirtschaftslehre."

44   Andreas Reckwitz, *Unscharfe Grenzen: Perspektiven der Kultursoziologie*, 2., unveränd. Aufl., Sozialtheorie (Bielefeld: transcript Verlag, 2010).

same concept of culture and also accepts its premises. A restrictive and normative definition of the term limits it to an excessive *high culture*, i.e., a canon of aesthetic works and great artists, while marginalizing the everyday mass and popular cultures. Characteristic of the development of the modern concept of culture is the overcoming of a narrow, normative understanding of culture as *high culture* or *high literature*, which developed in the 19th century linked to German idealism within the bourgeoisie, by a broad, value-neutral culture concept, which includes high culture and folk culture.[45]

The *totality-oriented* concept of culture extends the complexity of the term culture by contextualization and historization. It tries to understand human communities depending on the conditions surrounding them. The analysis of the culture's character includes

"everything that people have created independently and that goes beyond nature"[46].

This holistic and contextualistic perspective allows it to use the term culture in a plural sense and thus, to compare cultures with each other. This results in a tendency to draw boundaries between cultures, whose certain way of life is homogeneous on the inside and closed like a ball or globe on the outside compared to other different globes. Tylor[47] established the theoretical principles of Victorian anthropology by adapting evolutionary theory to the study of human society. Written at the same time as Arnold's "Culture and Anarchy"[48], Tylor defined culture in very different terms:

"Culture or civilization, taken in its wide ethnographic sense, is that complex whole, which includes knowledge, belief, art, morals, law, custom, and any other capabilities and habits acquired by man as a member of society".[49]

---

45   Ansgar Nünning and Vera Nünning, eds., *Einführung in die Kulturwissenschaften: theoretische Grundlagen—Ansätze—Perspektiven* (Stuttgart Weimar: Verlag J. B. Metzler, 2008), 21.

46   Reckwitz, *Unscharfe Grenzen*.

47   Edward Burnett Tylor, *Primitive Culture: Researches into the Development of Mythology, Philosophy, Religion, Art, and Custom*, Repr, Cambridge Library Collection Anthropology (Cambridge: Cambridge Univ. Press, 2010).

48   Matthew Arnold and Jane Garnett, *Culture and Anarchy*, Oxford World's Classics (Oxford; New York: Oxford University Press, 2006).

49   Tylor, *Primitive Culture*, 1.

Here, culture refers to the learned attributes of society, something we already have obtained. Arnold's theory focused on the learned qualities that we should have obtained instead, which he prescribed as a way to improve the existing society.

According to such a non-normative, holistic understanding, which anthropology, ethnology, and folklore, still use for their purposes today, the term culture means the epitome of all collectively spread forms of belief, knowledge, and lifeform that people have acquired during the course of socialization and that makes a society different from others.

While the Anglo-American cultural studies primarily deal with phenomena of everyday and popular culture, the interest of European arts and humanities is equally focused on high- and popular culture. The relevance of everyday culture is above all that e.g., celebrations, festivities and other rituals that make a significant contribution to portray, visualize, pass on and renew the cultural values and norms of a society.[50]

The concept of cultural differentiation was influential for the sociology of culture in the 20th century but has little impact on cultural theories after the cultural turn and their understanding of cultural differences. In the differentiation-theoretical concept of culture, culture is understood as a functional subsystem of society, as a trustee system, which is institutionalized especially in arts and education, and which has the task of handing down and developing new interpretations of the world.

However, examples from divergent theoretical approaches would be the concept of the living environment by Habermas[51] or Parson's cultural system[52]. The subsystem of culture differs from other subsystems, such as those of law, politics, or economics, by a specific intrinsic value, for example by its own code, by a specific medium (in Parsons: the medium of value) or through a genuine form of rationality (in Habermas: practical rationality).

The universal pattern of the cultural conceptions made here shows, that culture is no longer primarily observed in its difference(s) to other cultures,

---

50   Ansgar Nünning, "Vielfalt der Kulturbegriffe—Dossier Kulturelle Bildung," bpb.de, 2009, https://www.bpb.de/gesellschaft/bildung/kulturelle-bildung/59917/kulturbegriff e.

51   Jürgen Habermas and Jürgen Habermas, *Zur Kritik der funktionalistischen Vernunft*, 4., durchges. Aufl., 24,5.-27,5. Tsd, Theorie des kommunikativen Handelns, Jürgen Habermas ; Bd. 2 (Frankfurt am Main: Suhrkamp, 1987).

52   Talcott Parsons, *Structure and Process in Modern Societies*. (Glencoe, Ill.: Free Press, 1960).

but rather being addressed in its social constitution as a complex of specific social communications as well as practices. In contrast to the normative and totality-oriented approaches to culture, the theory of concept of cultural differentiation has proven to be highly connectable for big parts of social
sciences. According to Reckwitz, however, it seems problematic that culture
(translated from the German language by the author)

> "is reduced to a certain field of action instead of as a social-theoretical cate-
> gory that points to the necessary symbolic conditions for every action".[53]

This appears is a different way in the meaning/knowledge-driven concept of
culture, which leads one step closer to the approach of this work:

The meaning/knowledge-driven concept of culture stands for a totaliza-
tion of culture. It is this meaning, knowledge and symbol-oriented understanding of culture that ultimately provides the foundation for the modern
cultural theories of recent decades. The meaning/knowledge-driven concept
of culture implies a theoretical argument: that human behavioral complexes
arise against the background of symbolic orders, of specific forms of world interpretation, are reproduced by sense systems and cultural codes.[54] The theoretical background for the meaning-oriented understanding of culture in
modern cultural theories can mainly be found in a series of social philoso-
phies of the first half of the 20th century, which, in their intensive themati-
zation of language, signs, knowledge and symbols, provided the impetus for
the change of perspective of the cultural turn in the humanities and social
sciences in the 1960s. They all provide the foundation for the sociological cultural theories that claim to explain and understand social order and human
action through recourse to symbolic orders.

In this alternative claim to explain and describe behavior via symbolic-
cognitive orders, cultural theories differ fundamentally from other social theories, especially from non-meaning-oriented social theories, from the model
of the interest-led homo economicus and from the model of the expectation-
oriented homo sociologicus. Cultural theories differ above all in this respect
of their localization of the meaningful, and this localization has remarkable

---

53   Andreas Reckwitz, "Die Kontingenzperspektive der ›Kultur‹. Kulturbegriffe, Kulturthe-
      orien und das kulturwissenschaftliche Forschungsprogramm," in *Handbuch der Kultur-
      wissenschaften: Grundlagen und Schlüsselbegriffe*, ed. Friedrich Jaeger and Burkhard Lieb-
      sch (Stuttgart: J.B. Metzler, 2011), 1–20, https://doi.org/10.1007/978-3-476-00468-0_1.
54   Reckwitz, *Unscharfe Grenzen*.

effects on the suggested understanding of cultural differences, that is, differences between systems of meaning. Ideally, three vocabularies are juxtaposed here: symbolic orders can be attributed at the level of mental structures and processes, they can be attributed at the level of discourses and texts, and finally they can be attributed at the level of social practices. Cultural theories and the cultural analyses that follow them therefore differ in terms of whether they are intellectually, textualistically or praxeologically oriented.[55]

However, the meaning/knowledge-driven concept of culture is contextualized one step before the three previously outlined cultural terms. By not focusing on cultural manifestations and their evaluation, analysis, or function, but asking which principles are used to create cultural manifestations. Not meanings, but the act evolving out of those meanings are examined. Thus, symbols, semantics, discourse structures and their respective narratives are now the focus of social science interest. As cultural meaning systems, they describe patterns of social knowledge and as a prerequisite for the perception, interpretation, and construction of social reality.[56]

Overall, the diversity of cultural concepts within the arts and humanities underlines the insight that culture is to be understood as a discursive construct that can be conceived, defined, and researched in the most diverse ways. An important function of culture is that it functions in an internally integrative, externally hierarchical, and exclusionary way.[57] On the one hand, culture contributes to the formation of individual and collective identity; and the standardizations of thinking, feeling, and acting that characterize cultures often go hand in hand with an exclusion of the other. The concept of culture tempts to perceive cultures too strongly as homogeneous communities and to neglect their internal heterogeneity. New approaches dealing with inter-, multi- and transculturality try to tackle this.[58]

---

55   Florian von Rosenberg, *Lernen, Bildung und kulturelle Pluralität* (Wiesbaden: Springer Fachmedien Wiesbaden, 2016), 76, https://doi.org/10.1007/978-3-658-06365-8.

56   Nünning and Nünning, *Einführung in die Kulturwissenschaften.*

57   Hartmut Böhme, "Vom Cultus zur Kultur(wissenschaft). Zur historischen Semantik des Kulturbegriffs.," in *Kulturwissenschaft—Literaturwissenschaft. Positionen, Themen, Perspektiven* (Wiesbaden: Glaser, Renate/Luserke, Matthias, 1996), 48–68.

58   Vera Allmanritter, "Multi-, Inter- und Transkulturalität (als Begriffe) in der empirischen Kulturbesucherforschung," in *Kulturelle Übersetzer*, ed. Christiane Dätsch (transcript Verlag, 2018), 339–54, https://doi.org/10.14361/9783839434994-022.

Social Practices and the Culture of Knowledge

It is practices that are act(ing)s, that can be observed as physical doings and sayings. They are not isolated actions, but collective patterns of routine actions, in whose temporal concatenation the *social* is produced. Practice represents a performative execution of an or more acts in which the ability to act and meaning are repeatedly produced by repetition and the exercise of those act(s).[59]

Building upon this, practices, strategies, and technologies for the production and also validation of knowledge can be defined as *Knowledge Cultures*.[60] Based on the aforementioned concept of the *cultural-scientific research program*, which taps into a variety of science fields, one must assume that very different knowledge cultures have developed within science, which often do not understand each other, do not recognize each other as equals, and thus have mutual prejudices. Often, these knowledge cultures also have very different, but interesting ideas about the questions regarding the definition of an experiment or what sources may be trusted. Hence, one must assume that there is a diversity of certain scientific cultures.

This multiplicity is then further extended by the fact that the concept of culture must be understood as a broad concept and cannot be restricted as in sociology, where it is very often broken down to a symbolic, normative or value level. In Knowledge Cultures, the level of practices is central to the concept of culture, but other categories that are of interest can also be understood as culture dependent. Hence, culture may also concern the ontological level in a sense that we can also regard the construction of reality itself as part of this culture. By no means, one can't be sure across different branches of science, that this reality is perceived in the same way.

In general, Knowledge Cultures are of great importance in our society, because our western societies are knowledge-based societies in which knowledge as an economic driving force became more important than capital and labor. The basic idea here is, that knowledge has penetrated and permeated all possible areas, self-evidently not always in the pure form of how natural

---

59   Theodore R. Schatzki, *Social Practices: A Wittgensteinian Approach to Human Activity and the Social* (Cambridge: Cambridge University Press, 1996), 22, https://doi.org/10.1017/C BO9780511527470.

60   Bernd Brabec de Mori and Martin Winter, eds., *Auditive Wissenskulturen* (Wiesbaden: Springer Fachmedien Wiesbaden, 2018), https://doi.org/10.1007/978-3-658-20143-2.

sciences tend to do, but always in professionalized forms. Returning here to this work's matter of research: Events like a festival, which are fabricated into a multi-sensory experience by a sophisticated mix of knowledge of different professional fields like psychology, engineering, economics, and physics are a suitable mirroring of an emergence of a certain knowledge culture.

Furthermore, practices of the involved sponsors, which partly refer to findings of sociology and/or brain research to successfully reach their marketing goals at these events represent the major theme of the concept of the cultural science research program. If such a wide range of penetration of knowledge is obvious, one must analyze these knowledge cultures!

If one extends these lines of thought to professional epistemic cultures, i.e., to cultures that are not concerned with basic natural scientific research, then it becomes particularly important to include some issues, such as questions of economics, profession, and questions about institutions. In professional epistemic cultures one is usually confronted with different categories of actors. In professional knowledge cultures, one usually must deal with multiple goals, practical applications, and also with financing conditions. One is surrounded by heterogeneous actors, who are located in different places and who deal with ideas and tasks in very different ways. Often the leading question is not one of truth, but of success which in a capitalistic world then may be: 'Is this how profit can be generated?' Hence, these practices also structure the meaning of an individual action and are simultaneously structured by it. This is the cultural side of practice in the narrower sense of the term, which has been dealt with most by cultural theories.[61]

Knowledge within the Investigation of Sponsorship Culture

"Cultures develop practices that include or presuppose knowledge required to do so."[62]

This quote from Böhme illustrates the necessary fusion of skill(s) and knowledge. Culture therefore has always been the object of knowledge-forms or

---

61   Andreas Reckwitz, *Die Transformation der Kulturtheorien: zur Entwicklung eines Theorieprogramms*, 1. Aufl. (Weilerswist: Velbrück Wissenschaft, 2000), 265.

62   Hartmut Böhme, "Stufen der Reflexion: Die Kulturwissenschaften in der Kultur," in *Handbuch der Kulturwissenschaften*, ed. Friedrich Jaeger and Jürgen Straub (Stuttgart: J.B. Metzler, 2011), 1–15, https://doi.org/10.1007/978-3-476-00627-1_1.

first order of sciences, which are in turn a part of this very culture. From this arises the figure of self-reflexivity, which is still unavoidable today: culture is the object level constructed from theoretical presuppositions and at the same time the last meta-level within cultural knowledge is determined. This is due to the fact that knowledge must be considered as a moment of comprehensive knowledge cultures and their history.[63]

Stehr describes knowledge as a capacity or ability for acting within a cultural definitional approach:

"I'd like to define knowledge as the ability to social acting, as the opportunity to set something in motion. Knowledge is a model for reality."[64]

Knowledge as the first step to action is capable of changing reality. And in doing so, it can enrich human ability (and interaction). Stehr's choice of terms is based on Francis Bacon's famous and fascinating thesis "Scientia Est Potential" or as this phrase has often, but misleadingly, been translated: Knowledge is power.

However, Bacon asserts that the special utility of knowledge is derived from its ability to set something in motion. The term potentia, ability, here circumscribes the *power of knowledge*. Knowledge is coming into being.[65]

The special significance of scientific and technical knowledge in modern societies, however, results from the fact that scientific knowledge, more than any other form of knowledge, permanently fabricates and constitutes additional (incremental) possibilities of action. Scientific knowledge thus represents possibilities of action that are constantly expanding and changing, producing novel opportunities for action that can even be privately appropriated, even if only temporarily. In short: In modern society, knowledge is the basis and motor of progressive modernization as a process of extension.[66]

Knowledge within sponsorship culture will be explored among all three formulated stakeholder groups. But especially in the case of the two stakeholder groups of organizers and sponsors, one does find himself conceptual

---

63   Böhme.

64   Nico Stehr, "Wissensgesellschaften," in *Handbuch der Kulturwissenschaften*, ed. Friedrich Jaeger and Burkhard Liebsch (Stuttgart: J.B. Metzler, 2011), 34–49, https://doi.org/10.10 07/978-3-476-00468-0_3.

65   Stehr.

66   Nico Stehr, *Die Freiheit ist eine Tochter des Wissens* (Wiesbaden: Springer Fachmedien Wiesbaden, 2015), https://doi.org/10.1007/978-3-658-09516-1.

as well as with regards to content within the internal corporate culture of the two actants.

The fact that corporate culture (in which a company's sponsorship culture must be embedded) is seen as a requirement for knowledge processes, is corresponding to current knowledge management and corporate culture literature.[67] This (cultural) knowledge influences employees' perceptions, thoughts, actions, and feelings. This is due to basic assumptions serving as a frame of reference for taking in and processing information, for setting priorities, and for selecting the right behavior in certain situations.[68] Therefore, the term *knowledge culture* was coined within economic literature as well, which is here characterized by employees sharing ideas and experiences because it is a natural thing to do and not because they have to. According to De Long and Fahey[69], four ways in which corporate culture influences knowledge processes:

a) Cultural assumptions drive views about what knowledge is and what knowledge is worth managing. Knowledge is in fact culturally transmitted and influences thought processes and language.[70]

b) Culture determines the relationship between individual and organizational knowledge, in particular the question of who owns which knowledge.

---

67   David W. De Long and Liam Fahey, "Diagnosing Cultural Barriers to Knowledge Management," *Academy of Management Perspectives* 14, no. 4 (November 2000): 113–27, https://doi.org/10.5465/ame.2000.3979820; William R. King, "A Research Agenda for the Relationships between Culture and Knowledge Management," *Knowledge and Process Management* 14, no. 3 (July 2007): 226–36, https://doi.org/10.1002/kpm.281; Richard McDermott and Carla O'Dell, "Overcoming Cultural Barriers to Sharing Knowledge," *Journal of Knowledge Management* 5, no. 1 (March 2001): 76–85, https://doi.org/10.1108/13673270110384428.

68   Sonja Sackmann and Bertelsmann Stiftung, *Erfolgsfaktor Unternehmenskultur: Mit kulturbewusstem Management Unternehmensziele erreichen und Identifikation schaffen—6 Best Practice-Beispiele.* (Wiesbaden: Gabler Verlag, 2013).

69   De Long and Fahey, "Diagnosing Cultural Barriers to Knowledge Management."

70   Rolf Franken and Andreas Gadatsch, *Integriertes Knowledge Management* (Wiesbaden: Vieweg+Teubner Verlag, 2002), https://doi.org/10.1007/978-3-663-05808-3.

c) Culture prepares the context, which plays a crucial role in knowledge and learning processes.[71] Especially for the exchange of tacit knowledge, context is essential[72].[73]

d) Cultural perceptions influence the processes by which new knowledge is created, legitimized, and distributed within the company. Initial trends usually show in theoretical considerations why cultural elements are important enablers.[74]

Quantitative studies have attempted to provide evidence of this influence and to identify elements that are critical to a knowledge culture (a summary of the cultural elements that impact knowledge processes is shown in Figure 3).

Figure 3 is a visual summary of the favorable and unfavorable characteristics of a knowledge culture based on Müller[75]. It is important to note that very few studies distinguish between different knowledge processes (e.g. knowledge sharing or knowledge creation) or between different types of knowledge used in this processes (e.g. tacit or explicit knowledge). However, recent qualitative case studies have focused on identifying how cultural characteristics influence knowledge processes.

---

71   J. Lave, "Situating Learning in Communities of Practice.," in *Perspectives on Socially Shared Cognition*, ed. Lauren Resnick et al. (American Psychological Association, 1991), 63–82.

72   For tacit knowledge to be passed on at all, it needs a common background of experience. Since the ownership of knowledge is not entirely clear, people are often reluctant to pass on their knowledge. Furthermore, the applicability of knowledge (especially the tacit dimension) is difficult for the recipients. The value of knowledge can therefore be difficult to assess, since it does not immediately yield a return.

73   Franken and Gadatsch, *Integriertes Knowledge Management*.

74   Julia Müller, *Projektteamübergreifender Wissensaustausch: Fehlervermeidung und organisationales Lernen durch interaktive Elemente einer Wissenskultur*, 1. Aufl., Gabler Research Strategisches Kompetenz-Management (Wiesbaden: Gabler, 2009).

75   Müller, 192.

Figure 3: Characteristics of Knowledge Culture

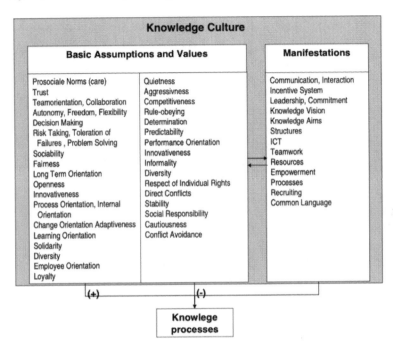

Müller, 192.

Reality Model(s) and Cultural Program(s) as Applicable Theoretical Merger

The different definitions and perspectives on culture presented in the previous chapter(s) suggest that a more comprehensive and multidimensional concept of culture is necessary for theoretically framing the term culture for this research work. Due to the fact, that in this work, three different stakeholder groups within sponsorship act and influence each other, a multidimensionality of a cultural concept is indispensable. Schmidt's definitional considerations presented in the following sub-section are intended to step in, since he divides his concept of culture into two different parts that yet influence each other:

The term *cultural program* was coined by media cultural scientist and philosopher Siegfried J. Schmidt. His concept of culture is derived from *systems theory* and is part of his theory of socio-cultural constructivism. Schmidt describes culture from the complex interrelationships of social and individual action and communication[76], which are oriented to the respective reality model.[77]

Reality models are to be understood as conceptual arrangements which individual experiences are made available to society. These arrangements make it easier for individuals (and society) to deal with their world. Culture, from this perspective, appears as a "program of socially practiced or expected references to models of reality."[78] Meaning, one reacts to the semantic categories and action-guiding orientations made available to us by society.

Semantic categories mediate not only distinctions, but also affects and beliefs, acceptance as well as rejection. Deciding for or against one side of a distinction is always a form of picking sides. It is a cognitive decision that could be made differently in each case. If such a decision is made by a society, then it must be (made) binding. This is done by linking the cognitive decision with moral and affective values, which have a forming-effect on identity in the socialization of the members. Thus, with a cultural program, the reproduction of society can be secured, and the individual can be controlled and/or rendered at the same time, because the program regulates the relationship between social orders and individual free spaces. The cultural program itself is to be understood as an invisible framework. It hides the fact that its semantic categories, moral value-settings, and the resulting instructions for action are only a selection of possible (value)settings that could in principle be made

---

76   Communication in the Schmidtian sense must be understood as reciprocal because communication within his considerations is seen as (a) small social system(s) with temporal-subjective-social reflexibility, which allows action(s) through interaction of communicants and differentiates social structures.

77   Siegfried J. Schmidt, "Eine Kultur der Kulturen," 2006, https://doi.org/10.25969/MEDIAR EP/1773; Edith Wienand, Joachim Westerbarkey, and Armin Scholl, eds., *Kommunikation über Kommunikation* (Wiesbaden: VS Verlag für Sozialwissenschaften, 2005), https://d oi.org/10.1007/978-3-322-80821-9.

78   Siegfried J. Schmidt, *Geschichten & Diskurse: Abschied vom Konstruktivismus*, Originalausg., Rowohlts Enzyklopädie 55660 (Reinbek: Rowohlt Taschenbuch Verlag, 2003).

differently. For semantic distinctions, value-settings and action-orientations are not alternatives of being, but only alternatives of observation.[79]

Seen in this way, the status of objects, concepts, actions, and affects becomes recognizable, i.e., their program-dependent assignments of meaning and attributions of value. With these, both cultural and subcultural[80] constructions of reality and identity are determined within a society. Against the background of these considerations, culture is not a referential value. Rather, it is a more or less binding and, above all, changeable collection of ideas and representations referring to respective valid models of reality. Schmidt's conceptualization of culture as the result of a program-specific reference to the respective reality models of a society is value-free.[81] Therefore, it is able to demonstrate the arising problematic when constitutive, i.e., hegemonic, cultural programs are absolutized—as in most societies—and appropriated for the maintenance of domination and power. The resulting tensions appear as avoidable effects that could be solved by re-decisions.

Therefore, Schmidt whose concept of culture—after much discussion and consideration—provides the appropriate concept of culture for this work, argues for more than three decades, that specifically knowledge as a segment of culture must be regarded as societal; as it is embodied in stakeholders, in and within processes, communications, contexts, and (sub-)cultures. It results from condensations of observations and experiences.[82]

However, with regard to the processes of perceiving, observing, thinking, or describing, according to Schmidt, two essential statements can be made: First, perceiving, thinking, observing, or describing are verbs of transitive nature that determine actions in a broader sense, in which only analytically (i.e., through change of observation) a distinction can be made between stakeholder(s), action completion, and action result. Second, these three compo-

---

79   Siegfried J. Schmidt, "Kultur als Programm—jenseits der Dichotomie von Realismus und Konstruktivismus," in *Handbuch der Kulturwissenschaften*, ed. Friedrich Jaeger and Jürgen Straub (Stuttgart: J.B. Metzler, 2011), 85–100, https://doi.org/10.1007/978-3-476-00627-1_6; Siegfried J. Schmidt, "From Objects to Processes: A Proposal to Rewrite Radical Constructivism," *Constructivist Foundations* 7, no. 1 (2011): 1–9 & 37–47.

80   In this case, subculture is understood as a sociological term standing for the deviant culture of the subgroup of a society or system. The degree of deviation may range from mere modifications to explicit counter-positions. In this way it thus behaves also with a linked reality model of the subculture.

81   Schmidt, "From Objects to Processes: A Proposal to Rewrite Radical Constructivism."

82   Schmidt.

nents, which are only analytically distinguishable from each other, form a process-system or an interdependency, which must be understood as fundamentally. If we speak of interdependency here, one must not think of causal relations; rather there is a self-constituting complementarity of conditions of possibilities.[83]

Schmidt opens up the twofold perspective on the term culture which, separates the theoretical composition of the term into a *reality model* and an (at the same time emerging and co-existing) *cultural program*.[84] In an ongoing step the concept of reality model and culture program are set in context to the investigation of sponsorship culture with emphasis on the university popular music festival market.

Sponsorship Reality Model and Sponsorship Culture Program

The following considerations on a process-oriented sponsorship culture concept start from the basic operation of all cognitive and communicative systems: observing qua distinguishing and naming.[85] Perceiving and recognizing operate with distinctions which are based on evolution as well as on socialization and which are communicatively consolidated with the help of language(s) as differential systems of naming; because in order to enable common action, the management of distinctions must be systematized and consolidated for all members of society.

In order for sponsorship culture actant groups to successfully orient themselves in their environment, with (sponsoring or organizing) partners in action, and with respect to social institutions, sense orientations are needed that (more or less tacitly) assumed are shared by all others (i.e., audience) involved. Meaning orientations can be theoretically conceived as an ordered semantic space consisting of a network (in principle made permanent) of semantic categories, which in a sense form the nodes of this network. Categories mark socially relevant dimensions of meaning, such as

83   Schmidt, "Kultur als Programm—Jenseits der Dichotomie von Realismus und Konstruktivismus"; Schmidt, *Geschichten & Diskurse*.

84   Schmidt, "From Objects to Processes: A Proposal to Rewrite Radical Constructivism."

85   Schmidt, *Geschichten & Diskurse*.

age and gender, music genres, food and clothing, power and goods, values, and emotions, etc.[86]

These dimensions of meaning are implemented semantically by a more or less large number of semantic differentiations, which can be two-digit (good/evil, old/young, sick/healthy, hostile/friendly), but also multi-digit (ice-cold/cold/lukewarm/hot). The term *differentiations* refers to the fact that these are processes during which, exactly according to the logic of positing and presupposition, a semantic dimension is differentiated in semantic space. In other words, the theory-building construction of this approach is 'self-supporting', meaning not to begin with the assertion of the existence of ontological quantities such as categories and differentiations, but rather the process of orientation in semantic space creates its own ontology (by collectively accepted presupposition).

When differentiations are used to make observations or descriptions, they must be transformed into side-specific distinctions—a man (and not a woman) is young (and not old) and sick (and not healthy). In other words, differentiations become asymmetrical distinctions or specific semantic options in use. Categories can therefore be described as unities of difference of semantic differentiations and distinctions.

Within these interaction of processes two directions of observation can be distinguished from each other: *Sense Orientation* and *Action Orientation*. Sense orientation concerns the time- and actant-neutral directional marking of actions, while action orientation concerns the time- and actant-bound processing of sense orientation possibilities in the form of concretely performed acts of differentiation in communication or action situations. The semantic categories can hardly be thought in an isolated and unconnected way but assign their functional possibilities to each other—like words in a word field. Models of reality can be theoretically defined as conceptual arrangements with the help of which individual experiences can be made socially visible and manageable. This model, which is (in each case only) partially built up and tested in the cognitive systems of the actants during socialization, does not have to be capable of consciousness (which is important for qualitative interview

---

86   Schmidt, "From Objects to Processes: A Proposal to Rewrite Radical Constructivism"; Schmidt, "Kultur als Programm—jenseits der Dichotomie von Realismus und Konstruktivismus."

studies) in the case of actants, nor does it have to be obligatory for them to be conscious.[87]

Reality models can be defined as systematized collective knowledge of the members of a community, which co-orients and thus communalizes their interactions via reflexive mechanisms (= expectations in the area of knowledge, imputations in the area of intentions and motivations).[88] Models of reality emerge through the construction and systematization of essential distinctions. Such essential distinctions concern five basic dimensions:

- the behaviors towards nature and environment such as event-venue, office(s), meetings (real/unreal, effective/effective, helpful/dangerous, above/below, outside/inside, etc.),
- towards co-actants such as co-workers, business partners, other members of an event audience (student/non-student, male/female, powerful/powerless, etc.),
- forms of socialization (institutions, organizations), i.e., openings for action or restrictions on action that actants accept or endure in the interest of common problem solving,
- in terms of norms and values (good/evil, sacred/profane, acceptable/unacceptable, etc.)
- as well as regarding the enactment of affects (happy/sad, loving/cruel, etc.).

These reality models of sponsorship culture can be theoretically determined as conceptual arrangements with the help of which all three stakeholder groups' individual experiences can be made socially visible and manageable—and vice versa. It's the collective knowledge of the members of a community such as a company or on the contrary a group of festival goers that has evolved from acting as well as communicating and is systematized by practice and communication and passed on through shared expectations and assumptions.[89] However, this shared common and collective knowledge can be obtained mostly by acting and doing. Reality models as systems of meaning categories for socially

---

87   Schmidt, *Kulturbeschreibung—Beschreibungskultur.*
88   Schmidt, "Kultur als Programm—jenseits der Dichotomie von Realismus und Konstruktivismus"; Schmidt, "From Objects to Processes: A Proposal to Rewrite Radical Constructivism."
89   Schmidt, *Kulturbeschreibung—Beschreibungskultur*; Jacke, *Medien(sub)kultur.*

relevant references of the stakeholders arise without a prior plan and on the way of the cognitive development of categories which have proven themselves and are therefore classified as practically essential. Schmidt concludes from this, that a society or a social system cannot be without reality models.

As mentioned above, according to Schmidt

"Such a reality model can only become effective if a practical program for its application, a culture program, emerges at the same time."[90]

These practical programs which he describes as culture programs balance and administer possible associations between basic semantic differentiations, their relevance, intuitive content, and their significance with regard to a socially binding aspect. They *render* the world view(s) and/or power structures in them of stakeholders in a socially effective way.

Sponsorship culture is the mechanism that allows these contingent selection performances to be carried out in an intersubjectively accessible way for actants as well as for the social systems of different stakeholder groups. Sponsorship cultural programs control which selections are realized, they relate the selection types, distinguish socially acceptable ones and sanction others. In this way, culture within sponsorship creates individual and social identity and compensates for the double contingency that determines communication. In other words, with the help of their (sponsorship) cultural program, stakeholder groups invisibilize the contingency of their practices.

---

90   Schmidt, "From Objects to Processes: A Proposal to Rewrite Radical Constructivism," 3.

Theoretical Perspectives Summary

The past four chapters provide the theoretical framing for this thesis. In the following, the described central themes of the different perspectives are summarized and serve to clarify the linkages between all highlighted issues, which ultimately support the empirical task(s) and necessity for the investigations laid out in the subsequent operationalization chapter.[1]

The demographic change faced by the Federal Republic of Germany is to be seen as the starting point for the theoretical considerations of this work and is discussed within the introducing part of the first theoretical perspective. With its sub-processes of aging, shrinking and internationalization of society, social structures as well as the economic inner-relations are going to change significantly. Due to the (partial) predictability of these transformational processes, the associated socio-economic implications represent an unprecedented upheaval for Germany in the coming years as they will affect many aspects of the socio-economic entity of the country and its society. These changes correspond to a complex socio-economic shift, which on the one hand involve socio-cultural changes in society. On the other hand, the economy and business world are entangled within an ongoing process of change as a result of flexibilization and globalization of production methods and a structural shift toward a service and knowledge society.

One (specific) identifiable outcome initiated by this development is the challenge of a cut-throat competition for residents, well-educated professionals and students between medium-sized German cities and municipalities, their local economy, communities as well as their local universities. With special regard to the (higher) educational system, the question arises as to what demand which educational service will continue to exist in the future since

---

1   References regarding the Theoretical Perspectives can be found in the corresponding chapters above.

the demographic change is spatially very different in its peculiarity. The number of students is going to fall at the majority of university locations in eastern Germany as well as in several regions of western Germany outside the metropolitan areas. Furthermore, as universities are becoming progressively important engines of economic and social development within their regions, this evolution goes hand in hand with the mentioned demographic challenges their cities and municipalities are facing.

Today's society has shifted to a knowledge (based) society in the last few decades, in which the 'older' approaches of location theories regarding the (industrial) secondary sector have mainly lost their importance. This shift from the primary and secondary economic sectors to the tertiary sector as well as the growing qualification of the employees also bring another aspect into the equation: the changed relation between work and leisure. Thus, soft location factors like the city- and landscape, the living as well as life quality or cultural life for the development of regions and cities gain in importance. Moreover, does the cultivation of a certain regional image and its marketing in and outside the municipality and regional area become more important.

Therefore, this inner-German competition between regions and their local academic institutions is very much embedded in the perceived external image of the entities. One response to prevail within this challenging environment is to utilize events within existing marketing mix(es). This has been observed in German city marketing offices for some time but has been increasingly adopted and applied by the executive committees of German universities as well.

The common thread between the first and second theoretical perspective respectively runs through the theme of events, their growing relevance and application within an eventized society.

Thus, the second theoretical perspective introduces Hitzler et. al's socio-economic concept of eventization which links the aforementioned (public) marketing efforts and its implementation of (cultural) events to a society which is increasingly characterized by the importance of the interior orientation of life. In an ongoing step, the conceptualization of eventization as a social development that is driven by the supply of cultural experience offers, is rediscovered within the German university landscape due to the changed attitude of universities and the admission of (marketing-) events within the university context.

In this frame of reference, it is not only the universities' effort to address and approach as many students as possible via (own or externally staged) events; to achieve a greater attention and emotionalization as well as form a well-received institutional image. At the same time, (advertising) enterprises increasingly rely on this same communication tool within the German university landscape as part of their marketing and PR activities. Student events are compelling for marketing and advertising activities, simply due to the face that today's students are most likely the higher-income earners of tomorrow. As a result of willingness and affinity for the use of events as an enhancement of the external image within university administration, the nowadays 'large-scale' music festivals on German university campuses are well developed events that have gained notoriety beyond the student body. Events against the background of marketing activities are particularly involved in motivational constructs and audience structure for precisely those event visits.

Accordingly, the latest motivational research for music event and festival attendance is discussed in the following chapter, as it is to be seen as an additional major theoretical layer for sponsorship culture within the university popular music festival market.

Furthermore, the subsequent chapter concludes the second theoretical framework of the dissertation and discusses the recent digital evolution of the music industry with high incorporation of liveness which today is strongly embedded in concepts such as the experience economy and the aforementioned inner-orientation of today's generation y audience.

The following chapter deals with the third theoretical perspective, which first defines and discusses different views and definitions on popular music (culture), to ultimately formulate it in a fitting manner for the purpose of this work and the incorporation of popular music in a festival sense. To establish the context within which the event's sponsorship and its stakeholders are situated, in an ongoing step, chapter 4.2 provides an outline of origins, academic literature, and research on music festivals in general as well as popular music festivals in particular. Furthermore, the preceding considerations from this work's second theoretical perspective regarding *eventization* and *interior orientation* as well as the definitional considerations on popular culture and popular music find their common overlap in this section.

An important enabling component of (popular) music festivals, especially within the university context and thus also ingrained in all mentioned issues is its sponsorship. The successive section is thus dedicated to the definition of the communication tool of event-sponsorship and its discussion within corporate communication as well as its specificity within a popular music festival context. Furthermore, sponsorship is contextualized within today's well saturated economic markets, which are characterized by purchasing restraints. Thus, sponsorship as a form of marketing and corporate communication tool plays a critical role in distinguishing a company's product or service from those of its competitors. The third theoretical perspective is finalized by a discussion of the special characteristics of music and festival sponsorship in chapter 4.5.

The fourth theoretical perspective explores literature surrounding different concepts, perceptions, and definitions of the term culture within interdisciplinary boundaries building a further theoretical layer for the research project. In contrast to other scientific research projects which exist in the thematic spheres of event management, event studies or event marketing, this approach tries to take an interdisciplinary look on things. Due to this interdisciplinary theme of this work, this is being done from both, an economic as well as from an arts and humanities viewpoint. The goal here is to equip the theoretical frame of this work with one fitting concept of the term culture. Since the 'culture of sponsorship' with all its actants and all their different perspectives on the matter, with everything they do and how they act, know, and deduce from this knowledge are located at this intersection of the scientific disciplines and needs to be understood as such. One additional reason for this lies in the junction of results as this dissertation encloses three separate studies.

As applicable theoretical merger for investigating sponsorship culture, the multidimensional concept of culture by Siegfried Schmidt is concluded in chapter 5.4. The twofold perspective on the term culture which, according to Schmidt separates the theoretical composition of the term into a reality model and into an (at the same time) emerging practical culture program builds the most useful way to filter (sponsorship) culture from the following three studies.

The thesis' main scientific objective is to explore and understand sponsorship culture within the German university popular music festival market with its three stakeholder groups. The discussed theoretical considerations form the foundation of the thematic discussion and at the same time the possibility to combine the results in accordance with Schmidt's multidimensional concept of culture.

Operationalization and Methodological Approach

The focus of this research is to filter an underlying sponsorship culture in accordance of an Schmidtian reality model and rendering practical cultural model of stakeholders within the German popular music festival market with emphasis on university popular music festivals. As mentioned above, if one tries to conceptualize the term culture, it can be stated that there is no uniform concept in economic scientific, nor arts and humanities research.

The lack of a unified conception of culture ultimately affects methodological implementation(s) in empirical research practice in this particular, as well as many other cases. It arises the question whether culture can be viewed as a conglomerate of objectively definable and operationalizable variables that theoretically act as a condition for cultural phenomena. In addition to the challenge of conceptualizing and operationalizing the term culture, the question of the description of processes that are set in motion when people design, plan, advertise, sponsor, visit or receive an event must also be asked. As mentioned above, Schmidt's cultural theoretical argumentations, which he has presented in a series of books and essays in the last four decades, systematize culture in the core of his considerations, not as objectivations, subject areas or to determine content, but rather to find out the mechanism(s) or orientation scheme(s) that are effective in the production of phenomena considered cultural in the broadest sense. For this work, this means exploring and trying to 'measure' reality model(s) of three acting stakeholder groups in the sphere of sponsorship within the German popular music festival market with emphasis on university popular music festivals. Furthermore, to stay aligned with Schmidt's cultural theoretical argumentations, regulating aspects of a simultaneously emerging (rendering) practical culture program needs to be addressed with regards to how the applications of mentioned models are rendered socially effective. The three stakeholder groups investigated in this dissertation are: sponsors, organizer, and the audience of the festivals.

Figure 4: Research Design

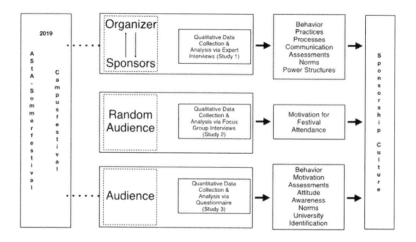

Figure 4 attempts to graphically depict the research design of this work. In the figure as well as, at several points in the research process, more practical issues evolved at the described interdisciplinary contact point of the disciplines. The chronological study sequence does not correspond to the numbering of the individual studies. The reason for this is that the results of Study Two were partially used in the creation of the questionnaire of Study Three, but for the flow of reading and better understanding of the three studies as an overall concept, it was more useful to list Study One first in the course of the work. The surveys of Study One and Study Three took place in parallel in 2019, Study Two was conducted in 2018.

"You win with mixed methods, i.e., you can understand a complex problem better if you illuminate both sides, the quantitative one of counting and the qualitative one of understanding meaning."[1]

---

1   Kuckartz, *Mixed Methods*, 53.

A number of reasons for investing effort into better understanding the sponsorship cultures within the German university popular music festival Market emerged from the four discussed theoretical backgrounds. In order to explore reality models, practical culture programs, stakeholder's motives, and their inner connections as well as assessments, (collective) norms, qualities, behavior patterns, beliefs and understandings, the following three studies were conducted. Study One is the first of its kind to explore and describe sponsorship culture within the German festival market excluding input from audience(s) and an emphasis on qualitative data gathered from interviews conducted with sponsors and festival organizers.

The second study of this dissertation is a qualitative approach and is employed to specifically explore and understand underlying motivational constructs for attending a (university) popular music festival in Germany using a focus group methodology. The second study has been conducted in a very early stage of the research process for this dissertation. As to not to overlook any motivational contexts at the time, wording was extended to popular music festival attendance, rather than focusing on solely university music festivals. Furthermore, results of this study are then utilized partially as a foundation to build upon in the questionnaire used in the third empirical section of this dissertation.

After having observed and analyzed professional stakeholders within sponsorship culture, namely sponsors and organizers of university popular music festivals, the third stakeholder group, the audience is shed a light on. To be precise, data of quantitative surveys consist of two separate examinations, each conducted within three weeks after the two biggest university popular music festivals in Germany in 2019: The *AStA Sommerfestival* in Paderborn and the *Campus Festival Bielefeld*. Quantitative surveys explore audience sponsorship culture with emphasis on university popular music festivals and outlines audience profile(s) to provide descriptive knowledge of the two biggest university popular music festivals held in 2019 in Germany. Furthermore, quantitative surveys aim at understanding motivational constructs for university popular music festival attendance by building upon results from focus group interviews (Study Two) and identifying a factor structure which stimulates members of an audience to visit these events.

Deduced from the outlined three empirical studies, the thesis employs a mixed-methodological approach that combines qualitative with quantitative research. Both methods are used to complement each other and bridge the gap between exploration, description, and inference. Naturally, the methodological structure must take the specifics of each research method into account because they differ in research goals, focus, procedure, data sampling, and analysis. There are multiple research methods to choose from. However, the choice to design a study that involved both quantitative and qualitative methods is based on the research need, the gap in the literature, the expected outcomes, and the research questions.

Qualitative research offers an insight into questions that address the way people think about a certain subject and how they feel rather than applying numerical data to their reports and reactions.[2] Qualitative research is often of an exploratory nature while it provides representative results mainly in accordance with the subject of investigation or a carefully selected target group. It does not yield towards a representative picture of the research population; nor does it allow confirmatory generalization of the results.[3] A classified sample is needed to make sure all possible views and opinions of the subjects can be expressed.[4] The goal of qualitative research is to describe processes as accurately as possible in verbal terms; therefore, the type of analyses usually employed for qualitative research are subjective and interpretative, such as Mayring's[5] content analysis.

Furthermore, an analytic-inductive process is rather found within a qualitative research process than a hypothetic-deductive process. Instead, analytic-inductive researchers begin by analyzing their data and when the data is analyzed, they develop theoretical concepts and propositions that may have derived from the analysis.

Quantitative research can be labeled as an explanatory method; a way to describe and explain data after it is collected. It aims at a validation of facts, estimates, relationships, and predictions using numerical calculations. Quantitative research uses a hypothetic- deductive approach that aims to test hypotheses rather than their formulation. Researchers begin with theoretical

2   Danny N. Bellenger, Kenneth L. Bernhardt, and Jac L. Goldstucker, *Qualitative Research in Marketing*, Monographs Series—American Marketing Association; 3 (Chicago: American Marketing Association, 1976).

3   Joseph F. Hair, Robert P. Bush, and David J. Ortinau, *Marketing Research: In a Digital Information Environment*, 4th ed (Boston: McGraw-Hill Irwin, 2009).

4   Ko de Ruyter and Norbert Scholl, "Positioning Qualitative Market Research: Reflections from Theory and Practice," *Qualitative Market Research: An International Journal* 1, no. 1 (April 1998): 7–14, https://doi.org/10.1108/13522759810197550.

5   Philipp Mayring, *Qualitative Inhaltsanalyse: Grundlagen und Techniken*, 11., aktualisierte und überarb. Aufl., Beltz Pädagogik (Weinheim: Beltz, 2010).

premises, predict a pattern of results, and examine their data to test their theory driven hypotheses. Statistical methods are used on a sample to infer facts and causal relations about the population.[6]

As mentioned, the project consists of two qualitative and one quantitative sub-study, which are arranged in parallel, and were partly carried out simultaneously. Therefore, the mixed method research design for this dissertation can be further defined as convergent design.

---

6   John W. Creswell and J. David Creswell, *Research Design: Qualitative, Quantitative, and Mixed Methods Approaches*, Fifth edition (Los Angeles: SAGE, 2018).

Study One: Qualitative Exploratory Interviews | Organizer and Sponsors

"Qualitative researching is exciting and important. It is a highly rewarding activity because it engages us with things that matter, in ways that matter. Through qualitative research we can explore a wide array of dimensions of the social world, including the texture and weave of everyday life, the understandings, experiences and imaginings of our research participants, the ways that social processes, institutions, discourses or relationships work, and the significance of the meanings they generate. We can do all of this qualitatively by using methodologies that celebrate richness, depth, nuance, context, multi- dimensionality, and complexity rather than being embarrassed or inconvenienced by them. Instead of editing these elements out in search of the general picture or the average, qualitative research factors them directly into its analyses and explanations. This means that it has an unrivalled capacity to constitute compelling arguments about how things work in particular contexts."[1]

Qualitive Methods are essential at several stages of developing a comprehensive research stream about many topics. They are particularly useful in exploring the depth of meaning about concepts and (un)hidden connections between issues, people, and culture(s). When, as in this dissertation, follow-up quantitative work will be conducted, the qualitative methods also help in adapting measures for concepts to the specific context in which research will be done, and in testing the survey instrument(s).

As prior discussed in the Theoretical Perspectives, culture(s) develop(s) practices, that embed required knowledge. This necessarily leads to a fusion

---

1   Jennifer Mason, *Qualitative Research* (London: SAGE, 2002), 1.

of skill(s) and knowledge. The qualitative approach taken in this study emphasizes discovery over confirmation and explores the sponsorship culture(s) within the German market for university festivals from a 'creator's perspective', meaning either festival's sponsors or organizers. This study aims to provide insight into relevant contexts and links between different aspects that eventually form a culture within the observed cosmos.

The qualitative interviews make it feasible to gain and analyze more information regarding the practical experience obtained by the experts over time and to examine the often subjectively influenced level of decision-making processes within the experts' 'territory' as well as decision-makers at the corporate level.

Based on these insights, a comprehensive conceptual framework of factors that create, amend, and influence these different culture(s) is developed. This forms the foundation for the subsequent steps in the research process and allows the relevant constructs to be operationalized in the quantitative studies.

The qualitative interview study addresses the following research questions:

a) How do professional stakeholders assess the market for university popular music festivals in Germany?
b) Which patterns about the procedural elements of sponsorship culture(s) exist?
c) What factors determine the existing company's communication and decision-making culture?

In particular,

•   How does (financial) support for an event come about?
•   What does the decision-making process look like?
•   What are the first steps after a sponsorship partner is accepted?
•   What are the interactions before, during and after the event?

d) What interrelations between sponsor and audience arise from the sponsorship engagement?

In particular,

- How good is brand recall after the event?
- How much does the perception of the sponsor's image change?
- How does the audience feel about sponsorship engagement?

e) How 'ticks' the audience of a university popular music festival?

In particular,

- Does the audience identify with its university?
- How can motivational constructs for festival attendance be described?
- What role plays social media regarding the festival experience?

Methodology—Semi-Structured Interviews as Instrument for Data Collection

This research study uses interviews as a method to capture the underlying dimensions of how either festival's sponsors or organizers perceive sponsorship cultures in their company as well as in the event branch. Lamnek & Krell define the qualitative research interview as a situation in which the interviewee "is to be moved to give verbal information about the lifeworld"[2]. The purpose of the qualitative interview is to gather descriptions with respect to interpretation of the described phenomena.

According to Lamnek & Krell, a qualitative research interview is characterized by the interviewee's undistorted and authentic information, that can be understood intersubjectively and reproduced at will. It is qualitative, descriptive, specific, impartiality, focused on certain themes and dependent upon the sensitivity of the interviewer.[3]

Technically, a qualitative research-interview is *semi-structured*, it is neither a free conversation nor a highly structured questionnaire. It follows an interview-guide, which rather than containing exact questions focuses on certain themes.[4] Throughout the interview, the researcher follows the rules of good

---

2   Siegfried Lamnek and Claudia Krell, *Qualitative Sozialforschung: mit Online-Material*, 6., überarbeitete Auflage (Weinheim Basel: Beltz, 2016), 212 f.

3   Lamnek and Krell, *Qualitative Sozialforschung*.

4   Lamnek and Krell.

interviewing such as using small encouragers like murmurs of understanding, maintaining eye contact, smiling expectantly during pauses as if expecting the interview to continue, using active listening technique of feeding back dialogue in the researcher's own words to check his understanding, and asking non-directive questions.[5]

In this study, face-to-face interviews with synchronous communication in time and place were conducted. This is the most common form of interview for integrating social cues in the interview analysis.[6] The interviews are aimed at gaining specific nuanced descriptions from different qualitative aspects regarding sponsorship culture in the field of music festivals with emphasis on university popular music festivals, at obtaining uninterpreted descriptions on how these cultures evolved and how they keep evolving. As such, the interviews are classified as theme-oriented rather than person-oriented, and data is collected based on what interviewees directly express as well as to what is 'said in between the lines'.

Qualitative Content Analysis as Instrument for Data Analysis

To analyze the interview material, this study uses the qualitative content analysis method.[7] Content analysis consists of a set of techniques for systematic text analysis. Mayring states that:

> "Qualitative content analysis defines itself … as an approach of empirical, methodological controlled analysis of texts within their context of communication, following content analytical rules and step by step models, without rash quantification."[8]

The material is to be analyzed step by step, following rules of procedure, devising, and summarizing the material into content analytical units.[9] Following the research questions, emerging aspects of text interpretation are put into

5   David Carson, *Qualitative Marketing Research* (London; Thousand Oaks, Calif.: SAGE, 2001).

6   Uwe Flick, *Qualitative Sozialforschung: Eine Einführung*, Originalausgabe, 8. Auflage, Rororo Rowohlts Enzyklopädie 55694 (Reinbek bei Hamburg: Rowohlts Enzyklopädie im Rowohlt Taschenbuch Verlag, 2017).

7   Mayring, *Qualitative Inhaltsanalyse*.

8   Mayring, 5.

9   Mayring, 6.

categories, which are carefully chosen and revised within the process of analysis. As with most qualitative oriented procedures of text interpretation, the inductive approach of category development is central to an exploratory study design.

The main idea of the inductive category development, as shown in Figure 5 is, to formulate a coding definition for each category derived from the theoretical background and guided by the research questions. Following these coding guidelines and the tentative categories, a step-by-step process is started. Within the feedback loop, the categories are revised, eventually reduced to main categories, and then checked with respect to their reliability.[10]

Figure 5: Own illustration of the Inductive Approach of Qualitative Content Analysis

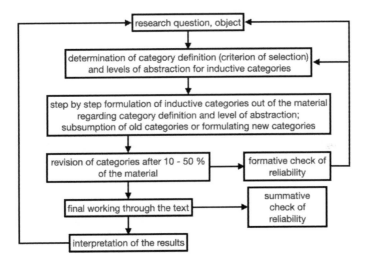

Mayring, Qualitative Inhaltsanalyse.

Validity and Reliability

As noted, qualitative approaches are very appropriate in the beginning stages of developing knowledge about unfamiliar situations. Healy and Perry argue that qualitative methods are essential in the early stages of theory building within what many researchers call the realism paradigm. This shall be closely connected to the quality of a qualitative study according to Healy and Perry.[11] However, validity and reliability are often regarded as the cornerstone of any research[12]. Thus, many qualitative researchers avoid the terms validity and reliability and use terms such as credibility, trustworthiness, truth, value, applicability, consistency, and confirmability, when referring to criteria for evaluating the scientific merit of qualitative research.[13][14] Other researchers develop a re-definition of validity and reliability in qualitative research and claim that validity and reliability in qualitative research can be achieved through forms of cross-checking.[15]

In the field of qualitative research, validity is mainly linked to the fact that constructs or emerging topics are closely aligned to their real-life context.[16] Thus, results become meaningful to the researcher if they are in a certain relation to the respondent's everyday reality. In this sense, de Ruyter and Scholl claim that qualitative research offers the possibility of *ecological validity* instead of construct validity or internal validity. The ecological validity of data collection depends on the purpose of the study.[17]

---

11   Marilyn Healy and Chad Perry, "Comprehensive Criteria to Judge Validity and Reliability of Qualitative Research within the Realism Paradigm," *Qualitative Market Research: An International Journal* 3, no. 3 (September 2000): 118–26, https://doi.org/10.1108/13522750010333861.

12   de Ruyter and Scholl, "Positioning Qualitative Market Research."

13   Yvonna S. Lincoln and Egon G. Guba, *Naturalistic Inquiry* (Beverly Hills: Sage Publications, 1985).

14   Marilyn R. McFarland and Hiba B. Wehbe-Alamah, "Leininger's Theory of Culture Care Diversity and Universality: An Overview With a Historical Retrospective and a View Toward the Future," *Journal of Transcultural Nursing* 30, no. 6 (November 2019): 540–57, https://doi.org/10.1177/1043659619867134.

15   Sally Rao and Chad Perry, "Convergent Interviewing to Build a Theory in Under-researched Areas: Principles and an Example Investigation of Internet Usage in Interfirm Relationships," *Qualitative Market Research: An International Journal* 6, no. 4 (December 2003): 236–47, https://doi.org/10.1108/13522750310495328.

16   de Ruyter and Scholl, "Positioning Qualitative Market Research."

17   de Ruyter and Scholl.

External validity addresses the degree or extent to which such representations or reflections of reality are legitimately applicable across groups and if they can be generalized to a population beyond the immediate study context.[18] The purpose of qualitative research is not to validate generalizations from a sample of population but rather to it serve more for genesis than for testing theories. Only based on the results of the data collection and following use of techniques of interpretation and evaluation, the researcher comes up with typified statements. Through these, the theoretical concepts about constellations of social reality are formed.[19] Reliability is concerned with the consistency, stability and repeatability of the informant's accounts as well as the investigators' ability to collect and record information accurately.[20] The reliability of qualitative research, in the sense of comparability of reproducibility, is often questioned.[21] Stenbacka claims that reliability issues related to measurement are of no relevance to qualitative research.[22] De Ruyter and Scholl claim, however, that a deeper insight into the motivations and perceptions of the respondents does not primarily require reproducibility, but rather depends on a systematic procedure.[23]

At this point it shall be stated once more that the quality of a qualitative interview study depends on how well the design of the study was conceived. To ensure the highest validity and reliability according to the sense of the prior discussed thoughts, the eight most suitable practices in qualitative study design recommended in literature were employed in this study. These are broken down into three main groups. First, to establish meaningful consistent respondent perceptions tied to real life contexts, the following recommendations were adhered to:

- Face-to-face-interviews were conducted in the respondent's own environment;[24]

18   William Emory and Donald R. Cooper, *Business Research Methods*, 4th ed (Homewood, IL: Irwin, 1991).

19   Lamnek and Krell, *Qualitative Sozialforschung*, 330.

20   Emory and Cooper, *Business Research Methods*.

21   Lamnek and Krell, *Qualitative Sozialforschung*.

22   Caroline Stenbacka, "Qualitative Research Requires Quality Concepts of Its Own," *Management Decision* 39, no. 7 (September 2001): 551–56, https://doi.org/10.1108/EUM0000 000005801.

23   de Ruyter and Scholl, "Positioning Qualitative Market Research."

24   de Ruyter and Scholl.

- Interaction between interviewer and interviewee was allowed for questions, verification, and to scrutinize statements;[25]
- During the interviews, carefully worded questions were raised that looked at sponsorship cultures within the German university popular music festival market from different angles.[26]

Due to this study's explorative attempt to understand the interrelation between audience, organizers, and sponsors:

- Interviewees with different perspectives on sponsorship cultures were selected to ensure that a cross-section of opinions was obtained.[27]

In qualitative research the requirement of reliability does not yield to reproducibility but rather should ensure inferability of the research findings. In this thesis, these demands were secured by the means of the following four tactics:

- The interviews were conducted in a flexible manner, e.g., it was possible to change research questions during the interview to look behind the facts and follow interesting emerging themes;[28]
- Questions were built on existing literature and concepts[29]
- Repeated listening to recorded interviews and multiple coding to foster intra-personal;[30] and
- Independent coding checked by another person and evaluation of intercoder reliability[31].

Field Phase—Sample Selection

As previously discussed, qualitative research does not intend to validate generalizations from a sample for society. It aims at discovery of typical themes,

---

25   Lamnek and Krell, *Qualitative Sozialforschung*.
26   Healy and Perry, "Comprehensive Criteria to Judge Validity and Reliability of Qualitative Research within the Realism Paradigm."
27   Lamnek and Krell, *Qualitative Sozialforschung*.
28   de Ruyter and Scholl, "Positioning Qualitative Market Research."
29   de Ruyter and Scholl.
30   Mayring, *Qualitative Inhaltsanalyse*.
31   Mayring.

processes, or patterns by which social reality is produced in its meaningful structure.[32] Thus, sample theoretical considerations in a probabilistic sense, such as the question of representativeness, only play a minor role in the qualitative interview. Therefore, a theoretical sampling procedure[33] was used to recruit the study's interview partners. The main goal was to ensure "typification instead of representativeness"[34] and to develop a certain diversity of knowledgeable people from both perspectives on sponsorship cultures (organizers as well as sponsors). Furthermore, it was a certain seniority and experience-level within their field of expertise has been ensured.

Participants were identified through the authors business network of people in the industry that grew substantially during his five-year long engagement as head of the AStA Festival in Paderborn. The possibility to be able to use an existing network and being able to utilize these contacts for the study's research had several advantages. First of all, existing relationships with some participants made it even possible in the first place to get in contact with the mentioned seniority level of a company. Furthermore, a trustful relationship regarding the topic was already present or could be established. To assure results that are valid beyond one specific sponsor scenario, a company outside the specific university popular music festival context, that specializes on campus marketing activities in general was also selected for data collection. All interview partners participated voluntarily in this study and were not paid for participation.

The exploratory study was conducted from June to October 2019. In sum five individuals were interviewed in person representing five different companies.

32   Lamnek and Krell, *Qualitative Sozialforschung*.

33   Barney G. Glaser and Anselm L. Strauss, *The Discovery of Grounded Theory: Strategies for Qualitative Research*, 4. paperback printing (New Brunswick: Aldine, 2009).

34   Lamnek and Krell, *Qualitative Sozialforschung*, 336.

Table 3: Interviewees

Participant	Function	Business Field	Exp. Level	Gender	Place
MBG International Premium Brands GmbH	International Brand Manager	Alcoholic Beverages	high	Female	Paderborn
VIBRA Agency	Project Manager	Event Management	high	Male	Bielefeld
Warsteiner	Music and Lifestyle Sponsoring	Beer	Very high	Female	Düsseldorf
Anonymous	Field Marketing Manager Southwest	(Anonymous)	Very high	Male	Frankfurt
UNICUM	Manager NRW	Marketing Agency	high	Female	Bielefeld

These companies included the organizing company of the two biggest university popular music festivals in Germany as well as companies who were involved in sponsorship activities on these events. Furthermore, one company that had no specific sponsorship connection to the festivals but specializes on *Campus Marketing* in general was also interviewed. The descriptive characteristics of all participants are shown in *Table 3*.

After interviewing the fifth subject, the need for further interviews ceased when it was apparent that a point of information saturation had been reached and that unique findings were no longer expected to be obtained under the used interviewing procedure.

Field Phase—Interview Situation and Questionnaire Design

All interviews lasted between 60 and 80 minutes. Each interview was conducted at the participant's place of business. The interview situation depended on the on-site actualities. All interviews were conducted with single participants and no person else in the room. Every interview was conducted by the author himself, the language spoken was German.

In each face-to-face conducted interview situation, the author aimed at creating a positive atmosphere to enable a forthright conversation regarding sponsoring cultures between experts. All participants were assured of confidentially and anonymity if participants preferred (see *Table 3*). According to Lamnek and Krell, most of the questions that arose during the process of the interviews were context-specific and assured presuppositionlessness. To guide the participants' flow of ideas, however, a small set of structured questions was used in the interviews. Questions were carefully worded to cause participants responses in a non-directive manner. For example, interviewees were asked to think of students' sense of identification with their educational institution and whether they have experienced.

Despite and because of the recording equipment, the discussion situation was designed by the researcher in such a way that the technical devices were forgotten. This was most likely achieved through active listening and confirmation from the author, so that the recording became a peripheral phenomenon.

The interview guideline comprises a set of questions based on the findings from the literature review as well as from the author's experience as an event manager and aims at exploring the general sponsorship culture in the context of campus festivals in the company including the market for university popular music festivals itself, communication, and decision culture as well as the underlying themes of *image* and audience(s). Deeper themes like for example 'the role of social media during event visit' or 'motives for event attendance' were meant to be explored preferably, when the interviewee brought the topic up himself during the course of the interview. This was mainly the case due to the logical interconnection between topic points. In some cases, the deeper themes were directly pointed out by the author himself to assure all interview partners were at some point talking about the same issues.

Two variants of the interview guideline were used to capture the expert's insights regarding sponsorship cultures in the university popular music festival market (see Appendix). Both comprise the same central themes and questions but were adjusted to the different perspectives of either sponsor or organizer. While the questions provided a general framework, they were followed up with additional questions requesting clarifications, examples, and more details into potentially interesting ideas if the situation gave chance to it.

Category Development and Coding

A total of five interview sessions were audio taped and transcribed verbatim in German. One participant declined the request to be named himself as well as the company for the reason of the sensitive nature of the subject and company policy. Thus, for the sake of analogousness, all interviewees were anonymized in the text. The transcribed versions of the interviews and notes constitute the material for the subsequent interpretation of meaning via qualitative content analysis.[35]

An inductive study design was chosen as it is a compelling way to investigate an understudied empirical phenomenon such as sponsorship within the German university popular music festival market.[36]

While in the process of data collection, analysis of the data began simultaneously. Following the inductive method, with the use of the qualitative coding software MAXQDA coding and extracting informant statements from all transcribed interviews was conducted without paying attention to pre-established theoretical codes. Instead, the analysis was started by open coding and aiming to create as many codes as possible from each informant perspective. For example, a code for *Personal Beliefs* was created.

The source material was coded implementing an inductive approach of category development according to the qualitative content analysis.[37] The categories were formed in an iterative process with constant revision of the coding and the tentative categories. The final coding scheme consists of five main categories and eleven subcategories. In sum, 172 statements—text units which can include one or more sentences—from the source material were related to the subcategories. The structure of the coding categories together with the number of statements attached to those categories as well as a description of those categories are shown in *Table 4*.

---

35   Mayring, *Qualitative Inhaltsanalyse*.
36   Mason, *Qualitative Research*; Rao and Perry, "Convergent Interviewing to Build a Theory in Under-researched Areas."
37   Mayring, *Qualitative Inhaltsanalyse*.

Table 4: Coding Categories of the Qualitative Interview Study

Category	Subcategory	References
First Step Process	/	6
Practices	Communication-Culture	11
	Decision-Culture	13
	Fingerspitzengefühl	19
Knowledge Management	/	17
Assessments	German Market for UPMF	28
	University Identification	13
	Motives for Attendance	18
	Consumer Budget	7
	Sponsorship Awareness and Attitude towards Sponsorship	11
	Social Media	8
Personal Beliefs	/	21

Study Results

Due to the anonymization of the interviews, each interlocutor is provided with a certain code, whereas the sponsoring companies are marked with the letters S1, S2, S3, S4 and the organizing company is marked O1.

In the following text, three points in square brackets, i.e., (...), indicate all statements that have been left out in the description.

Structure of Results

The major themes that emerged from the interviews with sponsors as well as festival organizers form a conceptual framework for understanding the factors that influence sponsorship culture in the festival market. Furthermore, the combination and pure existence of all aspects being described by the interviewees form this vibrant cosmos of culture. The framework is shown in figure 6. It depicts the grouping and relationship between the relevant issues and themes regarding sponsorship culture.

These themes represent the major results discovered through the process of inductive category development. The following sections explain in the individual results and the derivation of the conceptual framework. This chapter is structured by following each of the major themes that form the framework.

Figure 6: Own Illustration of Conceptual Framework Resulting from Qualitative Study

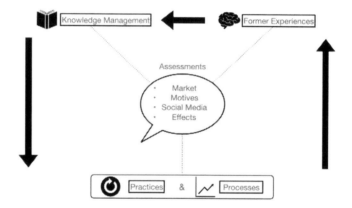

First Step Process

One can argue about the exact difference of definitions of practices and processes. However, this is not necessary for the essence of this study. What's key for understanding culture, is that a process within a culture can be described as a broader term that includes the underlying practices within. In contrast to practices, processes are more fixed and represent a sequential of actions by stakeholders and some of which may be technically amended or supported.

When discussing the matter of sponsorship culture, participants often referred to the word *process* when they were describing the mentioned sequential of actions or practices or when they meant to describe an existing culture or what they felt would fit for this term around their field of work.

Participants were asked to describe what first procedural steps after a sponsorship agreement is reached look like.

In order to seal the mostly verbal agreement between the stakeholders, a contract has to be drawn up. on the one hand this is important to have a kind of security for both parties, on the other hand this process is often lengthy and has to be carried out parallel to the first work. Accordingly, this harbors a certain risk for both parties:

> "Indeed, the contents of the contract. Just so we can talk about the same approach. As I said, we have 360-degree support in one person, so I can't talk about an event five times. I've been doing this for seven years now and it has to be done relatively quickly." (S1)

> "Contract and contract drafting. This is also a process that should not be underestimated. Ultimately, you only need it when something doesn't work, but it makes sense to design it cleanly. But there is also no point in only starting when the contract has been signed. That's not even possible in this business, so you do a lot of parallel work." (S2)

One interviewee described the moment of the agreement as a kind of mechanism that triggers the first step process including the contract as well as several steps that are alike with every project:

> "If we decide to take part, there is first a meeting with the organizer, where the (contract) measures are then discussed with each other. Somehow that starts with an event delivery (...). You then skin that into our system, where the shipping company is commissioned. I think that's the first step. After that, of course, you distribute jobs internally and say we now have a festival here with 10,000 people etc. (...) So all people who are somehow involved in this project are brought on board and the order is placed" (S3)

Practices

> "Online marketing is a clear-cut case, due to the posted ads. Offline it's way more complicated" (S3)

As described in the Theoretical Perspectives of this dissertation, stakeholder's practices can mirror how things are done within a certain environment or in certain situations. Hence, the analysis of these practices delivers a first glimpse on sponsorship culture regarding the sponsors as well as the organizer of a university popular music festival.

As stated above, practices are broken down into the three subcategories of decision-culture, which is embedded in the second subcategory of communication-culture as well as the more complex and tougher to grasp subcategory *Fingerspitzengefühl*.

Beginning with the way of how a decision is made to 'justify' or express the need for a possible sponsorship cooperation with an event is seen complex by the interviewees, because as stated before, sponsorship in comparison to other marketing engagements is very complex to valuate, and all interlocutors were aware of this circumstance :

> "Normally you screen the market for assets or communication opportunities, engagements, collaborations, sponsoring that make sense for the brand. Obviously, you always have guidelines, either you are looking for a certain target group or a certain region (...) We have designed some kind of dashboard which records various KPIs and aggregates them on one level and then spits them out like a traffic light system. Because brand activation sponsoring is incredibly difficult to capture in KPIs." (S2)

However, interviewees of sponsoring companies fully comprehend the fact that, at first glance, music festival sponsorship looks like a 'bad move' in terms of pure economic figures. Thus, the appropriate weighting of the underlying, and hard to measure effects of sponsorship needs to be considered and communicated within the decision-making process in an ongoing step:

> "A Festival per se is actually not a good case for the company (...) because you always lose money (...) unless you add a 'million equivalence value' to it. You can generate this value once and then have to generate it again and again for your definition (...) but then you can just say 'Look here guys, if we had advertised for the same value (on TV), it would have cost us so much money and now we have collected (even more) in the context of this festival.' And then, of course it's fun again, and the case looks completely different." (S2)

For one interviewee the decision to engage as a sponsor at the event, is linked to the characteristic emotions of the university popular music festival itself:

I believe that campus festivals have a higher reference than all the other open airs (...) I'm basically home to party (...) Because I know that people do it with a different kind of emotion. (S1)

Furthermore, this also leads to a 'safe bank' in terms of ticket sales, which then assures the support for the sponsorship within the (sponsoring) company:

At a (regular) Open-Air, the visitor decides kind of spontaneously (if I go) and prefer to buy the ticket rather later than as an 'early bird'. But the decision in terms of going to a campus festival is not even a question. (Because they go) Ticket sales are also important for me as a sponsor and if x-numbers are expected, then that's usually really the case." (S1)

The same interview partner described the decision-making culture with the word 'focus', which here generally is a term that's rather tagged with a time limit. It can either mean that the company is ("at the moment") focusing its brand activities on certain areas or it shall be focused of a slightly changing orientation or direction of the brand in general. These company backgrounds therefor influence decisions as well and incorporate short- and medium-term thinking from the responsible sponsorship manager:

"We always orientate ourselves according to the (current) focus (...) The focus is on 'cities', 'orientation' etc. For example, my brand takes place all over Germany, i.e., wherever there is a party. For me, every university party or campus could be relevant (...) You have to plan everything in advance, so that discussions for the coming season would definitely have to take place in September. But we (also) usually plan at very short notice too." (S1)

The person representing the biggest company in the interviews, stated that the term sponsorship is actually being tried not use within his firm. Furthermore, a pure financial engagement is avoided. He explained that his employer's brand wants to rather be perceived as a partner to event organizers. In the end, this shall lead obviously to a sponsorship partnership with linked marketing activities, but according to the company's motto, it's the goal to being known as a companion that helps the events in order to build a long-term and sustainable relationship with each other. This then forms the basis for long-term goals of both companies and hopefully fuels growth for everyone involved in the project. The decision for a partnership emerges therefore organically by the student employees (of the company) who are already working on the campus as brand ambassadors , who report requirements for certain event activities to the sponsorship manager and then involve him at some point when it seems necessary:

"As long as we can, we try to keep the financial issue out of the picture. Our product is just a functional product and that is very important to us. (...) Especially with our slogan—in this case it is a metaphor—which should help you to do something better, to become even bigger, to become faster and that is the DNA of our marketing concept. (...) We always try to help people to do something better (...) That is our approach. We try to deal with such a festival individually and then discuss: What kind of needs do you have? What do you really need? The simplest would be the Sparkasse (local bank) style, they open the wallet and hang their logo everywhere. But nobody remembers that afterwards, nobody gives a damn, and it doesn't help. (...) We then sit down with the organizer and ask explicitly: What do you need? Is it functional tools? Then someone has costs for bar equipment, which someone has to borrow. Or you need a system for another genre-floor that you want to make somehow." (S3)

On the other side of the spectrum, the organizer sees the process a bit more simplistic, although a successful acquisition of sponsors can be described as mandatory for making a festival financially feasible.

The organizer also endeavors to ensure that brand appearances in whatever form, by and large, have to be compatible with the image of the festival. Thus, when trying to understand how a decision-making culture is to be described, according to his main motive it can be interpreted as a direct or indirect incentive to foster revenue. In this case, the organizing company has been active in the event industry for more than 2 decades. Thus, when dealing with future desirable sponsorship cooperation, the involved employees can already rely on a solid number of known sponsorship-partners:

"In general, this (sponsor-acquisition) is actually part of the entire preliminary planning. We have had festival experience with the "Serengeti Festival" since 2004, so we also know that such festivals cannot be financed without sponsors. Before we deal with certain festivals, we talk to sponsors or agencies in between to see how exciting it would be for them, so that we then have a rough calculation that shows us what sponsorship performance can be achieved." (O1)

As mentioned in the theoretical perspectives regarding an ongoing eventization of the university campuses, a certain professionalization in regard to on-site campus (event-)marketing in general was described. It's these specialized marketing firms who channel sponsorship-endeavors from willing companies directly into the market, which is normally very hard to get into due to the regulation policies of the universities. These 'little helpers' in combination with the positive image-narrative the festivals hold within the universities make it way easier and more lucrative for sponsors to engage in the process. Thus, it is from great help for the organizer of a music festival that is held on a campus. This in turn benefits the organizer:

> "Exactly, it is actually the case that there are also university-marketing-agencies. (...) In addition, it is incredibly difficult for the brands to get to the universities in order to advertise there. When I think of Redbull for instance, who try with all means to advertise there, which is absolutely impossible because the universities exclude that. If you do that in a fundamental festival context, then it looks very different again. The universities in Bielefeld and Paderborn are also 100 % behind their festivals, which is then also part of university marketing or city marketing and then suddenly a lot is possible for the brands to present themselves there." (O1)

The second subcategory of practices can be described as communication-culture and again includes both sides of the sponsorship engagement of sponsors as well as the organizers of the festival.

All interviewees of this study stated to work in a work environment where some sort of a flat hierarchy is incorporated. This goes either for the smaller or bigger firms as it is the case for sponsors and organizer. These hierarchic structures are mostly based on the fact that the employees have a specific authority over their work area. This also includes a certain budget (for sponsors) which shall be managed and utilized for sponsorship activities. The budget, is the issue where sponsorship managers hold total responsibility on the one hand, but on the other hand is mainly the point of issue where despite of the flatness of hierarchy, the supervisor, or the next higher manager needs to be consulted in a case of exceedance:

> "We have a very flat hierarchy (...) I have a budget for regional events, support or whatever in my budget for 2020, for example. And within this budget I then decide myself which events I do (support) and to what extent. It would be pointless to go through everything with the managing director and the marketing manager. That is why it is easier for everyone involved that there

is a clear message that I know my strategy. But I could also talk to them at any time when I have a cool event and run out of money." (S1)

"In general, I am already responsible for the content of my area. In the case of particularly large commitments, you coordinate with your superiors in accordance with the business plan." (S2)

The transfer of responsibility was described particularly distinctive with interviewee three. The interviewee justified this, like many other statements during the interview, with the special corporate and communication culture of the company. In this aspect, the founder of the firm has always seen itself as an innovative and leading player in the event marketing sector.

"Exactly, we have flat hierarchies and what is also very important at our company, is a certain transfer of responsibility. In many companies, you have a marketing goal, you have a budget for that and then you get instructions on how to achieve your marketing goal under this budget. Then you are a robot that works according to scheme F. At our company it's different. There is also a goal and a budget, but you trust the person completely because they know how things are going. The company entrusts the person with the budget so that the person can go to work with their expertise." (S3)

On the organizer's side, the conclusion of sponsoring contracts is usually the responsibility of the company owner. This is due to the fact that long-term relationships usually exist here and can thus be maintained at the same time during personal meetings:

"Then it's more the bosses or the brand representatives who speak directly with each other. But then they (the sponsors) have already received a release of money or a budget that they can spend and then they distribute it to the various festivals. From the point of view of the brand, it is often the case that the representatives are sent out with a budget for the next year and then they should present this brand at ten festivals. They then just have to see to get this budget distributed that way … Sometimes it's really just a phone call or an accidental meeting of a good friend (of the boss) in the sauna or at another event." (O1)

However, ongoing sponsorship relations between the organizer and sponsors do also exist on lower hierarchy levels. These are being reestablished when the next festival is coordinated between the personas who know each other, although the different events hosted by the organizing company are each assigned to different specific employees:

"No, for Bielefeld that's 'Person A'"s responsibility. In the general sponsorship market, of course, we split it up by existing personal relationships, so 'the boss' does a little something, I do a little something and 'Person A' does a little something. It is not very clear now that only one person really does sponsorship." (O1)

When asked if there are any specifics regarding communication within the event management branch, O1 admits to the ongoing 'craziness' someone from outside the branch is probably not familiar with. This fact needs to be considering especially when dealing with potential sponsors as these persons might be scared away by the conventions of the branch:

"Difficult to say as the industry is actually very weird. When I think of such a classic local bank employee who could (during the process) gets caught up in typical 'festival communication', it might be a bit overwhelming because he doesn't know it that way. Everyone also is on first-name basis with external folks, which might also be unusual for him. Otherwise, it is sometimes so chaotic that everyone is somehow special." (O1)

Subsequently to the specifics of communication-culture is the third expressed subcategory: Fingerspitzengefühl.

During the conversations, interviewees often used this German expression, when they wanted to make clear, that certain behaviors when dealing with stakeholders in the music festival branch require a mix of certain experience, touch and some kind of 'pokerface'. Something or some skill not really measurable but certainly important. When it comes to this sure instinct, on where certain practices are originated, interviewees explain their 'doing' with some kind of an instinct feeling which is rooted in experience. This feeling was an always present, underlying description of why and especially how interviewees are acting within their practices. One major circumstance where this was expressed, was by interviewee two, when the often-difficult process of convincing decision-makers of a (big and risky) possible future sponsorship engagement.

"You talk a lot (when explaining or defending a sponsorship engagement within the company) about 'Yes, I think' or 'Yes, I mean' and then there are a lot of personal tastes from the decision-makers (influencing the process).

> That's really terrible and you have to somehow put it on stable feet to make it transparent and understandable for everyone." (S2)

Another aspect was the description of possible complications in the operational implementation of the sponsorship. The changing correspondence with the organizer was especially underlined by S1:

> "(...) change of the contact person on site and the agreed structure is no longer known. Or the event team didn't deliver what you ordered. At one festival, you don't believe how pissed I was because none of it was built up as agreed. Those are the implementation problems that you often have, especially at open air events. You try to set it up (the company's branded equipment) a day in advance and you can't organize everything the way it should be. You then have to give up a certain part because you know it in your gut that it will be done that way and 70-80 % of the time it will not be done that way." (S1)

Strongly connected with the concept of Fingerspitzengefühl is trust between the different parties. All interviewees stated the always occurring goal of sustainable partnerships. The foundation for these relations is trust and due to the parallel running processes, such as contract management and initial operational procedures, trust is an important factor that is difficult to measure right from the start:

> "(...) contract and contract drafting. This is also a process that should not be underestimated. Ultimately, you have to trust and only need it when something doesn't work, but it makes sense to design it cleanly. But there is no point in starting when the contract has been signed. That's not even possible in this business, so you do a lot of parallel work." (S2)

> "(...) and trust is an absolute key element" (S3)

Knowledge Management

The processing and archiving of gained experiences in sponsorship activities plays a major role for either the sponsors or the organizer of music festivals. It justifies how the company, and their employees behave currently and in the near future. Hence, knowledge management can be stated on the one hand as the underlying foundation of the above-described practices and other hand represents a key element of the companies' sponsorship culture which is simultaneously is fueled by experiences made from these practices. The particular kind of ways this issue is approached by, is differentiated by how 'big' the interviewee's employer is. For instance, S1 who works in the smallest corporation (based on annually revenue) described the knowledge archivization process from previous sponsorship engagements as a combination of revue talks and a sort of archive filing:

> "First by looking through the contract's filing, where you will then know what I've actually been doing. Additionally, I have my bullet points describing things like a bad setting … this and that must be improved and so on. There is also still a review conversation with the organizer if possible. With someone I had one after the 'Tausendquell'. I then save everything in my system and can then use it for other brands as well." (S1)

S2 has established and developed the company's own internal Sponsorship-KPI-System, which has been proven its value for a couple of years already:

> "I introduced a modeling [system], which then works more or less like a dashboard and records various KPIs, aggregates them on a level that it ultimately spits out like a [red, yellow, green] traffic light system." (S2)

S3's employer has gone a couple of steps further and uses an internal reporting tool that is implementing not only written knowledge but also connects ongoing project-communication as well as on-site documented media in the archiving process(es):

> "In any case, that's [archiving] super important! We have such an online tool. That is called *companyname*-University. It is structured in a similar way like Facebook, so you have such a forum where all employees [dealing with sponsorship engagements] in the world have access to. They all have the same reporting guideline under their account, where you can upload your report via an entry. These are then an exact documentation of what you exactly did. Photos or recap videos are also uploaded there. Each individual entry is then also associated with working hours that the respective employee must then also report to us and that is then also associated with direct feedback from us (…) Everything happens at the festival level, but what is also important for us is internal reporting. So, the employee does this using the mentioned online tool and we have to report to our bosses in Munich. You can then have a quick phone call, which alone doesn't show that much impression, or you can prepare a really nice PowerPoint presentation. We always have photographers

and videographers with us, and we use these recordings to build these re-caps. And with that we show exactly what we have done awesome with our budget (...) So this reporting really always captures the most impressive picture of the event. This shows that something was really going on and there is also a description. When did it take place, where it was and how many people were there? And the listed measures once summarized. Ideally, this is all a highlight clip and at the end of each presentation there is a slide with learnings on it. What went well? What do we definitely have to do again? What needs to be improved? It's generally just a collection of knowledge for us. Mistakes can happen, but not for a second time." (S1)

Next to the actual data regarding e.g., experiences or beliefs, what became very clear during the interview was how sensitive these gathered information seem to the companies. The constant amendment and updating of the experiences made in past engagements imply a great value for competing in this branch:

"And it's also very clear that we have to protect our ways of thinking. Because sometimes they are very specific. This is not top secret and if you deal with it, you will find it out on your own, but there is still this executive order that I am not allowed to speak in public on behalf of my employer." (S3)

Furthermore, the sponsoring companies rate the archiving process of much higher than the 'receiving stakeholder' of sponsorship engagements, the organizer of a festival. Hence, the focus here lies more on 'satisfying the sponsor' shortly after the festival with the intention to continue the sponsorship engagement at future events:

"First you look at how the process worked, especially with such large sponsors you look again explicitly. (For example) With the crane in Paderborn, the Sparkasse (Local Bank) thought that every visitor who got on, would receive a white ribbon with a Sparkasse logo. That was not discussed in advance and unfortunately this white ribbon was identical to the backstage ribbon, which of course caused confusion for the security. Such points are of course addressed, but also when we have provided the sponsors with material on how it works. And then, what's of course much more important for the sponsor is, how the overall process was for him. Whether his goals were achieved, which are of course also defined in advance." (O1)

All interviewees expressed that the companies have understood that the constantly evolving knowledge will reflect a key element in the future marketing activities of the companies. This is especially the case in times of high fluctuation, it is very important for companies to secure and archive this 'capital' in order to benefit from it in the long term.

Assessments

As above illustrated in Figure 6, the conceptual framework of this study incorporates assessments of all interviewees as a constantly evolving construct influencing all other aspects of their individual (inter)acting, experiencing and knowledge regarding sponsorship culture between sponsors and festival organizer.

The individual assessments that were addressed in the interviews are very different from one another with regards to content. Therefore, the individual sub-categories are listed as individual sub-chapters accordingly.

Market for University Popular Music Festivals in Germany

As mentioned in the theoretical perspectives section, one might still describe the market for university popular music festivals in Germany despite the eventization of university campuses as niche. As active stakeholders in this market, it was therefore of interest to understand how the interviewees explain and evaluate market.

All interlocutors described the market for university popular music festivals as a niche market within the market for popular music festivals in Germany. This description is mainly based on huge differences in terms of revenue or visitor numbers when comparing a university popular music festival with e.g., *Rock am Ring*. Furthermore, although a variety of pop music is performed at the events, one interviewee would not describe university festivals as being mainstream.

Nevertheless, sponsors value the importance in regard to the city and/or university and the 'image-boost' of these events especially in mid-sized German cities:

"I think the campus festivals have a higher reference than all the other open airs you could do in many cities." (S1)

"(...) the niche could be expanded there. But you could never make it completely mainstream." (S1)

Due to the mentioned smaller audience of around 15,000 to 18,000 (at the biggest events in Germany) people, S2 rates university popular music festivals still as 'boutique', meaning an event with strong local connectedness and unique character. Furthermore, the niche character of university music festivals may have negative consequences in the near future due to the current extrusion in the business. The interviewee predicts a tougher competition for all mid-size music festivals in terms of high-quality artist booking:

> "Precisely because EDM actually comes from a completely overpaid corner (of the business) (...) which makes it really difficult for small festivals to still afford artists." (S2)

S3 sees the current market for university music festival as a growing and very important market, especially from the viewpoint as a sponsor. In his considerations with regard to sponsorship-culture, students and (live) music are fundamentally linked. He justifies this with the fact that students in Germany already represent the largest proportion of festival attendees.

> "From the numbers, you could still call it a niche market (...) I think this is a growing, very important market. Students and music are two very big topics that go together. Lots of students already go to festivals, etc. (...)" (S3)

In addition, he states that university music festivals hold the vibe of teenager house parties:

> "Having a festival at your university is a bit like having a party at your home when you were younger, and your parents are not there and you can really freak out." (S3)

Furthermore, he predicts high professionalism with regard to the organization(s) behind the events. According to his experiences, the current different kind of existing university events across Germany seem to head in this direction. For potential sponsors, this means a better access to the market itself.

As an experienced stakeholder in the festival market, he also attributes a special characteristic or vibe to the university festivals due to their location and the audience which consists almost exclusively of student. This is very appealing for some artists, as many artists are looking for special performances in addition to the 'normal' festivals:

> "These are very different models. Is it now a student council or someone who now has an event agency? Seen through marketing and application glasses,

that's gold because you have the opportunity to suddenly be visible in the middle of the campus and to advertise your products." (S3)

Nonetheless, in some cases the sponsorship process may come to a certain point, where it collides with intentions of the university of city who also want to use the event as a marketing instrument:

"That's a fine line, of course. How much you (the event) cooperate with business(es) or not. Or how much you can do with yourself as a university or when it ends. That also varies a lot."

From the organizer's point of view, the market can be characterized with high growth potential due to (still) rising student numbers in Germany. Due to traditions of more than 20 years for some festivals, the events have reached a point of trademark understanding. In some cases, the popularity within the student community can then spill over to the rest of the city. The combination of localism and sure every year ticket sales then creates a specific vibe of every event for the organizer and the audience combined:

"(...) but also, quite specifically tailored to the cities (...) Then there is the environment of the respective students, as well as those interested in festivals in general. They will then also have a larger ore where they sell their tickets. (...)"

University Identification
When interviews were asked about their assessments, identification of students with their respective educational institution were of interest, as this issue can leverage the way sponsorship at a university popular music festival is handled and conceived.

Sponsors described this topic with caution or were assessing it without relies on experience or numbers. The general assumption of sponsors is an existing wide differentiation of identification over different faculties and departments within the universities. Nevertheless, sponsors as well as organizer see a certain appreciation among students in terms of the university's effort that benefits their view to the university and its executive committee:

"I believe that the bond is greater than I would personally assess." (S1)
"I think there are courses of studies which are very proud of its institution, others not so much I guess (...) and at campus festivals, which then take place at the university, there is a total identification of the university. Well,

if my university can organize such a big festival, then my university is awesome." (S4)

Sponsors assessed the identification context as utilizable for sponsorship activities if it is appropriately addressed. Thus, they see in this issue as yet untapped potential. Furthermore, in their considerations when debating university identification in regard to sponsorship culture, organizers draw a comparison with the identification culture of U.S. American universities and their students, which appears to be significantly higher. This is taken as a reason for a similar development in this direction in Germany as well:

"They (U.S. universities) also have a higher degree of identification to their university. They make significantly more money with their university merchandise etc. than over here; I believe we are heading in such a direction as well." (O1)

Motives for Festival Attendance

Understanding motives for festival attendance is key for designing sponsorship-activities in the market as well as creating the event and the embedded experience itself. Thus, interviewees gave deep insights into their understanding of why visitors attend the festivals, whereas different attempts in explaining those underlying motives became evident.

Comprehending these contexts is critical to the culture of sponsorship for these events, as the same interviewee describes:

"There is a completely different bandwidth of partying and experiencing than in classic nightlife for instance (...) That's what makes sponsorship here so exciting, you know exactly where to put the right accents." (S1)

University popular music festivals were described as events with a whole different bandwidth of experiences which includes the mentioned bond to the region as well as the university venue. According to one interviewee, this leads to a certain fear of missing out on something, which hence can drive people to attend:

"I believe that such an event is actually always a nicer experience than going to a dark disco on Saturday night (...) Very different emotions are set free (...) There are different kinds of moments at these festivals (...) Then there is also the connection to the region, and the fear of missing out." (S1)

The fear of missing out on something is based on socializing factors, which was also mentioned by every interviewee. Especially the fact, that one has the possibility to not only socialize with unknown people prior to the event, but to everyone from their individual daily life:

> "I believe, what's very cool is, that if you are firmly integrated in the university-life and know your 30-40 people, then a festival like this is always a special experience. Otherwise, you might always drive to another city, where only 3-4 people join. At the university festival on your doorstep, (...) you can possibly manage to go with all your friends." (S3)

One interviewee was extraordinary well read on the subject matter and cited marketing literature as well as scientific motivational research papers, that were also implemented in the theoretical perspectives of this dissertation. Based on this, the interviewee's company's hashtags connecting the event with the sponsoring brand as well as the suitability of the event venue for taking Instagram photos finds a way into the way sponsorship is tailored.

At some point in every interview, the conversation led to a point where music as a motive for festival attendance was discussed. This was either the case for seeing music consumption in general as a motive or the specific line-up as reason to visit the event. What sounds obvious at first, turned out to be a critical issue for sponsors. Thus, two interviewees stated to had developed an elaborate in-house assessment- and classification-system to differentiate types of audiences. In this way, any adjustments to sponsoring activities at events can be adjusted and refined prior to the actual event:

> "We also thought a lot about this! We actually defined three different music consumers for ourselves (...) the music diggers, the nerds who make music themselves or play instruments, who have an extremely high level of knowledge of the scene, but are only a very, very small percentage of the people. Then there are the 'semi-professionals' who are not that sick but already know what's going on in the music world. With their understanding of music, they can still assign artists and hypes. (...) The biggest ones are the live music followers. Their main focus is on partying, they don't care who is up there, they just want to freak out with friends, celebrate, drink (...) If you put an extremely expensive DJ on a festival where drinking is in the foreground, then that's absolutely wasted money and a stupid experience for this DJ. And you have to be careful how mainstream and how scene you do it in the end." (S3)

"You can't generalize that (...) There is also a very heterogeneous mix of visitor types. Also, clearly dependent on the music direction. Basically, the young target group has a positive attitude towards value-added sponsoring. They are aware of infrastructure and booking costing money and that this works much easier through cooperation with valuable partners." (S2)

However, music is seen definitely as the number one motive for festival goers by the organizer of the event:

"Fundamentally, firstly because people want to see the line-up. After all, we always book correspondingly well-known artists and that costs us a lot."

Consumer Budget

The financial budget of the festival's audience was described as rather low. This has been stated by all interview partners and has been not only assessed but also been explained by gained experiences in the market:

"Bad haha! According to our (internal) calculations, the willingness to spend money at such festivals is very low. You always hope that it might be around 20-40 €, but it's usually more like 10-15 €, unless the party escalates, and people lose track of things." (S3)

Prices for tickets for the university student festivals are also kept low by the festival's organizer themselves, to ensure that students as main audience group are able to afford a ticket:

"So, we're slowly testing prices to be a little more marketable. At such a normal day festival with bands you kind of pay double of that. We have always divided the prices into students, non-students, and employees. But we already have the feeling that we can't go over € 20 with a festival like this if it is supposed to be of that magnitude." (O1)

However, some interview partners expressed the assumption of a misleading interpretation of financial abilities of the current generation of students, as some interviewees are not only involved in the university music festival market but additionally in the general event branch as well as other music festival branches. As mentioned above, students also represent a big part of the consumers in these areas too. Interview partners expressed doubt why one should generally assume, that students have a low budget when it comes to university music festivals, when on the other hand they (students in general) spend a lot of money on other events:

> "And on the one hand you are totally frugal, buy cheap clothes, but then suddenly spend 500-600 € on Parookaville etc." (S1)

Sponsorship Awareness and Attitude towards Sponsorship

Whether or not a sponsorship engagement at a university festival is being accepted seems to be very depending on how intrusive it is designed and or carried out. Especially when the sponsor is actively getting in touch with the festival visitors, interview partners state a necessity for sure instinct and intuition for the specifics of the individual target group. One sponsor explicitly linked these 'specifics' of an audience to the genre of the festival (if it is to be called).

> "You can't generalize that and say the same about all festivals. There is also a very heterogeneous mix of visitor types. Also, clearly dependent on the music direction." (S2)

However, if interview partners had to define the current (generation y) group of festival attendees, they described them leaning towards sponsorship-favorable due to the existing common background knowledge regarding a festival's funding structure:

> "Basically, the young current target group has a positive attitude towards value-added sponsorship. They are aware that infrastructure and booking also cost money and that this works much easier through cooperation with valuable partners. But of course, there are always those complainers who then say, now I'm going there and then have to look at this branding for five days." (S2)

The general assumption that students are more likely to lean left in their political opinions than the general population, is still an issue when designing a sponsorship cooperation with a university music festival. Organizers try to communicate this issue to sponsors, to avoid possible criticism linked to the sponsorship which ultimately could then be linked to the festival itself:

> "So, I think everything that takes place on the poster is a bit more critical (...) for universities, because that seems a bit more capitalistic." (O1)

However, one interviewee stated that although some students still seem to have this kind of skeptical attitude towards ('capitalistic') festival sponsorship, he experiences students (on social media) becoming more favorable to the topic, when they are aware of the (valued) add-on the sponsorship can have on the festival experience and the benefitting and often necessary funding for the festival:

> "In Mainz we had a case where it really polarized because our logo couldn't be overlooked there. Then there were a few who railed against the commercialization of their university and criticized why an advertising company was given access to the university this way. On the other hand, there were also students on a Facebook post who defended it emphatically and declared it was the best campus festival that ever existed, and it was clear that it was not only financeable through the beverage-revenue."

In addition to the acceptance of sponsorship activities, the quality, and the way how they are communicated and designed also influence the effectiveness of the cooperation, according to the interview partners. Due to the differences in experiences with the specifics of the festival market, especially 'one-time sponsorships' are rated negatively:

> "So, I don't think that you can consolidate a brand at a festival with a one-time sponsorship. If you are not yet firmly established (...) then I would not enter into such a commitment. I cannot assume that someone with 1.7 per mille will still remember that I had a great big pink cube and that he won a crown there." (S4)

Furthermore, the growing overflow of information and overstimulation of daily life is seen as challenge(s) for sponsorship activities. Fishing for attention is led by smartphone apps as well as the digital and analogue marketing industry and challenges sponsorship to find better subliminal ways to communicate to the audience of a music festival. In that case, branding therefor is seen as one effective way to meet these challenges due to its subliminality and its link to be perceived as festival funder:

> "(...) then you just had a beer. But if there is a stage around it and special artists have also performed. Then it may be remembered as supporter" (S2)

Social Media

When asking the interviewees very openly about their first thoughts in relation to impact of on-site social media usage with regards to music festival sponsorship, two main themes emerged. First, the current (technical) situation on festival venues usually doesn't really allow smart phone use and thus data-intensive apps like social media consistently. This is due to the network being overloaded by a large number of people in a confined space:

> "I don't see that as a problem (right now). At a lot of festivals, the network coverage is bad anyway. Sooner or later the cell phone will be gone anyway." (S2)

Furthermore, this issue has even been addressed as a sponsorship idea itself:

> "There are sponsorship models that incorporate this. Often it is actually still the case that you have little or no reception at such festivals. I remember that Deutsche Telekom once took advantage of that (...) They simply set up a mobile tower and used it as a marketing-gag" (O1)

However, all interview partners are aware of this (technical) state will possibly change in the medium term and on-site social media usage will increase. This scenario is rather seen as an opportunity than a problem. The possibility to expand the social-media-reach of the festival to people who were not at the festival at all, offers the sponsors the chance to digitally link the positive experiences of the event (experienced by the audience) with their brand or product for third parties. Additionally, the gained sponsorship effects from the festival are also preserved on social media for a much longer time:

> "Reach is always a very strong argument. Whether you have reached 10,000 people on site or all of them post their stuff. Then the range increases very quickly, of course. That has mind blowing potential." (S3)

Another point that was noted was the prevailing 'show what you have' mentality in the Instagram app. Therefore, a festival visit can be also understood as a status symbol that is worth sharing. Hence, the sponsors' thoughts go in the direction (similar to travel agencies) to design certain (sponsorship) locations on the festival venue in such a way that they are perceived offensively as good and suitable Instagram photo spots and are then ultimately used as a motive by the visitors:

> "Young kids in particular always hold their cell phones up horizontally. People go to festivals to talk about them and the Instagram world in particular is structured in such a way that it almost points in the direction. I show my followers what I experience. All the stories that are made at such festivals are then absolute status symbols. We just have to see how we integrate." (S3)

Personal Beliefs

Across all interviews, participants stated different descriptions and opinions on basic habits, practices, knowledge, and standards that shape the culture of sponsorship between the organizer of the university festivals and potential festival's sponsors. Due to the semi-structure of the interviews, sometimes interviewees reported things, circumstances or opinions that were taken out of context of the on-going discussion at various points during the conversation. Therefore, during coding it became clear to sum-up these scattered answers as own *Personal Beliefs* code themselves, which now forms a round off of the results as closing chapter before concluding the study.

All participants expressed the general need for recognizing, understanding, and implementing possible consequences of social developments in their doing. This is key for avoiding mistakes and protect the fragile construct of reputation of their employer:

> "Yes, understanding both target groups and preferences. A few years ago, we had a survey at a festival, when we weren't really perceived as natural partners for them. In fact, it is now the case that people who were then able to get enthusiastic about our assets at festivals also statistically buy more of our product. This naturally supports the 'favorite brand' preference." (S2)

> "(...) but you have to discuss that with the artists and yes, I've been accompanying these festivals for four years now and we do really need to notice the shift in behavior" (S1)

Following the issue of societal developments, interviewees described the current audience (in 2019) as difficult to comprehend as a whole. Terms like *individualization* and *ungroupable* were used to express the adversity to communicate via sponsorship at a festival:

> "I find this generation difficult to understand anyway." (S1)

> "It is so much more complex to 'talk' to these folks" (S3)

Participants describe this generation as stingy demanding consumers who are only willing to spend money if they get something really special in return, an experience:

> "But then they stand on the shelf and definitely want the cheapest product. And best of all, free entry to discos, etc. Money is only spent when its tailored especially 'to you' and when it enhances or improves your current state (of mind)." (S4)

Therefore, the main goal of sponsors is to include the festival's experience narrative, where they can and link these positive individual emotions to their brand or product:

> "It's a very emotional asset and it's wonderful when you can develop something like that. That should actually always be the objective (...) I am a fan of the fact that messages should always be tailored to the target group, activation should also offer added value for the organizer, as well as for the target group, as well as for us." (S2)

This is especially important when companies or brands have their sponsorship debut. One participant expressed the necessity for emotion as the number one preference when entering the first sponsorship deal and risking a total waste of money when not doing so:

> "But then you also have to look which brands are at festivals. These are mostly brands that have accompanied you quite often in your everyday life (...) It makes no sense for me to launch a product at a festival without linking it to the atmosphere, emotions only arise when I will associate something with the brand." (S1)

Next to the mentioned activation of the brand, the overall challenge in the sponsorship business was addressed by all participants: sustainability. In times of sub- and subsubcontracting, sponsorship manager can oversee the fact that the more a process is cut into pieces and delegated to numerous external partners, the more the underlying sponsorship goals lose their significance in their doing:

> "In my opinion, some organizers don't quite get it right. Where you always feel a bit abandoned as an industry, is when they hand it over to a caterer and the caterer hands it on to another company. *The content of the event has to be prepared by the organizer, whereby I would have clear ideas of how everything*

should work. Then you can't suddenly say during the planning that our brand is not to be seen on all counters after all. Then you will come to an agreement on monetary terms, there is a contact price, after which a contract is drawn up that includes all the measures that are important for both sides." (S2)

This behavior and the lack of commitment often forces the sponsors to re-work themselves and to check the organizer's implementation of the needed actions:

"Yes, they don't activate it. *That's exactly what I mean. If you just buy your rights and push your product through, it won't work in Germany." (S2)*

"The main thing is to have a banner hanging somewhere, haha. (...) *The brand manager doesn't know sometimes either, etc. This is how it is, I'm the one who imagines it in my head, sees it implemented and can then initiate changes." (S1)*

Discussion of Results

The qualitative interview study delivers unique insights because it is the first qualitative study focusing on the culture of sponsorship in the German popular music festival market. It identifies not only beliefs of the sponsors as a single belief group, but also incorporates the organizer of popular music festivals which enables a holistic view on the underlying culture existing between these two stakeholder groups. Based on the interview analysis, a comprehensive conceptual framework was developed which includes six factors that are relevant for the multi-layered connection between organizer and sponsors. The framework summarizes the findings of the qualitative study and is presented in Figure 6.

The conceptual framework of factors influencing sponsorship culture comprises descriptions by both groups nested in four main categories that are amended by the assessments of six environment issues and the personal beliefs by participants. All categories as well as the assessments and personal beliefs are affected by each other and are discussed below:

First Step Process(es): The first steps after a by both sides preferred deal are shaped by legal actions. Basically, a legal framework is intended as a kind of safeguard in the event of things going wrong. But especially in this case it is particularly important due to two contractual partners involved pursuing completely different goals: on the one hand, there are marketing and sponsoring goals such as visibility or brand activation, and on the other stands the success of the event and the monetary intentions of the organizer in the foreground. Already in this first process of rapprochement between the two contractual partners, it became clear that sometimes rather unusual attempts to deal with the situation are being used. In most cases one cannot await contract drafting or signing, due to time limits and pressure. Trust therefore plays a role right from the start and encourages all parties to think long-term in order to build an upright relationship with the other. In addition to the contractual matter, first steps are the planning and pre-organizing of the sponsorship obligation, orders are given, tasks are assigned to both sides and communication channels are defined. Also regarding with this issue, existing relationships between the contractual partners are seen as great value because progress is made much faster, as you can rely on and refer to well-established customs and known persons.

Practices: Practices were divided into three subcategories, decision-culture, Communication culture and the overarching term *Fingerspitzengefühl*. The decision culture covers the practices up to the point where a decision for or against a sponsorship deal is made. This includes either actively screening the market or being approached by a possible business partner. The bigger the sponsoring company, the more sophisticated these practices are. Utilizing campus ambassadors to receive the ongoing happenings on and inside the campus or managing an internal KPI System for rating particular festivals in regard to the fitting of the brand. Sponsors try to find festivals that incorporate a vibe or experience which fits the sponsoring brand or company. The way how the festivals are being sponsors is also very different from sponsor to sponsor and varies from a simple transfer of money to being seen a holistic event management partner of the festival. The embodiment of this practices, this became very clear during the interviews, is very much connected to the overarching incorporated company culture of the sponsors.

The communication-culture is overall coined by flat hierarchies, this is the case for the sponsoring companies as well as for the organizer. Nevertheless, the field of sponsorship seems to be of rather great interest within sponsorship companies, bringing even the CEO to the table. The reason for this lies in the incalculable value of such an engagement. The mentioned KPI Systems are also tied to this instance, because very often it needs rather *Fingerspitzengefühl* than complex calculations to sell a sponsorship agreement within the company. *Fingerspitzengefühl* is a German expression for sure instinct that was used frequently during the conversations. Next to inner-company explanation of sponsorship deals it is needed in various situations by sponsorship managers ranging from first encounters with new business partners to having a feel for the fit of sponsoring brand and sponsored event.

Knowledge Management: The term knowledge management which has been intended for this work can be seen as the process of creating, sharing, using, and managing the knowledge and information of an organization. Therefore, when following point (2), knowledge management, in a sense may also be understood as a combination of certain practices as the term management evidently forms a cycle of adopted actions. However, due to its archiving narrative it is being analyzed as a standalone issue. Interviews revealed its multidisciplinary approach to achieve organizational objectives by making (the best) use of past gathered experiences ultimately forming knowledge. As described above in the theoretical framework, knowledge is a major part which fuels the culture of an entity.

Knowledge management in regard and as part of sponsorship culture between the organizer and the sponsor of a university popular music festival incorporates a review process of the contract's content and what was then implemented or actively carried out at the event. Participants assessed the specific timing of this procedure as important to be as early after the event as possible to be able to recall as much as possible.

Building upon these insights, findings in regard to how knowledge is then being transformed and archived, again, varies in complexity depending on the company's size(s).

However, the intentions of altering the newly obtained knowledge and the newly gained experiences with business partners lie in shaping the way how participants will act in a similar setting in the future. Furthermore, the abovementioned kinds of (KPI) System(s) also utilize newly gained benchmarks for influencing future decisions on similar possible sponsorship deals.

Assessments: As shown in figure 6, subjective assessments by participants regarding environment as well as thematically expanding and related areas of sponsoring cultures represent a certain meta level influencing all above mentioned issues of sponsorship cultures.

Participants were asked directly and specifically about some issues according to semi-structure. However, in some cases, at different points in time during the interviews, other (better) opportunities emerged to discuss and debate participant's assessments. This methodologically particularity shows (once again) the entanglement and influence of personal assessments on the related issues.

The assessments can be separated into six sub-categories: Market for university popular music festivals in Germany, university identification (of attending audience), motives for festival attendance, budget (of the audience), sponsorship—approval and impact (on audience), social media.

The market for university festivals is a rapidly growing niche market within the event industry and is vaguely described as non-mainstream by participants. One reason for this is seen in the image effect of such a festival on the university, its city, and its region. This strong involvement with the university as well as its city and municipality harbors enormous potential in terms of public and legal approval and support, which can have an indirect positive effect on sponsoring activities on the events.

The special vibe of the festivals emerging through their special on-campus location, is another feature which can release special potential within sponsorship engagement if it is correctly refined. The size of the festivals can be described as medium-sized (boutique) compared to the big players of the superior festival market. In the medium term, the normally very difficult access to the university audience is easier due to specialized marketing companies such as *Unicum*. Organizer structure is seen very professional.

The student's personal relationship with their university and the associated identification with it is an issue which can be utilized for sponsorship activities. In particularly by understanding the linkage between the similar image motives of the university and the municipality. Sponsors as well as organizers have recognized this topic and assign a decent potential to it.

There were two main Motives for festival attendance specified by participants. Due to the local bond a university music festival has with its city and region can be seen as the root for a motivational aspect when fearing to miss out on something. Socializing with fellow student or friends is seen as the number one motive by the sponsors, though it is complicated to channel this context into actual sponsorship activities due to a different and unique kind of event setting. The second mentioned motive was music and is rather seen critical due to the differentiation of today's audience(s). Music as motive for festival attendance is seen as number one motive for the organizer whereas sponsors value it second.

Visitor's budget for university popular music festivals is estimated to be very low on average due to the high student share of the audience. Participants called it to be ranging between 10 € and 25€ after having paid the ticket.

Sponsorship approval is closely linked to the differentiation of target groups within the festival audience. As mentioned above this differentiation of generation y audience(s) requires intuition, sure instinct and experience of the person involved with the designing of the sponsorship content. To put it very cautiously, generation y student audiences do seem to be favorable and open for music festival sponsorship in general, due to an existing understanding of the financial necessity of sponsorships for the event. However, student audiences are politically characterized as a bit left leaning which in some cases requires special cautiousness when designing sponsorship activities with regards to (anti-)capitalistic narratives. Assessments regarding the effectiveness of sponsorship engagements with university popular music festivals strongly depend on how sponsorship is designed in relation to the growing information overflow caused by smart phone use. Furthermore, sponsorship sustainability with respect to a long-running nature of a sponsorship commitment with a festival, is important to ensure meeting marketing goals. One time sponsorship deals are assessed as very ineffective.

Assessments regarding social media within the context of music festival sponsorship is still affected by a limited use of the mobile network on-site due to overload. However, it can be assumed that these restrictions will be solved in the medium term. Therefore, a holistic view on social media is seen as an opportunity within sponsorship culture in the music festival market. This is mainly due to the possibility to expand the sponsorship engagement beyond the actual festival site(s). Furthermore, a visit to an event and/or music festival can be interpreted as a certain status symbol in today's experience society. In particular, the app Instagram actively picks up on this issue of exhibition and can thus be utilized within a sponsorship context.

Personal beliefs of sponsorship stakeholders (sponsors and organizers) constantly fuel and bias decisions and practices. Repeating practices manifest themselves within knowledge structure(s) as well as within believe systems. Personal beliefs are closely linked to recognizing, understanding, and implementing possible consequences of social developments in their acting and behaving. Personal beliefs range across a variety of meta-themes that stand in direct influence on sponsorship within the music festival market. Specifically meant here, is the individualization and ungroupability of the current visitor structure of popular music festivals. The fundamental inclusion of an emotionalizing festival narrative within the sponsoring context as well as a constant determination to reform and maintain sponsorship culture within the sponsoring or organizing company is seen as mandatory for long term success.

However, qualitative studies have shown that by engaging in inductive research, scholars can illuminate understudied phenomena that may bear unexpected discoveries. Therefore, findings from qualitative studies contribute to marketing, economics, event management as well as popular music studies literature by discovering the substantial issues affecting sponsorship culture within and between sponsors and organizers of popular music festivals with emphasis on university popular music festivals. Also, it sheds new light on the dynamic interrelations between practices, knowledge, assessments, and personal beliefs of involved stakeholders. In an ongoing step, qualitative studies' results will together with results from Study Two build a part of the foundation of the quantitative questionnaire of Study Three of this dissertation.

Study Two: Focus Group Interviews | Audience

An understanding of all stakeholder's motivational constructs plays a major role when dealing with sponsorship cultures.[1] Thus, in the second study of this dissertation a qualitative approach is employed to specifically explore and understand underlying motivational constructs for attending a popular music festival in Germany using a focus group methodology. This study has been conducted in a very early stage of the research process for this dissertation. As to not to overlook any motivational contexts at the time, wording was extended to popular music festival attendance, rather than focusing on solely university music festivals.[2] Furthermore, results of this study are then utilized partially as a foundation to build upon in the questionnaire used in the third study of this dissertation.

Methodology—Focus Groups as Instrument for Data Collection

Focus groups are a suitable and relatively resource-efficient qualitative survey tool for involving a limited number of citizens in a discourse process. They encourage group interaction on a topic predetermined by the researcher, and allow for the open discussion of participant viewpoints, as well as the sharing of any dissenting positions and alternative viewpoints. The discussed subject matter is set by means of a stimulus, for example by a short film, an image, a

---

1   Bruhn, *Sponsoring*.
2   Although the question regarding motivational constructs was broadened in this study, the discussion nevertheless reached a point several times at which the Paderborn or Bielefeld Festival were discussed without the moderator forcing it.

homepage or as in this case, a short lecture.[3] Therefore this method has been selected and identified as particularly suitable for exploring consumer motivational constructs prior to the collection of these motivational constructs which forms one part of the questionnaire in the quantitative studies. The aim was to recruit a cross-section of adults who are familiar with and had attended at least one popular music festival in the last two years which met the criteria of the study. Participants were selected from responses to an e-mail advertising the study. A 25€ Amazon voucher was used as an incentive. The focus group participants, therefore, formed a convenience sample of potential audience of such an event with an age range of 18–35 years. Three focus groups were conducted, with a total of 18 participants. As with all dialogue processes, group effects should be minimized due to seniority or status. Because focus groups work best when they are put together homogeneous in terms of socio-economic and demographic characteristics, so that all participants can and are willing to talk to each other well in an unprejudiced way.[4]

Thus, participants were divided into three focus groups according to their current individual career status.

The process of the focus groups is divided into three main parts. The *first part* deals with establishing the research question, defining the group(s) as well as the preparation of the focus group with regard to the content and organization:

- Defining the problem and the research question: The main goal of the focus group interviews conducted prior to the questionnaire is to explore motivational constructs for popular music festival attendance and to confirm or repel existing motives for cultural consumption which had been drawn from literature.

- Determination of the group: When composing the participants of a focus group, the socio-demographic variables have to be considered. As with all dialogue processes, group effects should be minimized due to seniority or status. Thus, focus groups work best when they are put together

---

3   Marlen Schulz, Birgit Mack, and Ortwin Renn, eds., *Fokusgruppen in der empirischen Sozialwissenschaft* (Wiesbaden: VS Verlag für Sozialwissenschaften, 2012), https://doi .org/10.1007/978-3-531-19397-7.

4   Corinna Pelz, Annette Schmitt, and Markus Meis, "Knowledge Mapping as a Tool for Analyzing Focus Groups and Presenting Their Results in Market and Evaluation Research," *Forum: Qualitative Social Research* 5 (2004); Flick, *Qualitative Sozialforschung*.

in a way that all participants are willing to talk to each other without restraint. Therefor focus groups are usually made up homogeneously regarding socio-economic and demographic characteristics. In addition to the communicative aspect, there is also a content advantage of homogeneous groups. People with similar backgrounds may find a common ground faster and identification/fraternization processes stimulate more honest and open-hearted responses. Usually, it is better for the quality of the discussion, if the participants do not know each other personally. To meet the mentioned requirements different focus groups are put together by the 'individual career stage', meaning 1) *in education* 2) *career entrant* 3) *career sophisticated*

- Selection and briefing of moderator: As moderator for the focus group interview Ms. Lea Hansjürgen has been chosen, Lea works as a research assistant and network manager for the startup centre *garage 33* which is closely linked to the University of Paderborn. In addition to her academic career, she has worked in several think tanks dealing with cultural development in German cities, where she has already gained a lot of experience as a moderator.
- Focus group guide preparation and stimulus determination.
- Recruitment of participants: The number of required focus groups varies with the scope and differentiation of the question. Closely defined problems—especially if they target only a very specific part of the population, such as a small group of experts—can be adequately dealt with in a single or very few focus groups.

The undertaken discussion by the focus group can be named as the *second part* of the process. According to literature a focus group discussion is set to last between 90 minutes and three hours, this was also the case in this study. The focus group's quality depends largely on the moderator's ability to involve all people equally, to keep any troublemakers in bound and to encourage reluctant people to actively participate, which was certainly the case in all three Groups. In addition to the moderator, an assistant was required who was responding to any concerns of the participants (e.g., get coffee) and keep an eye on the time, write down central theses and assign them to the participants accordingly. This task was taken over by the author himself which gave him a first peek of feeling regarding the discussions of the focus groups.

The execution of the focus groups can be divided into six individual steps:

a) Greeting
b) Introduction by participants (name, profession etc.)
c) Introduction to the topic by the moderator by short lecture and a Power Point Presentation
d) Asking key questions: "Why did/do you buy tickets for a university popular music festival", "What are the driving motives to attend a university popular music festival"
e) Additional (explaining) questions: Define 'motive-areas' such as *Music, Escape, Environment, Social Interaction*
f) Prioritize motives with the help of index cards as individual participant and as focus group

All focus groups were digitally recorded, transcribed, with transcripts then checked against the recordings. A clear assignment of persons and statements in retrospect has been achieved. No video recording was made due to the increased quality of a study with a certain proximity to the everyday world of the respondents:

Knowing about the video recording can cause uncertainty among the participants and have a not inconsiderable influence on the detail or depth of their answers. The effect of the various technical devices and materials commonly used in dialogue processes, such as flipcharts or overhead transparencies, have not yet been clearly investigated. This can certainly increase the impression that the situation is professional, but possibly with the undesirable side effect of noticeable reluctance on the part of individual participants.

The *third part* is formed by the data analysis, interpretation, and presentation of the results. To this day, there is no standardized procedure for evaluating focus groups. The analysis is usually based on a transcript of the conversation. Thus, all social science evaluation methods from hermeneutic to contingency-analytical to frequency-analytical methods are available.

According to the main goals of the focus groups, it is less the individual contributions to the discussion than the range of opinions of the entire group that are of interest.[5] Digital audio recordings and protocols serve as the basis, but also checked transcripts and symbolic outputs (e.g., index cards). If several materials were used in one focus group, all were taken into account in the evaluation. Since these were developed during the focus group under

---

5   Pelz, Schmitt, and Meis, "Knowledge Mapping as a Tool for Analyzing Focus Groups and Presenting Their Results in Market and Evaluation Research."

the critical eye of the participants and Lea, the communicative validity of the findings was amended.

The evaluation based on transcripts can basically take place on two different levels, on the one hand on the relationship level when the process of forming an opinion is the focus, which is not the case for this study. In this case the content plays the main role, meaning the group output is relevant. This form of evaluation includes the identification of central topics of the conversation as well as a description and explanation of the various opinions and also additionally (as described earlier in step six of the individual execution of the focus group) the output regarding the motivational constructs formed by the whole focus group. Topics were obtained inductively from the discussions during the focus groups.

Study Results

A number of key themes were identified, whereas three themes are individually connected to related (sub-)themes. Analysis of these themes led to the development of *Table 4*, which summarizes the key insights gained regarding Motivational Constructs for popular music festival attendance. Each of these themes as well as subthemes are explained further in *Table 5*.

Table 5: Motivational Constructs for University Popular Music Festival

Escape	Seeking distraction from everyday life, routines responsibilities (e.g., university, school, work, family).
Uninhibited Behavior (Escape)	Social behavior that may be unaccepted in a 'normal' setting such as alcohol and drug consumption or abuse.
Social Interaction	To interact and socialize where thinking, acting, or feeling are mutually related.
Meet Friends (Social Interaction)	To interact and socialize with known people and to feel part of a group.
Meet New People (Social Interaction)	Meet and befriend new people who may or may not be alike.
Music	Listen to and enjoy music that is performed live
Dance (Music)	Physically feel and move to the performed (live) music
Local conditions/ Location	Enter an isolated world
Fun & Enjoyment	Be put in a fun state of being—no matter how

Escape

A number of participants in each focus group expressed being motivated to attend a university popular music festival providing a means of escape from daily life. One participant stated that 'escape' in this matter is to be seen as something positive although the word in general sticks with a negative connotation. Another participant described the idea of a future escape from his life while buying tickets way in advance as a very pleasant anticipation. Discussions revealed that people "like a chance to get out of the norm". Furthermore, the world *dreamworld* was used several times when lamenting about *escaping* the known daily world.

Uninhibited Behavior (Escape)

When analyzing transcripts, it was found that the motivation of *Escapism* was closely connected to the subject of *Uninhibited Behavior* in focus group discussions. Thus, it is described as subtheme of this matter:

A large number of participants conveyed that their main motivation for attendance to some festivals was at times just to 'go nuts', with one participant stating, "it is the only place in the world, where I can dance my butt off in a total crazy way without the guy standing next to me thinking, 'What's wrong with him?'"

The opportunity for uninhibited behavior was deemed an important aspect of the festival experience, where participants expressed desires of drinking, dancing, and the fact that the chances of seeing new met people again are very small.

Another behavior that participants believe allow them to feel uninhibited at festivals was in relation to what they choose to (not) wear. One participant stated:

"You can be as you want there and then just behave in that way. When you decide to walk around topless, you know it's not something you would do elsewhere, but in that moment, you know it's fine."

Some participants also explained temporary changes to their personality and behavior, with one participant relaying that "a certain drug consumption" is also part of the process that intentionally leads to uninhibited behavior.

Social Interaction

A number of social motivations for festival attendance were revealed in the focus groups. It was described as the attendees' need for 'socializing' meaning interacting with other (known) people or other groups of (known) people, meeting new people or just 'to be' with their friends. Participants expressed the desire to feel "part of a group" who "liked the same music" they did, with some even describing these events as 'community like'.

In all focus groups, Social Interaction was rated higher than the motivation to experience music:

"Because of the circle or group of (new) friends you have a great time, even more than because of the music."

Furthermore, the Social Interaction motivator could additionally be amended by two connected subthemes:

Known Group Socialization (Social Interaction)

The majority of participants had attended festivals at times only for the "sake of being together with the old clique". For some participants it is the number one motive for buying a ticket in advance not knowing about the line-up of the festival:

> "Most of all, I'm actually looking forward to seeing people again I went to high school with. Many from my hometown are spread across all Germany. Then I just know that we will have a longer period of time together where we can meet."

External Socialization (Social Interaction)

The second subtheme of the Social Interaction motive is the interaction with strangers meaning the external socialization with people who were unacquainted with the visitors prior to the festival.

Having in mind that in terms of music, alike people with similar interest being at the venue, visitors seek out to connect to them. One participant specifically described:

> "Especially because I'm the only one in our circle of friends who listens to electronic music, it's just cool if you are only with people for 3 days who listen to the same music as you do."

Most participants described the External Socialization as especially exciting due to the shortness of the befriending with alike groups or individuals. Furthermore, participants appreciated the diversity of the external people introduced to them:

> "For a weekend you have all kinds of different people who celebrate together. Doctors, students, you name it, and everyone then drink beer together and celebrate. That's just something completely different than going on vacation."

Music

The obvious motivation or motive to attend a festival when giving the title of this work a first glance is of course: Music.

Participant's discussions about Music as a specific motivation for festival attendance had different dynamics from focus group to focus group. Some participants described Music as the shared theme everyone attending the festival has, which also connects this theme partly to the social motivation described above. One participant concluded:

> "a person who has a certain taste for Music, often holds a certain view of things in life, meaning if someone has the same taste in Music, he most certainly will think about things the way I do".

Music also was the certain 'something' which can be described as the non-attend-motive, as one participant describes it:

"I would obviously not go to a festival where I don't like the style of music."

Nevertheless, the line-up of the festival seems to not play that big of a part, whereas it often is not even revealed when people are able to buy tickets for it.

Another motivation revealed in the focus groups regarding *Music* was attending festivals for an opportunity to experience new music and music that can only be heard at live events such as a festival or a concert. For some participants, new music referred to

"actually seeing bands or music that I haven't actually seen before"

and for others this meant

"hearing songs from their upcoming album that you could not hear yet."

For the majority, however, it was primarily about the opportunity to hear music from a particular artist where attendance to the festival is the only means of experiencing some aspect of the artist's performance. This included hearing music that had not yet been released or recorded,

and other unique performances such as hearing cover songs, instrumental riffs, stripped down acoustic versions of songs, and improvisations. To sum it up, one participant explained that their motivation for attending some festivals was mainly to hear

"stuff you won't normally listen to on your headphones."

Dance

One may discuss whether *Dance* needs to be described as a 'stand-alone' (sub-)theme of *Music* here. Nevertheless, when it was mentioned and discussed by focus group participants, it was always mentioned in context of the music genre or the genre of the festival:

"There are festivals where the music actually is put into the background, e.g., at Dockville, in contrast to techno festivals, where I then really go and dance massively for several days."

Local conditions/Location

The place where the event is hosted was discussed by participants of focus groups as a potential motive for going to a festival. It is, though, depending on the festival itself only sometimes a real motive rather than a positive (or negative) byproduct within the whole motivational structure, meaning every festival site has its own positive character. The organizers always put a lot of effort into this.

Fun & Enjoyment

Fun as a named motive for the attendance of a Music festival or as one participant described it:

"Fun. It is a very general statement, but it applies to me."

was mentioned by all participants of the focus groups. There seems to be a certain effect combining all aspects of a festival as a whole which generates a motivational energy to go there in this combination.

Furthermore

"knowing the fact that everyone at the venue will be having fun, is also motivating everyone else in the first place to also have fun which then creates a good kind of a vicious circle",

was also a general statement through all focus groups.

Discussion of Results

The findings from the focus groups show that motivational constructs for popular music festival attendance in Germany seem to differ partially from mentioned previous existing research regarding other cultural events such as concerts as well as other genre festivals in other countries (for example, concert attendance[6] or a festival organized by a non-profit organization[7] with more emphasis on cultural exploration and family togetherness).

Although existing research for similar events have identified similar motives such as escape, social interaction, uninhibited behavior (especially when

---

6   Kulczynski, Baxter, and Young, "Measuring Motivations for Popular Music Concert Attendance," July 25, 2016.

7   Crompton and McKay, "Motives of Visitors Attending Festival Events."

attending a concert), this research facilitated the development of more appropriate context-festival-specific definitions (presented in *Table 5*) and the construct description of the connection between the individual motives. Earlier research suggesting uninhibited behavior was a particularly important motive for other types of cultural consumption like concert attendance[8], this study showed that this seems also to be the case regarding popular music festival attendance.

Specifically, this study reveals 9 motives, 4 of which are subthemes of the other 5, that drive people to attend popular music festivals.

When wrapping up the focus groups, Lea, the moderator asked all participants to rank their individual's motivations explaining their personal attendance and write them on a list. In the following step, she discussed and then prioritized motives with the help of index cards as together as a focus group. Through this process it became clear, the most reoccurring motives were made very visible to everyone.

Social Interaction and Escape were here named the most, as well as ranked the highest on every focus group's index card. Furthermore, those two motives can be described as the least interwoven with each other. Social Interaction, either happens internally and satisfies the desire to spend time with friends in a known group or external with new unknown people. Both types display the social dimension(s) an event attendance can have and determine its atmosphere intuitively.[9] This could be repeatedly confirmed by his study. What stood out was the often-mentioned context of getting together with old (high school) friends to visit the (same) festival year after year. Additionally, the get together with old acquaintances from the past is often seen as the only way to keep these relationships alive, which makes it very meaningful to that individual.

The partial overlapping of motives for recreational leisure and festival attendance was also affirmed due to the variety of different experiences offered to the visitors. These characteristics were also discussed as powerful enough to sometimes even replace a vacation in the same year.

---

8   Kulczynski, Baxter, and Young, "Measuring Motivations for Popular Music Concert Attendance," July 25, 2016.

9   Manolika, Baltzis, and Tsigilis, "Measuring Motives for Cultural Consumption"; Steven Caldwell Brown and Don Knox, "Why Go to Pop Concerts? The Motivations behind Live Music Attendance," *Musicae Scientiae*, 2016, 1029864916650719.

The second highest ranked motive on the index cards, escape and its linked subtheme uninhibited behavior, was also a reoccurring over all focus group discussions. Seeking distraction from everyday life, routines responsibilities was named by almost every participant and often centered around a social behavior that may be unaccepted in a 'normal' setting, especially when it includes alcohol and drug consumption at the venue. It did not seem as if participants were unhappy or generally bored with their everyday life and in need of a change for a brief period of time. But it displayed the shared intrinsic desire to forget conventions of society during their visit and to draw strength from it at the same time.

In 2005 Bowen and Daniels published a much-quoted article[10] regarding the motivations for visiting a county fair and music festival hybrid. Using their controversial title "Does the Music matter" does fit very well when discussing the third motive of the focus group index card in this study. As stated by Bowen and Daniel's article, one might assume that *music* should be named as number one motivator when going and experiencing a music festival. In contrast, this study also reveals that this seems not to be the case, although live music does have a certain expressed specialty to participants and the subtheme *Dance* was also named in connection to the liveness of the event. Liveness was also described as the opportunity to experience new music and music that can only be encountered at a live event such as a festival. Listening to songs or performances that have not been released yet is a feature always named in context to this matter.

Local conditions and the location itself were named also on all index cards. Naming this as a motive for attendance, it was often centered to the escapism aspect. A well decorated location or a location that by itself gives the audience the feeling of 'entering a different world' amends and intensifies desire of escape. As other event specific factors, the location does not always serve as a motivator due to the fact that some festivals are just 'being held on regular meadow'.

If there was a generic term for all the mentioned aspects of the focus groups, it would be something as *Fun*. Because all of the mentioned motives obviously may be defined or identified as *Fun* in some way. However, in discussions one often came to the conclusion that the festival visit's existing underlying combination, entanglement and dynamics of all aspects could also

---

10   Bowen and Daniels, "Does the Music Matter? Motivations for Attending a Music Festival."

be seen as a stand-alone motive itself. Therefore, *Fun* also appeared on the index cards of the group discussions.

These qualitative findings serve as an additionally source of data next to literature findings, used to design an instrument for measuring popular music festival attendance. The development and evaluation of this instrument is discussed in the following quantitative studies of this dissertation.

Study Three: Quantitative Surveys | Audience

The following section forms the third and final empirical element dealing with this dissertation's research field of sponsorship culture within the German popular music festival market with regard to university popular music festivals. After having observed and analyzed professional stakeholders within sponsorship culture, namely sponsors and organizers of popular music festivals, in the following, the third stakeholder, the audience is shed a light on. To be precise, data consists of two separate surveys, each conducted within three weeks after the two biggest university popular music festivals in Germany in 2019: The *AStA Sommerfestival* in Paderborn and the *Campus Festival Bielefeld*.

The study aims at amending the existing research results from exploratory qualitative study (Study One) and focus group study (Study Two) as well as existing research literature on the topic.

As previously indicated, the majority of sponsorship studies conducted with regard to festival sponsorship, focused on sponsorship awareness and attitude towards the on-site sponsorship activities of companies. By combining results from the present three different studies examining three different fields of sponsorship stakeholders, the dissertation serves a unique purpose of capturing a holistic understanding of existing sponsorship culture in the German popular music festival market with emphasis on university popular music festivals.

In order to achieve this, this study pursues two objectives:

Research objective one Provide descriptive knowledge of audiences who attended the two biggest university popular music festivals held in 2019 in Germany. Building on this data, outline Generation Y audience profiles that exploratively describe audiences' behavior, assessments, former event experiences, collective knowledge, institutional identification, norms and accepted moral orientation with regard to the two festivals.

Furthermore, this study shall generate results for reviewing statements from the qualitative interview study (Study One) by comparing them to the following quantitative findings in the Overall Discussion of the dissertation:

a) Single motivators for festival attendance (13 items)
b) Festival visit as (social media) status symbol (4 items)
c) Sponsorship awareness (2 items)
d) Attitude towards sponsorship (6 items)
e) University identification (1 item)

Additionally, point (3) sponsorship awareness, point (4) participants' attitude towards sponsorship and point (5) university identification are analyzed with regards to differences among event attendees.

Research objective two Understanding motivational constructs for university popular music festival attendance by building upon results from focus group interviews (Study Two) and identifying a factor structure which stimulates members of an audience to visit these events.

Furthermore, differences in motivational constructs between popular music festivals in Germany in general and specifically university music festivals shall become evident. The reason for putting much effort into understanding visitor's motivational constructs is due to their importance for designing product offerings, planning event programs and effectively marketing them to potential audiences within the event industry.[1] Furthermore, this is logically and directly linked to the organizing stakeholders of such festivals and additionally entangled with the sponsors due to the constant knowledge exchange of understanding and designing underlying experiences between the two stakeholders.

Methodology

In this chapter, the research methodology is outlined. It provides an overview of the research design, pursued research objectives, targeted participants and

---

1   Kulczynski, Baxter, and Young, "Measuring Motivations for Popular Music Concert Attendance," July 25, 2016.

sampling procedures, participant demographic characteristic statistics, experiential item statistics, description of instrumentation and statistical procedures used.

Research Design

Two quantitative research surveys using survey methodologies were conducted. This design assists in data collection and provides numeric description of trends, attitudes, or opinions of the population under study.[2] Considering the purpose of the investigation, two survey studies were identified as the most appropriate research method.[3] This approach was consonant with previous motivational research in the event sector.[4]

As in Study Two, the same use of descriptive language regarding the issue of motivational constructs is used.

With the goal of developing a holistic understanding of motivational constructs, the current research has used exploratory factor analysis to discover the underlying structure of observed variables.[5] In other words, exploratory factor analysis was a useful way to summarize and interpret underlying relationships and patterns in the data.[6] It was the most appropriate since

"the researcher has no expectations about the number of common factors or which measured variables will be influenced by the same common factors"[7].

In short, the exploratory factor analysis should reveal the underlying dimensions related to motivational constructs for university popular music festival attendance. Additionally, descriptive statistics were calculated and/or presented for all other variables alongside the motivational construct(s). These descriptive statistics were analyzed to obtain a sense of the overall characteristics regarding the audience(s) and its/their visit.

---

2   Kuckartz, *Mixed Methods*.

3   Creswell and Creswell, *Research Design*.

4   Kulczynski, Baxter, and Young, "Measuring Motivations for Popular Music Concert Attendance," July 25, 2016.

5   Kulczynski, Baxter, and Young.

6   An Gie Yong and Sean Pearce, "A Beginner's Guide to Factor Analysis: Focusing on Exploratory Factor Analysis," *Tutorials in Quantitative Methods for Psychology* 9, no. 2 (October 1, 2013): 79–94, https://doi.org/10.20982/tqmp.09.2.p079.

7   Leandre R. Fabrigar and Duane Theodore Wegener, *Exploratory Factor Analysis*, Understanding Statistics (Oxford; New York: Oxford University Press, 2012).

Description and History of the Events

In the following, the history of two biggest university popular music festivals held in Germany in 2019 is outlined. Special attention is paid to the different growth development of the two events, which are important as background knowledge for methodology as well as for the discussion of the results. In 2019, the AStA Sommer Festival of the University of Paderborn with 15,000 and the Campus Festival Bielefeld with 18,000 visitors presented themselves as the two largest German music festivals on a university campus. Both events featured multiple stages and served a diverse range of genres. Both grounds are completely fenced off during the event and can only be entered upon presentation of the festival ticket starting at 3:30 p.m., with events officially ending at 11:30 p.m. According to tradition, there will be an additional performance by a DJ in a part of the indoor area of Paderborn University from 6:00 p.m.—11:00 p.m. (Building G with a capacity of 800 people). The event in Paderborn was completely sold out, in Bielefeld this was not the case with 18,000 visitors, the maximum capacity here would have been 20,000 people. Both festivals offer a wide variety of musical genres on several stages.

AStA Sommerfestival (Paderborn)

The AStA Sommer Festival is annually held on campus of the University of Paderborn. The institution is a campus university in North Rhine-Westphalia, Germany and was founded in 1972. With over 20,000 students (as of winter semester 2018/2019), it is one of the medium-sized universities in Germany. The University of Paderborn has 254 professorships, 1,270 scientific employees and 747 non-scientific employees (incl. trainees). It offers around 70-degree programs. The AStA Sommer Festival looks back on a 20-year history and has enjoyed a nationwide reputation since the MTV Campus Invasion cooperation with the event took place in the early 2000s. As an organically grown event—as the name suggests—the AStA of the University of Paderborn plays a much bigger role in the yearly conception and organization of the event than it is in other comparable cases such as the event in Bielefeld, for example. The reason for this is the aforementioned history of the event and the fact that the event was originally also founded by the AStA of the university itself.

Due to increasingly complex security and liability structures for these kind of events with more than 5,000 people, which developed, among other things, due to the Duisburg Love Parade accident in 2010, one became more cautious in Paderborn over time and accordingly liability-shy(er). This was followed by cooperation with professional booking and event agencies based on Europe-wide tenders to incorporate these agencies, let them participate in the project, let them take the major risks and to let them profit economically from it. In this way, all decisions are still made together with the AStA, the entrepreneurial risk in all its facets in relation to a major event with now 15,000 visitors is transferred to the organizing agency.

Up to this day, the AStA Sommer Festival is seen by the university and the city of Paderborn as a flagship event with a supra-regional impact for its habitants as well as for city marketing purposes.

Line Up AStA Sommerfestival Paderborn:

- 'Stage 1': RIN, Von wegen Lisbeth, Querbeat, Massendefekt, BLVTH,
- 'Stage 2': Nura, Drunken Masters, Salwa Benz, BRKN, Majan
- 'L'Unico Stage': Driftwood, Cut Spencer + Panorama, Figur Lemur, Hal Johnson, Katastrow, Summery Mind, Aire
- 'Fairytale Forest Stage': Snads, Averro, Patrick W., Boj Angler, DJ Dan

Campus Festival Bielefeld

50 km away, in neighboring Bielefeld, the development of the Paderborn event has always been observed with some envy; especially with regard to the supra-regional success of the event and the associated positive effects on the external image of the city of Paderborn.[8] Bielefeld University is a German campus university founded in 1969 in North Rhine-Westphalia and the largest research institution in the region of East Westphalia-Lippe. With more than 25,000 students (in the winter semester 2018/19), Bielefeld University is the largest of the six universities located in Bielefeld.

In Bielefeld, however, when a decision was made to create a university popular music festival as well, a somewhat 'faster path' compared to Paderborn was taken. In 2015, the university presidium decided to set up a festival format of similar size and complexity and commissioned the Bielefeld concert agency *VIBRA Agency* to do so. Due to this composition, the organizer structure is therefore different from the ground up compared to the structure in

---

8   This circumstance was brought to the author's attention in several discussions with presidium staff of the university of Bielefeld as well as municipal administration staff.

Paderborn since the student body via AStA is only involved to a minimum extent.

Furthermore, the Bielefeld campus is, strictly speaking, home to two different institutions: Bielefeld University, which has already been mentioned, and Bielefeld University of Applied Sciences.

Bielefeld University of Applied Sciences is the largest state university of applied sciences in Ostwestfalen-Lippe, with 11,000 students, 272 professors and lecturers for special tasks, and around 568 other employees. Bielefeld University of Applied Sciences has its headquarters in Bielefeld. Further locations are in Minden and Gütersloh. The range of courses offered includes 68-degree programs (38 Bachelor's and 25 Master's programs as well as five certificate programs), which are spread across six departments.

Both institutions sharing the campus for the event are legally separate and independent from each other. However, in terms of the campus and the event, they are spatially and visually very much interwoven with each other.

Line Up Campus Festival Bielefeld:

- 'Main Stage': Alexander Marcus, Fil Bo River, Grossstadtgeflüster, Donots, Fritz Kalkbrenner
- 'Stereo Stage': Punch Drunk Poets, Moped, BRKN, Sondaschule, Nura
- 'Hertz 87,9 Stage': Dünamit, Provinz, Magical Creatures, Nevermeant, The Wild Rumble
- 'Red Bull Electronic Floor': Ivans, Dirk Siedhoff, Matjoe, Dirty Doering
- 'Slam Stage': Various poetry and lecture hall slams

Sample

In this section, information regarding the targeted population and sampling frame are presented. Since participants demographic descriptive statistics are a matter content in terms of content, they are not included in this section, but will be presented in the results section of the study.

Targeted Population

Potential participants for the printed questionnaire[9] were the Paderborn University students who visited the 2019 AStA Sommerfestival in Paderborn on June 6th. The event was completely sold out and was visited by a total number of 15,000 visitors, students representing the biggest visitor group. Potential participants for the (online) *LimeSurvey* questionnaire were either Bielefeld University or Bielefeld University of Applied Sciences students who attended the 2019 Campus Festival Bielefeld on June 27th. The event was nearly sold out and was visited by a total number of around 18,000 visitors, students representing the biggest visitor group. Since both events took place three weeks in a row and both cities are located only 50 Km apart, it is theoretically possible that participants who were questioned via *LimeSurvey* after the Bielefeld Festival could have attended both festivals.

The faculty statistics in the summer semester 2019 were composed as follows at the three institutions:

Figure 7: Faculty Statistics Bielefeld University of Applied Sciences

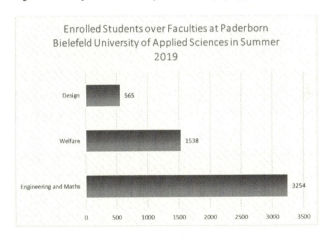

---

9   LimeSurvey (Online) and Offline questionnaires are fully provided in the appendix of the dissertation.

Figure 8: Faculty Statistics Paderborn University

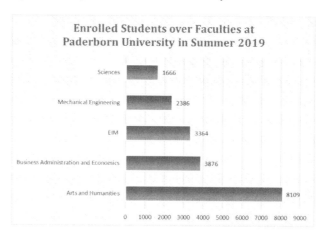

Figure 9: Faculty Statistics Bielefeld University

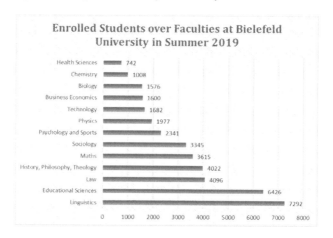

Sampling Procedures

Due to online data collection in Bielefeld and offline data collection in Pader-born, probability sampling had to be adjusted between both cities as different results across faculties were expected. In Paderborn a stratified sample was conducted to ensure a fitting sampling according to distribution of students across all faculties.

In Bielefeld a voluntary response sample was conducted by sending out the questionnaire via e-mail to all enrolled students at Bielefeld University and Bielefeld University of Applied Sciences. Due to the fortunate response rate, it was possible to ensure a distribution of responses across all faculties, which corresponds to the distribution of student numbers across the faculties of the institutions. Following this process, a representative sample of the entire institutions in Bielefeld across all faculties can be achieved.

In Paderborn, a written questionnaire was distributed in seminars, exercise courses and lectures. In Bielefeld, the questionnaire was distributed digitally with the help of an online tool. More information regarding the data collection follows in chapter 10.1.6.

Sampling Adequacy

For an interpretable factor structure to emerge, research suggests using at least five to ten participants per survey variable/item.[10] Given there are 46 items on the questionnaire, about 230 participants were required. With an actual sample size of 914 for combined results, it was sufficient for exploratory factor analysis.[11]

However, during the process of creating and structuring the instrumentation of the study, several reasons emerged speaking in favor of considering results from both surveys at least in parts differentiated from one another. First, as this study is the first of its kind with regard to the German student audience(s), potential differences of audience behavior, motivation, critique etc. would be of great interest in general and in concluding results as a whole with respect to sponsorship culture. Second, the festival in Paderborn has

---

10   Nyaradzo H. Mvududu and Christopher A. Sink, "Factor Analysis in Counseling Research and Practice," *Counseling Outcome Research and Evaluation* 4, no. 2 (December 2013): 75–98, https://doi.org/10.1177/2150137813494766; B. S. Everitt, "Multivariate Analysis: The Need for Data, and Other Problems," *British Journal of Psychiatry* 126, no. 3 (March 1975): 237–40, https://doi.org/10.1192/bjp.126.3.237; Richard L. Gorsuch, "Exploratory Factor Analysis," in *Handbook of Multivariate Experimental Psychology*, ed. John R. Nesselroade and Raymond B. Cattell (Boston, MA: Springer US, 1988), 231–58, https://doi.org/10.1007/978-1-4613-0893-5_6.

11   Andrew Laurence Comrey and Howard B. Lee, *A First Course in Factor Analysis*, 2nd ed (Hillsdale, N.J.: L. Erlbaum Associates, 1992); Mvududu and Sink, "Factor Analysis in Counseling Research and Practice."

been around for more than two decades and has grown steadily and organ-ically until it has reached its annual 15,000 visitors, whereas the festival in Bielefeld was held for the first time in 2015 and started with approximately the same number of visitors in the first year. And third, both festivals are be-ing organized by the same company with nearly the same network of sponsors which induces a favorable setting for comparison of results.

The mentioned 914 participants across both audiences are split into 688 from Bielefeld and 226 from Paderborn. Thus, both data sets individually as well as a combined are sufficient for exploratory factor analysis.

Instrumentation

The item development process began with the creation of items to assess the construct under examination. These items can be generated inductively, by generating items prior to deriving scales, or deductively, using theory to gen-erate items.[12] In this study items with the exception to the motivational con-struct, were developed inductively, as the phenomenon of sponsorship culture within the German popular music festival market is a fairly under examined phenomenon and the study's purpose is considered explorative.

Furthermore, results from the focus group study (Study Two) were used to amend the motivational construct items and results from the qualitative interview study (Study One) were utilized to amend items regarding the re-maining parts of the questionnaire.

To establish face and content validity, items were revised based on the feedback from an expert review conducted with a panel of six professionals that are experts in the fields of counseling and conduct research on event management, economics, marketing as well as popular music studies. These scholars had varying expertise. Two of the six were university-level profes-sors, four were university-level counselor educators. The panel was asked to judge the content relevance, representativeness, and clarity of items. One of the reviewers helped examine each of the items and assisted in the merging of the results from the previous as well as simultaneously conducting qualita-tive research with the literature findings. Reviewers provided feedback on the

---

12   Timothy R. Hinkin, J. Bruce Tracey, and Cathy A. Enz, "Scale Construction: Developing Reliable and Valid Measurement Instruments," *Journal of Hospitality & Tourism Research* 21, no. 1 (February 1997): 100–120, https://doi.org/10.1177/109634809702100108.

language used and improved the balance between descriptive, professional, and colloquial wording.

As the time frame of item development was partly overlapping with obtaining data for the qualitative study, this process ensured a seemingly transition of information.

Based on the feedback from the expert review and on further examination of literature, items associated with genre specifics were eliminated from the survey.

Both questionnaires consisted of six sections: (a) 2019 visit consisting of six items, (b) critique—consisting of six items, (c) motivational construct—consisting of 13 items, (d) external value of visit—consisting of four items, (e) sponsorship awareness and attitude towards sponsorship—consisting of eight items, (f) demographics including university identification—consisting of nine items. Below, each of these sections is discussed further.

The final instrument consisted of 46 total items. Of these items, 28 require participants to respond a five-point Likert scale, six items required a response via German school grading system (ranging from one to six, one being the best grade), one item required a yes and no response, three items required a response of a number, one item requires the choice of a sponsoring brand, and one item requires the choice of a certain place at the event venue. The five-point Likert scales either ranged from 1—*does not apply* to 2—*does rather not apply* to 3—*neither* to 4—*rather applies* to 5—*does apply* or ranging from 1—*I don't agree* to 2—*I rather don't agree* to 3—*neither* to 4—*I rather agree to 5—I agree*, depending on the matter of subject.

In addition, seven items were added examining the respondent's demographics.

The top front page of all questionnaires included a statement explaining the purpose of the study, a statement of confidentiality, and an approximation of the time necessary to complete the questionnaire. Furthermore, an attention-check question to ensure participants reading the questionnaire before answering was implemented.

In the following chapters the individual questionnaire sections are explained in more detail:

2019 Visit

As this investigation is of descriptive character aiming to understand and analyze the visitors' componential element within sponsorship culture, the basic behavior throughout the 2019 visit of either the event in Paderborn or Bielefeld had to be examined. This necessity became further obvious during the qualitative interviews as well as in the focus groups as several differences in behavior before the actual event visit were discussed. Especially the visitor's increasing entry time to the event venue and the suspected relation to prior attended private preparties by the participants were noticed as sort of negative influences on sponsorship awareness and on-site revenue by organizer as well as by the sponsoring partners.

Furthermore, participants were specifically asked about their (evolving) music festival experience, meaning how many music festivals they are likely to attend in 2019 (in addition) to the university popular music festival they just had attended. Additionally, number of visits to the Paderborn or Bielefeld festival prior to 2019 were retrieved. As the survey was conducted in June of 2019 and the festival season in German had just started, participants were asked to guess rather than being 100 % certain about this topic.

Critique

Being able to describe the current culture of sponsorship, systematic framework information regarding the topic as a whole needed to be conducted. Therefore, creating items regarding the general assessment of the event experience(s) by the visitors, was managed by focusing on issues such as the general critique regarding the event visit, the organization at the motivenue, the general program, the atmosphere, the sensed marketing campaign of the event and the campus venue itself.

However, when creating these items as well as in the revision process of them, the assumption was that this basic assessment and evaluation of the experience(s) ought to be significantly related to almost all other items in the questionnaire, since evaluation(s) of experience(s) may interpret the reasons for action and vice versa.

Motivational Construct

As described in the theoretical perspectives above, motivational research in the event management literature is well established. Studies on motivational constructs exist in reference to attendance at sporting events, business events, and various types of festival events such as, jazz festivals, cultural festivals, performing arts festivals, music festivals and events in general. These studies have revealed varied motivational constructs for event attendance. The fact that motivational constructs that drive event attendance have been shown to differ between not only disparate, but also similar events made it necessary to conduct the focus group study after literature review and prior to the item development for this study. In this way, the 'basic' visitor motivations found in literature, which often overlapped between the different types of events, were either confirmed or rejected by focus group results and then amended or expanded by specific motivators for visiting one of the two biggest university popular music festivals in Germany.

External Value of Visit

The section aiming at external valuing the 2019 festival visit, consisted of four items. As mentioned in the theoretical perspectives, social phenomena such as the experience society (*Erlebnisgesellschaft*) by Schulze[13] or economic concepts such as the experience economy by Pine and Gilmore[14] suggest an increasing appreciation for personal leisure experiences and an associated higher valuation of these experiences compared to materialistic belongings. *External Value* in this sense means the value of the event attendance for the person who has attended; externally in relation to others.

Building on this, audience research literature as well as findings from qualitative interview studies suggests event attendance as status symbol[15][16], as something with which visitors may even brag about or differentiate themselves from others and/or friends. Furthermore, this circumstance seems to be heavily fueled by social media use and in particular by the app Instagram. This was encouraged by expert's review and confirmed in the focus groups. Thus, items were designed to tackle these issues by asking specifically about the importance of sharing the festival visit in social media, defining it as a

---

13   Schulze, *Die Erlebnisgesellschaft*.

14   Pine, Gilmore, and others, "Welcome to the Experience Economy."

15   Martin Gannon, Babak Taheri, and Hossein Olya, "Festival Quality, Felf-Connection, and Bragging," *Annals of Tourism Research* 76 (May 2019): 239–52, https://doi.org/10.1016/j.an nals.2019.04.014.

16   Chei Sian Lee et al., "Instagram This! Sharing Photos on Instagram," in *Digital Libraries: Providing Quality Information*, ed. Robert B. Allen, Jane Hunter, and Marcia L. Zeng, vol. 9469, Lecture Notes in Computer Science (Cham: Springer International Publishing, 2015), 132–41, https://doi.org/10.1007/978-3-319-27974-9_13.

status symbol, seeing the visit as something to be used to brag about and whether participants utilize the visit to differentiate themselves from others. At this point it needs to be further noted, that external value of visit items may (also) be part of a motivational construct for event attendance at some level. However, in this case, questionnaire items were categorically formulated differently from one another to draw a clear line between items for motivational construct as well as external value purposes. (For further clarification, see appendix)

Sponsorship Awareness

The section dealing with sponsorship awareness is designed to investigate two separate issues. At first, two items test participants' recollection regarding on-site sponsoring brand appearances by asking to mark the brand which they can remember the most (including the answer 'none of the mentioned') and second, which brand they link to a specific stage. However, the question regarding the best recollection of a sponsoring brand did not include brands that were actually present on the venue. The reason for implementing the question in this way was twofold, a sensitive matter on the one hand and gave a chance to be very insightful on the other.

First, one of the main sponsors of the festivals was a beer brand that had just been attained by the organizer one year earlier. This new sponsoring partner's engagement with the festival and especially how it managed the sponsorship, was being described to the author in the expert interview as poorly executed. Second, the beer brand that had been sponsoring the event prior to this new partner, had been doing so for over a decade. Therefore, it seemed to be inviting in the research process to name the old sponsoring beer brand in the recollection question instead of the new one, to maybe able to display the underlying (poor) sponsoring strategy by the new sponsoring beer brand.

The second part of the section aims at examining the attitude of participants towards sponsorship activities at the festival in general, the critical review of sponsoring companies and the apprehension for financial sponsorship necessity for the organizer of a music festival.

As partly mentioned above, the item creation process for this section was profoundly affected by the qualitative research study results.

Demographics

The questionnaire consists of nine items examining basic demographic qualities related to the respondent's gender, age, marital status, children, and income. The items also assist in gathering information on the participants' university matriculation and participants' identification with the institution (e.g., semester, faculty, identification with university and faculty).

Pilot Testing

Upon receiving approval from the expert reviewers, the survey was piloted with 10 students at Paderborn university prior to data collection. This was done to assure content adequacy and to provide preliminary support for construct validity as it allows the deletion of items that may be conceptually inconsistent.[17] In addition, qualitative feedback from participants via brief individual interviews was sought. Changes in the questionnaire were made based on their feedback. Specifically, the researcher received input from participants' understanding of the items. Some modifications in the language used to describe certain terms were required. For example, the wording of explaining certain motivations for attending the festival were rephrased in a more colloquial style.

Data Collection

Data was collected using both electronic and written paper questionnaires. To ensure a decent level of participant's recollection of the event experience(s), within three weeks after the festival in Paderborn, the interviewees were selected, and a written survey was carried out using printed questionnaires. As a doctoral student at the University of Paderborn, the author was able to take advantage of a corresponding network of lecturers and professors at the institution. This allowed the active survey process via written questionnaire to be carried out much more feasibly. Thanks to cooperative lecturers across all faculties, it was possible to locate visitors of the 2019 AStA Sommerfestival in lectures, seminars and exercise courses and ask them to participate in the survey. The willingness to fill out the six-page questionnaire was very high (> 90 %).

---

17   Hinkin, Tracey, and Enz, "Scale Construction."

Using experiences from similar studies[18], the stipulation was set to complete at least 200 to 250 questionnaires. The questionnaire was a single-sided, unfolded DIN-A4 sheet of paper with a length of six pages. The processing time was an average of five to ten minutes; the questionnaire was processed at the seats in the lecture hall or seminar room. An incentive was not used, which makes the high level of voluntary willingness to participate in the survey described as even more positive.

In Bielefeld, due to the author's lack of a network of personally known lecturers and professors, a different approach had to be chosen. Foremost, the language of the questionnaire was adapted to the Bielefeld Festival and the questionnaire was digitally created with the online survey application *Limesurvey*. Subsequently, with the help of the Bielefeld university marketing department and the university's own campus radio (*Hertz*), an e-mail distribution list was used to 'call for help' in the scientific survey regarding the university's campus festival. As well as in Paderborn, no prospect of an incentive was communicated in the request. According to the Bielefeld university marketing and Hertz radio staff, the questionnaire was able to reach almost every enrolled Bielefeld student following this procedure. As in Paderborn, the time frame for participating in the survey was set to be within three weeks after the festival was hosted.

Data Analyses

Prior to analyzing descriptive data and exploratory factor analysis, quantitative data from Paderborn questionnaire was entered by hand into SPSS 26.0. As quantitative data from the Bielefeld questionnaire was conducted online via *LimeSurvey*, the transition of data was fluid. Descriptive statistics and frequencies of all questions were computed in order to check plausible and data entry errors. Respondents who left many items unanswered or failed the attention check at the end of the questionnaire were deleted from the data set.

Screening and Data Cleaning

Participant responses were checked to ensure they all were within the range on the Likert scale. All the data inputting errors were corrected. Additionally, the recoded items were relabeled for clarification purposes. The data were scanned for missing responses and certain cases were deleted that have

---

18   Otte, "Die Publikumsstrukturierung eines Open-Air-Festivals für elektronische Musik."

about 5 % missing data.[19] Descriptive statistics were computed to check the normality of the item distributions. Based on the descriptive statistics, valid responses were identified.

Parametric Properties of Questionnaire Items

The parametric nature of each item was also inspected. Histograms, box plots, and QQ plots were viewed to identify outliers and any other irregularities in the data distribution. Items with a skewness and kurtosis values of less than an absolute value of 1 can be considered normally distributed for statistical analyses.[20]

Descriptive Data Analysis

Descriptive statistics, including mean, standard deviation, maximums, and minimums were calculated for all variables measured in the study. These descriptive statistics, such as data distribution of the whole sample and each participant group (online and offline), were analyzed to obtain a sense of the overall characteristics of the participants and each group variable.

Exploratory Factor Analysis (Motivational Constructs)

Exploratory Factor Analysis (EFA) tests the number of common factors that influence measures and tests the strength and relationship between each common factor to the corresponding measure.[21] Researchers use EFA to identify the nature of constructs that underlie responses given in a questionnaire, determine sets of items that interconnect, demonstrate the depth and breadth of measurement scales, classify the most important features of a group of items, and generate factor scores that represent the underlying constructs.[22] Because EFA is a multivariate statistical approach, it is appropriate for reducing the number of factors, examining relationships between categories, and evaluating the construct validity of a measurement scale.[23]

Exploratory factor analysis involves a series of statistical analysis steps. The first is the planning phase, where it is determined if the data is suitable

---

19   Andy P. Field, *Discovering Statistics Using IBM SPSS Statistics: And Sex and Drugs and Rock "n" Roll*, 4th edition (Los Angeles: Sage, 2013).

20   Field.

21   Fabrigar and Wegener, *Exploratory Factor Analysis*.

22   Comrey and Lee, *A First Course in Factor Analysis*.

23   Gorsuch, "Exploratory Factor Analysis."

for EFA by selecting the sample size then after collecting the data, creating a correlation matrix, and testing for adequacy. The second step is to extract factors. The third step is to determine the number of factors to retain. The fourth step is factor rotation. The fifth step is to interpret the factor structure.[24]

In the following, the described steps that were taken are summarized. These included an analysis of the initial reliability, intercorrelations, and assumptions underlying principal axis factoring (PAF or principal factor analysis) and oblique rotations. The following steps were taken for motivational construct items for all respondents (n=914) as well as for each event separately (Paderborn, n=226 and Bielefeld, n=688).

Initial reliability analysis To determine whether the 13 items represented an internally consistent measure, the researcher computed an overall Cronbach alpha (α) coefficient.

Correlational analysis An analysis of the inter-item Pearson Product correlations was conducted. Items with consistently low (approximately < .20) or high (> .80) inter-item correlations were deleted.

Verifying assumptions In verifying assumptions prior to rotation, the researcher computed the Bartlett's Test of Sphericity and a Kaiser-Meyer-Olkin Measure of Sampling Adequacy.[25] A significant sphericity ($p < .05$) suggests that the data set, and thus, the correlation matrix is factorable.[26] In addition, the researcher is looking for a KMO ranging between .60 and .90.[27] These results will indicate whether it is an identity matrix. The Bartlett's Test compares the correlation matrix to the identity matrix (i.e., it checks whether there is a certain redundancy between the variables that we can summarize with a fewer number of factors). Therefore, if the items are highly correlated, only one factor is most likely sufficient.

Extraction methods After the requirements for performing a factor analysis have been checked, the choice of extraction method and the number of factors

24   Field, *Discovering Statistics Using IBM SPSS Statistics.*
25   Field.
26   Mvududu and Sink, "Factor Analysis in Counseling Research and Practice."
27   Mvududu and Sink.

to be extracted must be discussed. Common methods are principal component analysis (PCA), principal (factor) axis analysis (PAF or PFA) and maximum likelihood analysis (MLA). As for MLA a normal distribution is mandatory, it is not considered for this study.[28] PCA is concerned only with establishing which linear components exist within the data and how a particular variable might contribute to that component. With 30 or more variables and communalities greater than 0.7 for all variables, different solutions are unlikely; however, with fewer than 20 variables, and any low communalities (< 0.4) differences can occur.[29] Consequently, a trade-off must be made between PCA and PFA at some point in the process. These techniques differ in the communality estimates that are used. Factor analysis derives a mathematical model from which factors are estimated, whereas PCA decomposes the original data into a set of linear variates. As such, only factor analysis can estimate the underlying factors, and it relies on various assumptions for these estimates to be accurate. As components analysis is only a data reduction method, it became common decades ago when computers were slow and expensive to use; it was a quicker, cheaper alternative to factor analysis.[30] It is computed without regard to any underlying structure caused by latent variables; components are calculated using all of the variance of the manifest variables, and all of that variance appears in the solution.[31] As previews research on motivational constructs for event attendance is available a vague a priori idea about how the variables are related was existent. Therefore, a factor analysis is suggested preferable to principal components analysis. Initially, however, both principal component analysis (PCA) and principal (factor) axis analysis (PAF or PFA) were computed on the data set to confirm mentioned issues regarding both techniques.

The items were examined for high and low factor loadings. The minimum acceptable factor loading was set at .30 according to Field.[32]

---

28   Helfried Moosbrugger, Helfried Moosbrugger, and Augustin Kelava, *Testtheorie und Fragebogenkonstruktion*, 2., aktualisierte und überarbeitete Auflage, Springer-Lehrbuch (Berlin: Springer Berlin, 2012).

29   Field, *Discovering Statistics Using IBM SPSS Statistics*.

30   Gorsuch, "Exploratory Factor Analysis."

31   Field, *Discovering Statistics Using IBM SPSS Statistics*.

32   Field.

Factor rotation To determine the number of factors to rotate, the following criteria were used: the amount of the explained variance for each derived factor (over 10 %), factor eigenvalues greater than 1, and from the results of the scree test. In addition, a parallel analysis was computed, as it is a more rigorous method for determining the number of factors to rotate.[33] Orthogonal and oblique rotations were compared. More specifically, varimax rotations (i.e., a form of orthogonal rotation that rotates in 90° angles) for PFA was examined for simple structure. However, PFA is especially well-suited for determining potential latent constructs in the data set and provides a more accurate estimate of the item correlations. Therefore, analyzing the data using PFA was suggested to be favorable as mentioned above.

In addition, according to Field[34], oblimin rotation (i.e., a form of oblique rotation that rotates the eigenvectors in less than 90° angles) should be used when there is an expected correlation between factors. Since the items were developed based on existing literature review and focus group results, different dimensions such as socialization, escapism, and music etc. a certain correlation between factors was expected prior to the analysis. Furthermore, oblimin rotation was conducted as it is appropriate for the current data set, because it is logical to assume that factors are correlated given the subjective nature participants' perceptions and experiences.

Post-rotation Post-rotation initial factors were extracted from the matrix, that is, the common or shared variance of each variable is partitioned from its unique variance and error variance to identify the underlying factor structure[35] and to determine simple structure. The communalities (h2) and explained variance for each item were examined. The percentage of total variance explained is crucial in determining factors and in combination should explain >50 % of the variance.[36] Items that have cross loadings (i.e., items that load substantially on two or more factors) were deleted if the loadings were weak (< .30). Items that did not load on any factor were deleted. The analysis was redone without those items to establish a simple structure. Lastly, the factors were named based on the content of the factor items.

---

33 Field.
34 Field.
35 Mvududu and Sink, "Factor Analysis in Counseling Research and Practice"; Field, *Discovering Statistics Using IBM SPSS Statistics*.
36 Field, *Discovering Statistics Using IBM SPSS Statistics*.

Summary

In this chapter, the methodology used to explore sponsorship culture within the German university popular music festival market with emphasis on the audience is explained. After explaining the purpose and research questions guiding the study, the researcher detailed information on data collection, sampling, participant demographic characteristics, instrumentation, and statistical procedures. Appendices are provided to review the instruments used in the study.

Study Results

In the following chapter, results from quantitative surveys including both research objectives are outlined.

Research Objective One (Descriptive Data Analysis)

Visitors of the two biggest university popular music festivals in 2019 in Germany comprised 914 participants for both surveys. The participants consisted of two groups: visitors of the AStA Sommerfestival at the university of Paderborn (n = 226), and visitors of the Campus Festival Bielefeld at the university of Bielefeld (n = 688). In the following, descriptive data results regarding (1) participants demographic characteristics (five items), (2) participant rating of the event (six items), (3) participant basic festival behavior (six items), (4) motivators for festival attendance, (5) external value of visit (four items), (6) sponsorship awareness (two items), (7) attitude towards sponsorship (six items), (8) university identification (two items) are outlined. Results are presented according to their individual rationale; complete results can be found in the appendix. Additionally, results with regards to differences among events are outlined for point (6) sponsorship awareness, point (7) participants' attitude towards sponsorship and point (8) university identification.

Participant Demographic Characteristics

In Paderborn, a student sample of n = 226 was collected via a written questionnaire with participants enrolled over five faculties. In Bielefeld a student sample of n = 588 was collected via a *LimeSurvey* (online) questionnaire with participants enrolled over 18 faculties in two institutions (Bielefeld University,

Bielefeld University for Applied Sciences). Tables three through six provide descriptive statistics for reported age range, gender, faculty, university status (semester) and attended music festivals per year. Statistics are sorted as well by type and location of the enrolled institution. Descriptive statistics of participant gender is presented in *Table 6*.

Table 6: Participant Gender

	AStA Festival 2019		Campus Festival Bielefeld 2019			
	Paderborn University		Bielefeld University		Bielefeld University for Applied Sciences	
	Fre-quency	%	Fre-quency	%	Fre-quency	%	To-tal
Fe-male	130	57.5 %	421	73.3 %	67	58.8 %	618
Male	94	41.6 %	150	26.1 %	45	39.5 %	289
Di-verse	2	0.9 %	3	0.5 %	2	1.8 %	7
Miss-ing	0	0 %	0	0 %	0	0	0
Total	226	100 %	574	100 %	114	100 %	914

Descriptive statistics of participant faculties is presented in *Table 7*. Results show, as expected the diversity of faculty structural composition between the institutions.

Table 7: Participant Faculties

	Paderborn University	Bielefeld University	Bielefeld University for Applied Sciences	Percent (across both events)
Arts and Humanities	116			12.7 %
Business Administration and Economics	78			8.5 %
Mechanical Engineering	28			3.1 %
EIM[37]	3			0.3 %
Natural Sciences	1			0.1 %
Educational Sciences		134		14.7 %
Business Economics		74		8.1 %
Psychology and Sports		64		7.0 %
Law		49		5.4 %
Sociology		43		4.7 %
Linguistics		36		3.9 %
Health Sciences		35		3.8 %
Economics and Health		33		3.6 %
Technology		22		2.4 %
Biology		22		2.4 %
History, Philosophy, Theology		20		2.2 %
Math		16		1.8 %
Chemistry		11		1.2 %
Medicine		8		0.9 %
Physics		7		0.8 %
Engineering and Math			45	4.9 %
Welfare			44	4.8 %
Design			25	2.7 %
Total	226	574	114	100 %

Descriptive statistics of participant age structure is presented in *Table 8*. Comparing results over both events reveal similar composition of age structures.

Table 8: Participant Age Structure

	AStA Festival 2019		Campus Festival Bielefeld 2019			
Age	Paderborn University		Bielefeld University		Bielefeld University for Applied Sciences	
	Frequency	Percent	Frequency	Percent	Frequency	Percent
16-19	40	17.7 %	64	11.1 %	6	5.3 %
20-23	132	58.4 %	296	51.6 %	61	53.5 %
24-27	40	17.7 %	143	24.7 %	34	29.8 %
28-31	9	4 %	46	7.8 %	6	5.3 %
> 31	5	2.2 %	28	4.7 %	7	6.1 %
Total	226	100 %	574	100 %	114	100 %

Descriptive statistics of participant semester is presented in *Table 9*. Comparing results over both events reveal not only differences over the events but interestingly over the two Bielefeld institutions as well. Whereas almost every participant from Bielefeld university is enrolled in semester 1-3, the majority of participants from Bielefeld University of Applied Sciences are enrolled in semester 1-6.

Table 9: Participant Semester

| Semester | AStA Festival 2019 | | Campus Festival Bielefeld 2019 | | | |
| | Paderborn University | | Bielefeld University | | Bielefeld University for Applied Sciences | |
	Frequency	Percent	Frequency	Percent	Frequency	Percent
1-3	122	54 %	553	95.5 %	47	41.2 %
4-6	50	22.1 %	14	2.4 %	49	43 %
7-9	14	6.2 %	5	0.9 %	11	9.6 %
> 9	36	15.9 %	2	0.3 %	7	6.1 %
Missing	3	1.3 %	0	0 %	0	0 %

Descriptive statistics of participant marital status is not presented in a table due to similar numbers and links to expected figures in the follow-up to table 6 whereas more than 96 % of all participants have indicated to be single.

Participant Rating of the Event

Participants varied in their response to six experiential items rating the festivals in general, their sensed organization on-site, the general program, the atmosphere, the general marketing campaign as well as the festivals' venue. Participants had to respond by German school grades ranging from "Very good" representing "1" to "Insufficient" representing "6".

Descriptive statistics of participant general critique of the individual event is presented in *Table 10*. Comparing results suggest an average better rating for the event in Paderborn. This is mainly due to the fact that the event in Paderborn was given a grade of one or two by more than 65 %. In Bielefeld, the majority of respondents rated average.

Table 10: Participant General Critique of the Events

| | AStA Festival 2019 | | Campus Festival Bielefeld 2019 | | | |
| | Paderborn University | | Bielefeld University | | Bielefeld University of Applied Sciences | |
	Frequency	Percent	Frequency	Percent	Frequency	Percent
1	20	8.8 %	36	6.3 %	9	7.9
2	132	58.4 %	182	31.7 %	39	34.2
3	60	26.5 %	199	34.7 %	38	33.3
4	11	4.9 %	100	17.4 %	20	17.5
5	3	1.3 %	41	8.2 %	8	7
6	0	0 %	10	1.7 %	0	0 %
Miss-ing	0	0 %	0	0	0	0 %
Total	226	100 %	574	100 %	114	100 %

Descriptive statistics of participant sensed organization on-site is presented in *Table 11*. Comparing results over both events suggest a better rating of the (sensed) local event organization in Paderborn. Differences can be seen in the best grades as well as in worst scores. The average grade assignment (Grade 3) seems comparable.

Table 11: Participant Sensed Organisation on-site

| | AStA Festival 2019 | | Campus Festival Bielefeld 2019 | | | |
| | Paderborn University | | Bielefeld University | | Bielefeld University of Applied Sciences | |
	Frequency	Percent	Frequency	Percent	Frequency	Percent
1	52	23 %	73	12.7 %	10	8.8 %
2	113	50 %	266	46.3 %	53	46.5 %
3	49	21.7 %	148	25.8 %	30	26.3 %
4	9	4 %	62	10.8 %	17	14.9 %
5	3	1.3 %	20	3.5 %	4	3.5 %
6	0	0 %	5	0.9 %	0	0 %
Missing	0	0 %	0	0 %	0	0 %
Total	226	100 %	574	100 %	114	100 %

Descriptive statistics of participant review on general program is presented in *Table 12*. Results suggest an increased willingness to rate the festival better in Paderborn than in Bielefeld. The proportion of participants who rate the festivals with the best grade are more or less comparable.

Table 12: Participant Review on General Program

| | AStA Festival 2019 | | Campus Festival Bielefeld 2019 | | | |
| | Paderborn University | | Bielefeld University | | Bielefeld University of Applied Sciences | |
	Frequency	Percent	Frequency	Percent	Frequency	Percent
1	14	6.2 %	31	5.4 %	9	7.9 %
2	91	40.3 %	164	28.6 %	26	22.8 %
3	77	34.1 %	168	29.3 %	48	42.1 %
4	33	14.6 %	128	22.3 %	19	16.7 %
5	8	3.5 %	71	12.4 %	10	8.8 %
6	2	0.9 %	12	2.1 %	2	1.8 %
Missing	1	0.4 %	0	0 %	0	0 %
Total	226	100 %	574	100 %	114	100 %

Descriptive statistics of participant review on atmosphere campaign is presented in *Table 13*. Comparing results over both events suggest a similar to almost equal feeling with regard to the individual atmosphere of the events.

Table 13: Participant Review on Atmosphere

| | AStA Festival 2019 | | Campus Festival Bielefeld 2019 | | | |
| | Paderborn University | | Bielefeld University | | Bielefeld University of Applied Sciences | |
	Frequency	Percent	Frequency	Percent	Frequency	Percent
1	67	29.6 %	143	24.9 %	34	29.8 %
2	122	54 %	274	47.7 %	57	50 %
3	27	11.9 %	106	18.5 %	13	11.4 %
4	9	4 %	39	6.8 %	9	7.9 %
5	1	0.4 %	11	1.9 %	1	0.9 %
6	0	0 %	1	0.2 %	0	0 %
Missing	1	0 %	0	0 %	0	0 %
Total	226	100 %	574	100 %	114	100 %

Descriptive statistics of participant review on marketing campaign is presented in *Table 14*. Comparing results over all institutions suggest similar to almost equal feeling with regard to the individual marketing campaign of both events.

Table 14: Participant Review on Marketing Campaign

| | AStA Festival 2019 | | Campus Festival Bielefeld 2019 | | | |
| | Paderborn University | | Bielefeld University | | Bielefeld University for Applied Sciences | |
	Frequency	Percent	Frequency	Percent	Frequency	Percent
1	19	8.4 %	64	11.1 %	12	10.5 %
2	94	41.6 %	285	49.7 %	59	51.8 %
3	74	32.7 %	163	28.4 %	34	29.8 %
4	24	10.6 %	45	7.8 %	5	4.4 %
5	6	2.7 %	14	2.4 %	2	1.8 %
6	2	0.9 %	3	0.5 %	2	1.8 %
Missing	7	3.1 %	0	0 %	0	0 %
Total	226	100 %	574	100 %	114	100 %

Descriptive statistics of participant review on venue is presented in *Table 15*. Results suggest a slightly better evaluation of the site in Paderborn. Furthermore, there is little to no significant differences between visitors' reviews.

Table 15: Participant Review on Venue

| | AStA Festival 2019 | | Campus Festival Bielefeld 2019 | | | |
| | Paderborn University | | Bielefeld University | | Bielefeld University for Applied Sciences | |
	Frequency	Percent	Frequency	Percent	Frequency	Percent
1	68	30.1 %	122	21.3 %	22	19.3 %
2	110	48.7 %	282	49.1 %	56	49.1 %
3	35	15.5 %	11	19.3 %	24	21.1 %
4	12	5.3 %	40	7 %	10	8.8 %
5	0	0 %	14	2.4 %	2	1.8 %
6	0	0 %	5	0.9 %	0	0 %
Missing	1	0.4 %	0	0 %	0	0 %
Total	226	100 %	574	100 %	114	100 %

Participant Basic Festival Behavior

Participants varied in their response to six experiential items describing their behavior around their visit of either the 2019 AStA Sommerfestival in Paderborn or the 2019 Campus Festival Bielefeld. Furthermore, past visit frequency to the events as well as to other festivals were requested.

Descriptive statistics of participant estimate 2019 music festival visits is presented in *Table 16*. Results suggest little differences over all institutions with regard to expected visits next to the event, participants had just attended.

Table 16: Participant Estimate 2019 Music Festival Visits

	AStA Festival 2019		Campus Festival Bielefeld 2019			
	Paderborn University		Bielefeld University		Bielefeld University for Applied Sciences	
	Frequency	Percent	Frequency	Percent	Frequency	Percent
0	94	41.6 %	152	26.5 %	17	14.9 %
1	72	31.9 %	152	26.5 %	22	19.3 %
2	33	14.6 %	117	20.4 %	36	31.6 %
3	14	6.2 %	83	14.5 %	20	17.5 %
4	3	1.3 %	37	6.4 %	7	6.1 %
>4	10	4.4 %	31	5.4 %	8	7.1 %
Missing	0	0 %	2	0.3 %	4	3.5 %
Total	226	100 %	574	100 %	114	100 %

Describes the estimated number of festival visits without visiting the respective university festival in Paderborn or Bielefeld.

Descriptive statistics of participant prior visits to respective event(s) is presented in *Table 17*. Results suggest differences between both events' participants having visited the festivals in the past. Results from Paderborn show a high proportion of first-time visitors in contrast to the event in Bielefeld. In addition, it needs to be mentioned, that the event in Bielefeld is still quite young and thus, data on participants with more than five visits is nonexistent.

Table 17: Participant Prior Visits to Respective Event

	AStA Festival 2019		Campus Festival Bielefeld 2019			
	Paderborn University		Bielefeld University		Bielefeld University for Applied Sciences	
	Frequency	Percent	Frequency	Percent	Frequency	Percent
0	111	49.1 %	144	25.1 %	31	27.2 %
1	24	10.6 %	90	15.7 %	25	21.9 %
2	24	10.6 %	140	24.4 %	26	22.8 %
3	24	10.6 %	121	21.1 %	21	18.4%
4	15	6.6 %	61	10.6 %	9	7.9%
5	13	5.8 %	18	3.1 %	2	1.8 %
>5[38]	14	6.2 %	/	/	/	/
Missing	1	0.4 %		0 %	0	0 %
Total	226	100 %	574	100 %	114	100 %

Descriptive statistics of participant number of visitor group members is presented in *Table 18*. Comparing results over all institutions suggest differences between group sizes over both events with bigger visitor groups attending the AStA Sommerfestival.

Table 18: Participant Number of Visitor Group Members

	AStA Festival 2019		Campus Festival Bielefeld 2019			
	Paderborn University		Bielefeld University		Bielefeld University for Applied Sciences	
	Frequency	Percent	Frequency	Percent	Frequency	Percent
0	3	1.3 %	9	1.6 %	1	0.9
1-3	33	14.6 %	106	18.5 %	30	26.3 %
4-6	62	27.4 %	276	48.1 %	48	42.1 %
7-9	35	15.5 %	88	15.3 %	14	12.3 %
>9	93	41.2 %	95	16.6 %	21	18.4 %
Missing	0	0 %	0	0 %	0	0 %
Total	226	100 %	574	100 %	114	100 %

Descriptive statistics of participant attendance to a preparty event is presented in *Table 19*. Results show very clearly that most festival goers do attend an event prior to the festival on campus. This is particularly evident in Paderborn, where this the case for more than 84 % of all participants.

Table 19: Participant Attendance to Preparty Event

	AStA Festival 2019		Campus Festival Bielefeld 2019			
	Paderborn University		Bielefeld University		Bielefeld University for Applied Sciences	
	Frequency	Percent	Frequency	Percent	Frequency	Percent
Yes	190	84.1 %	396	69 %	73	64 %
No	34	15 %	178	31 %	41	36 %
Missing	2	0.8 %	0	0 %	0	0 %
Total	226	100 %	574	100 %	114	100 %

Descriptive statistics of participant arrival at the individual festival venue is presented in *Table 12*. Comparing results over all institutions suggest participants do not enter the venue(s) on time. Especially in Paderborn, participants tend to enter the venue hours after the doors open.

Table 20: Participant Arrival at Festival Venue

	AStA Festival 2019		Campus Festival Bielefeld 2019			
	Paderborn University		Bielefeld University		Bielefeld University for Applied Sciences	
	Fre-quency	Per-cent	Fre-quency	Per-cent	Fre-quency	Percent
3:30 — 4:30 p.m.	32	14.2 %	175	30.5 %	31	27.2 %
4:30 — 5:30 p.m.	75	33.2 %	175	30.5 %	33	28.9 %
5:30 — 6:30 p.m.	76	33.6 %	166	28.9 %	37	32.5 %
6:30 — 7:30 p.m.	30	13.3 %	44	7.7 %	10	8.8 %
After 7:30 p.m.	13	5.8 %	14	2.4 %	3	2.6 %
Missing	0	0 %	0	0 %	0	0 %
Total	226	100 %	574	100 %	114	100 %

Descriptive statistics of participant budget across all events is presented in *Table 21*. Comparing results over all institutions suggest a budget between 10 € and 20 € for the majority of all participants, whereas for more than 50 % of all participants the budget is limited between 10 € and 30 €.

Table 21: Participant Budget

	AStA Festival 2019		Campus Festival Bielefeld 2019			
	Paderborn University		Bielefeld University		Bielefeld University for Applied Sciences	
	Frequency	Percent	Frequency	Percent	Frequency	Percent
<10 €	41	18.1 %	76	13.2 %	9	7.9 %
10-20 €	72	31.9 %	192	33.4 %	35	30.7 %
20-30 €	50	22.1 %	139	24.2 %	28	24.6 %
30-40 €	27	11.9 %	53	9.2 %	20	17.5 %
40-50 €	17	7.5 %	62	10.8 %	13	11.4 %
>50 €	19	8.4 %	52	9.1 %	9	7.9 %
Missing	0	0 %	0	0 %	0	0
Total	226	100 %	574	100 %	114	100 %

Motivators for Festival Attendance

Descriptive statistics of single motivators for festival attendance is presented in *Table 22* and sorted by relevance. To get an idea of how significant each single motivator for festival attendance was represented in the data sets, two of the highest values for every single motivator from the five-point Likert scale answers (4—*rather applies* to 5—*does apply*) were aggregated. Comparing results from both events suggest differences for all items but item 26 ("have fun"), item 21 ("spend time with friends"), item 24 ("experience music live"), item 28 ("drink alcohol") and item 20 ("flee from everyday boredom").

Table 22: Single Motivators for Festival Attendance Significance

	Motivators	Paderborn	Bielefeld	Combined
Item 26	Have fun	98.2 %	99.0 %	98.8 %
Item 21	Spend time w. friends	95.6 %	96.1 %	96 %
Item 24	Experience music live	85.8 %	88.8 %	88.1 %
Item 19	Experience sth. Special	75.2 %	81.8 %	80.2 %
Item 27	Dance	74.8 %	81.4 %	79.8 %
Item 28	Drink alcohol	58.4 %	57.3 %	57.5 %
Item 20	Flee from everyday boredom	50.4 %	48.8 %	49.2 %
Item 23	Party on campus	59.3 %	44.3 %	48 %
Item 17	Everyday life escape	42.9 %	47.7 %	46.5 %
Item 22	Meet new people	37.2 %	32.3 %	33.5 %
Item 25	Line-Up	23.9 %	30.4 %	28.8 %
Item 18	Behave inappropriately	14.2 %	8.7 %	10.1 %
Item 29	Consume drugs	8.0 %	3.1 %	4.3 %

External Value of Visit

Descriptive statistics of the external value of the visit(s) are presented in *Table 23*. To get an idea how significant the festival visit is valued with regard to the four items, a summary of all Likert scale frequencies is provided. Comparing results from both cities suggest mostly similar characteristics with Bielefeld results leaning towards a more likely share of the festival visit on social media than participants in Paderborn. Furthermore, approval over all four items can be described as low to very low with combined Likert scale values (1—*I don't agree* and 2—*I rather don't agree*) of more than 75 %.

Table 23: External Value of Visit

		Com-bined	Pader-born	Bielefeld
Item 30	Differentiate from others by visit			
1	I don't agree	60.5 %	61.5 %	60.2 %
2	I rather don't agree	16.6 %	14.6 %	17.3 %
3	Neither	15.6 %	16.8 %	15.3 %
4	I rather agree	5.8 %	5.3 %	6 %
5	I agree	1.4 %	1.8 %	1.3 %
Item 31	Brag with visit	Com-bined	Pader-born	Bielefeld
1	I don't agree	74.5 %	75.2 %	74.3 %
2	I rather don't agree	11.9 %	8.8 %	12.9 %
3	Neither	8.8 %	11.1 %	8.0 %
4	I rather agree	3.6 %	3.5 %	3.6 %
5	I agree	1.2 %	1.3 %	1.2 %
Item 32	Visit as status symbol	Com-bined	Pader-born	Bielefeld
1	I don't agree	77.8 %	78.8 %	77.5 %
2	I rather don't agree	12.3 %	10.6 %	12.8 %
3	Neither	7.1 %	8.8 %	6.5 %
4	I rather agree	2.5 %	1.3 %	2.9 %
5	I agree	0.3 %	0.4 %	0.3 %
Item 33	Share visit on social media	Com-bined	Pader-born	Bielefeld
1	I don't agree	55.6 %	60.6 %	53.9 %
2	I rather don't agree	18.7 %	18.6 %	18.8 %
3	Neither	10.7 %	11.1 %	10.6 %
4	I rather agree	12.3 %	8 %	13.7 %
5	I agree	2.7 %	1.8 %	3.1 %

Sponsorship Awareness

Descriptive statistics of sponsorship awareness are presented in *Table 24*. To get an idea how well participants would recall brands that were not even present at the venue (item 34), results are presented as 'correct' or 'incorrect'. Comparing results from both cities suggest significant difference in brand recollection and similar results with regards to connecting a certain sponsoring brand to a stage at the venue.

Table 24: Sponsorship Awareness

Item 34	Brand most recalled	Com-bined	Pader-born	Bielefeld
	Correct	66.2 %	45.5 %	73 %
	Incorrect	33.8 %	54.5 %	27 %
Item 35	Brand-stage connection	Com-bined	Pader-born	Bielefeld
	Correct	61 %	59.2 %	61.5 %
	Incorrect	39 %	40.8 %	38.5 %

Attitude towards Sponsorship

Descriptive statistics regarding attitude towards sponsorship are presented in *Figure 10*. For all items, Likert scale answers 4 ("I rather agree") or 5 ("I agree") were summarized in the table. Comparing results from both cities suggest differences between results with regards to item 36 ("There was too much advertising at the festival") and item 38 ("I question business practices of sponsoring brands"). Results for item 37 ('An event such as the AStA Sommerfestival/Campusfestival Bielefeld is only possible with sponsorship"), item 39 ("I'm not interested in which brand supports the festival"), item 40 ("I'd pay more for the festival ticket if fewer companies advertised on-site"), item 41 ("I want more non-musical offers/things to do at the festival") suggest similar characteristics.

University Identification

Descriptive statistics regarding attitude towards sponsorship are presented in *Table 25*. Results for both items are displayed and suggest differences across all Likert scale values with exception of answer "3" ("neither"). Item 48 ("Identification with university") suggests a high sense of identification of visitors with their institution in both cities.

Figure 10: Attitude towards Sponsorship

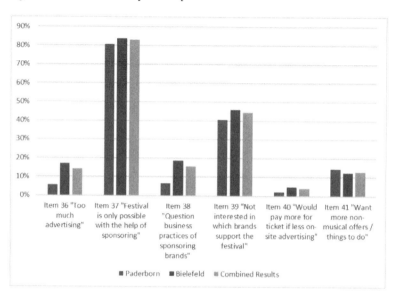

Table 25: University Identification

Item 48	Identification with university	Combined	Paderborn	Bielefeld
1	Doesn't apply	13.7 %	3.1 %	17.2 %
2	Rather doesn't apply	11.8 %	11.9 %	11.8 %
3	Neither	25.6 %	26.1 %	25.4 %
4	Rather applies	35.1 %	45.6 %	31.7 %
5	Does apply	13.8 %	13.3 %	14.0 %
Item 49	Identification with faculty	Combined	Paderborn	Bielefeld
1	Doesn't apply	14.3 %	8.0 %	16.4 %
2	Rather doesn't apply	10.8 %	14.2 %	9.7 %
3	Neither	24.8 %	26.1 %	24.4 %
4	Rather applies	34.0 %	38.9 %	32.4 %
5	Does apply	16.0 %	12.8 %	17.0 %

Summary

The description of results regarding research objective one in the previous chapters show that both events, despite spatial proximity, same organizer structure and fundamental similarity in terms of event identity and organizational proximity to the associated universities, differ in their outcome of their individual descriptive data analysis partly significant. At this point it should be pointed out that the two surveys are based on different methodologies. Whether mentioned differences are due to the different methodologies or not cannot be said on the basis of the presented data and results. In the ongoing step, research objective two is outlined and will be followed by the discussion of results in chapter 10.3.

Research Objective Two (EFA)

In the following, results regarding the second research objective are outlined. This is being done in a detailed manner, as the analysis consists of several consecutive steps which refined the statistical data for a usable interpretation.

Preliminary Analyses

In this section, the steps taken prior to rotating the factor matrices (n=914, n=688, n=226) are summarized. These included an analysis of the initial reliability, intercorrelations, and assumptions underlying SPSS's principal axis factoring (i.e., principal factor analysis).

Initial reliability analysis

To determine whether the 13 items represented an internally consistent measure, the researcher computed reliability statistics for the overall scale, generating a Cronbach's alpha of .613 for both data combined, .636 for Paderborn data and .624 for Bielefeld data.

In the item-overall scale correlations, there was no item that would significantly improve the Cronbach's alpha, if deleted. Based on an examination of kurtosis and visual inspection of the QQ plot, no items were deleted due to excessive skewness. Therefore, the researcher decided to compute the factor analysis with the initial 13 items.

Correlational analyses

An analysis of the inter-item Pearson Product correlations demonstrated at least one low-to-high association per item, ranging from .30 to .63 for combined results, .31 to .51 for data from Bielefeld and .31 to .50 for data from Paderborn. Items 23 ("celebrate on campus") and 29 ("consume drugs") did not correlate with any of the other items within this acceptable range 0.30-0.80 for combined data as well as for data from Bielefeld. Data from Paderborn showed no correlation with any other item for item 29 ("consume drugs") but did so for item 23 ("celebrate on campus"). However, the researcher decided to include them in the initial rotation to assess its suitability for the factor analysis.

Verifying assumptions
In verifying assumptions prior to rotation, the results of the Bartlett's Test of Sphericity for combined results, B (914) = 1597,303, $p < 0,000$ and a Kaiser-Meyer-Olkin Measure of Sampling Adequacy (KMO = .684) were computed. Results for the individual data computed for Paderborn, B(226) = 444,972, $p < 0,000$ and a Kaiser-Meyer-Olkin Measure of Sampling Adequacy (KMO = .668) and for Bielefeld, B(668) = 1258,688, $p < 0,000$ and a Kaiser-Meyer-Olkin Measure of Sampling Adequacy (KMO = .676). This latter finding indicated that the correlation matrices were favorable and not an identity matrix. This finding suggests that there is potential in the model to measure multiple constructs.

Unrotated Results
An initial analysis was run to obtain eigenvalues for each factor in the data. Combined results showed four factors having eigenvalues over Kaiser's criterion of 1 and in combination explained 53.37 % of the variance. Results from Paderborn data showed four factors having eigenvalues over Kaiser's criterion of 1 and in combination explained 54.07 % of the variance. Results from Bielefeld data showed four factors having eigenvalues over Kaiser's criterion of 1 and in combination explained 54 % of the variance. To further identify potential meaningful factors the scree plot was examined. The scree plots of combined data as well as for individual data were ambiguous and showed inflexions that would justify retaining either two or four factors. Four factors were retained because of the large sample size and the convergence of the scree plot and Kaiser's criterion on this value.

Additionally, a parallel analysis was conducted. The method compares the eigenvalues generated from the data matrices to the eigenvalues generated from a Monte-Carlo simulated matrix created from random data of the same size.[39] In doing so, each eigenvalue is being compared to an eigenvalue from a data set that has no underlying factors. Thus, eigenvalues from the factor analysis are compared with the eigenvalues from the parallel analysis, and eigenvalues for the fifth and subsequent components (factors) were nearly equal for combined and Bielefeld data, indicating eigenvalues of this magnitude could have been derived from a random sample of data. Therefore, only four factors were retained for further analysis for combined and Bielefeld data. Comparison of Paderborn data eigenvalues and eigenvalues from the parallel analysis suggested five factors. Cattell's scree test matched the above results, while Kaiser's rule would also have retained four factors. Thus, four factors based on the results of visual inspection of Cattell's scree test were chosen to rotate, the accounted percentage of variance and the results from the parallel analysis. The items examined for high and low factor loadings, and .30 was set as the minimum acceptable factor loading.[40]

Figure 11: Eigenvalue Comparison between Factor Analysis (FA) and Parallel Analysis (PA) for combined results

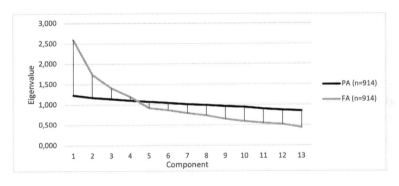

---

39   Field, *Discovering Statistics Using IBM SPSS Statistics.*
40   Field; Comrey and Lee, *A First Course in Factor Analysis.*

Figure 12: Eigenvalue Comparison between Factor Analysis (FA) and Parallel Analysis (PA) for Bielefeld results

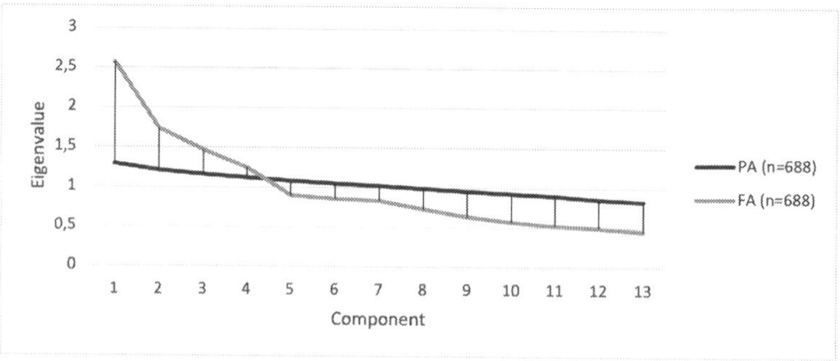

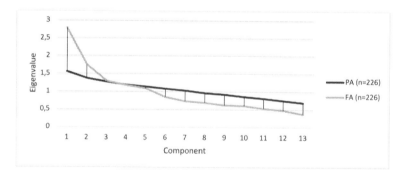

Figure 13: Eigenvalue Comparison between Factor Analysis (FA) and Parallel Analysis (PA) for Paderborn results

Rotation Results

Varimax rotations (i.e., a form of orthogonal rotation that rotates in 90° angles) for both PCA and PFA were compared and found similar variance in the models. This similarity between the PCA and PFA results suggests that both approaches represent a coherent and interpretable factor structure. However, PFA is especially well-suited for determining potential latent constructs in the data set and provides a more accurate estimate of the item correlations. According to Field[41] oblimin rotation (i.e., a form of oblique rotation that rotates the eigenvectors in less than 90° angles) should be used when there is an expected correlation between factors. Since the items were developed based on existing literature review and focus group results, different dimensions such as socialization, escapism, and music etc., a certain correlation between factors was expected prior to the analysis. Furthermore, oblimin rotation was conducted as it is appropriate for the current data set, because it is logical to assume that factors are correlated given the subjective nature participants' perceptions and experiences.

Based on a visual inspection of the oblimin rotation matrices using a PFA four/five-factor structure, the researcher selected the pattern rotation matrix for it provided the best interpretation of the factor structure with the least evidence of cross-loadings.

Communalities for combined results were reasonably strong, ranging from about 0.3 to 0.6, except for three items: Item 22 ("meeting new people"), item 23 ("celebrate on campus") and item 29 ("consume drugs"). Two of these items (item 22 and item 23) also did not load on any factor at the minimum level of 0.3. These items were deleted from the set, leaving eleven items. After deleting the above mentioned two items, the resulting factor structure accounted for 60.13 % of the total variance.

Communalities for Bielefeld results were reasonably strong, ranging from about 0.3 to 0.6, except for three items: Item 22 ("meeting new people"), item 23 ("celebrate on campus") and item 29 ("consume drugs"). One of these items (item 23) also did not load on any factor at the minimum level of 0.3. This item was deleted from the set, leaving 12 items. After deleting the above-mentioned item, the resulting factor structure accounted for 57.14 % of the total variance.

Communalities for Paderborn results were reasonably strong, ranging from about 0.3 to 0.6, except for two items: Item 22 ("meet new people") and item 23 ("celebrate on campus"). None of these items did not load on any factor at the minimum level of 0.3, leaving the set with 13 items. The resulting factor structure accounted for 62.46 % of the total variance.

Pattern matrix for combined results is shown in *Table 26* showing four motivational dimensions for festival attendance and incorporating all 13 items

---

41   Field, *Discovering Statistics Using IBM SPSS Statistics*.

of the survey. According to Field[42], structure matrix for combined results will not be interpreted as presented pattern matrix as underlying interrelations between factors are not given.

Table 26: Oblimin-rotated Component Structure (Pattern Matrix) based on Principal Axis Factor Analysis (13 items) for Combined Results

		F1	F2	F3	F4
Item 17	Everyday life escape	.769			
Item 20	Flee from Everyday Boredom	.638			
Item 19	Experience sth. Special	.371			
Item 26	Have Fun		.595		
Item 21	Spend Time w. Friends		.563		
Item 27	Dance		.504		
Item 22	Meet new people				
Item 23	Party on campus				
Item 25	Line-Up			.788	
Item 24	Experience music live			.517	
Item 18	Behave inappropriately	.320			.570
Item 28	Drink alcohol		.344		.526
Item 29	Consume drugs				.351

Pattern matrix for combined results is shown in *Table 27* showing four motivational dimensions for festival attendance incorporating reduced num-

---

42   Field.

ber of items from survey. According to Field[43], structure matrix for combined results will not be interpreted as presented pattern matrix as underlying interrelations between factors are not given.

Table 27: Oblimin-rotated Component Structure (Pattern Matrix) based on Principal Axis Factor Analysis (11 items) for Combined Results

		F1	F2	F3	F4
Item 17	Everyday life escape	.769			
Item 20	Flee from Everyday Boredom	.638			
Item 19	Experience sth. Special	.370			
Item 25	Line-Up		.684		
Item 24	Experience music live		.591		
Item 26	Have Fun			.626	
Item 21	Spend Time w. Friends			.575	
Item 27	Dance			.467	
Item 28	Drink alcohol			.361	.579
Item 18	Behave inappropriately	.323			.540
Item 29	Consume drugs				.346

Pattern matrix for Bielefeld results is shown in *Table 28* showing four motivational dimensions for festival attendance and incorporating all 13 items of the survey. According to Field[44], structure matrix for combined results will not be interpreted as presented pattern matrix as underlying interrelations between factors are not given.

---

43   Field.
44   Field.

Table 28: Oblimin-rotated Component Structure (Pattern Matrix) based on Principal Axis Factor Analysis (13 items) for Bielefeld Results

		F1	F2	F3	F4
Item 17	Everyday life escape	.777			
Item 20	Flee from Everyday Boredom	.633			
Item 19	Experience sth. Special	.423			
Item 25	Line-Up		.810		
Item 24	Experience music live		.541		
Item 26	Have Fun			.588	
Item 21	Spend Time w. Friends			.551	
Item 27	Dance			.492	
Item 22	Meet new people			.318	
Item 23	Party on campus				
Item 18	Behave inappropriately	.354			.542
Item 28	Drink alcohol			.360	.542
Item 29	Consume drugs				.318

Pattern matrix for combined results is shown in *Table 29* showing four motivational dimensions for festival attendance incorporating reduced amount of twelve items from survey. According to Field[45], structure matrix for combined results will not be interpreted as presented pattern matrix as underlying interrelations between factors are not given.

---

45   Field.

Table 29: Oblimin-rotated Component Structure (Pattern Matrix) based on Principal Axis Factor Analysis (12 items) for Bielefeld Results

		F1	F2	F3	F4
Item 17	Everyday life escape	.766			
Item 20	Flee from Everyday Boredom	.638			
Item 19	Experience sth. Special	.413			
Item 25	Line-Up		.691		
Item 24	Experience music live		.643		
Item 26	Have Fun			.600	
Item 21	Spend Time w. Friends			.574	
Item 27	Dance			.468	
Item 22	Meet new people			.302	
Item 18	Behave inappropriately	.328			.590
Item 28	Drink alcohol			.360	.502
Item 29	Consume drugs				.311

Pattern matrix for Bielefeld results is shown in Table 30 showing five motivational dimensions for festival attendance and incorporating all 13 items of the survey. According to Field[46], structure matrix for combined results will not be interpreted as presented pattern matrix as underlying interrelations between factors are not given.

---

46   Field.

Table 30: Oblimin-rotated Component Structure (Pattern Matrix) based on Principal Axis Factor Analysis (13 items) for Paderborn results

		F1	F2	F3	F4	F5
Item 19	Experience sth. Special	.656				
Item 22	Meet new people	.483				
Item 23	Party on campus	.331				
Item 17	Everyday life escape		-.974			
Item 20	Flee from Everyday Boredom		-.493			
Item 27	Dance			-.655		
Item 21	Spend Time w. Friends			-.616		
Item 26	Have Fun			-.572		
Item 24	Experience music live				.561	
Item 25	Line-Up				.502	
Item 28	Drink alcohol					.695
Item 29	Consume drugs					.504
Item 18	Behave inappropriately					.444

The correlation matrices for all results were reproduced to verify each factor solution. The content of the items for corresponding factor structure of Paderborn and Bielefeld do not resemble each other. Thus, factors for Bielefeld results and Paderborn results were labeled individually: escape, music, social, drugged escape (Bielefeld); Novelty, escape, social, music, drugged escape (Paderborn). Factor structure for combined results resembled Bielefeld results.

Mentioned four factors from Bielefeld results initially accounted for 54 % of the total variance. However, after deleting the above-mentioned item 23

("Party on campus") for Bielefeld results, it accounted for 57.14 % of the variance in the correlation matrix. Mentioned four factors from combined results initially accounted for 53.37 % of the total variance. However, after deleting the above mentioned two items 23 ("Party on campus") and item 22 ("Meet new people") for combined results, it accounted for 60.13 % of the variance in the correlation matrix. Mentioned five factors from Paderborn results accounted for 62.46 % of the total variance. The range of correlations between derived factors for the oblique rotation was between .014 and .232 for combined results, .073 and .229 for Bielefeld results and .017 and .369 for Paderborn results. In summary, an exploratory factor analysis of the questionnaire's items produced an interpretable four-factor structure for combined and Bielefeld results and an interpretable five-factor structure for Paderborn structure.

Table 31: Final Factor Inter-Correlation Matrix (combined results)

Factor	1	2	3	4
1		.114	.209	.221
2			.232	-.063
3				.014
4				

Table 32: Final Factor Inter-Correlation Matrix (Bielefeld results)

Factor	1	2	3	4
1		.108	.218	.185
2			.229	-.073
3				.096
4				

Table 33: Final Factor Inter-Correlation Matrix (Paderborn results)

Factor	1	2	3	4	5
1		-.232	-.369	.123	.242
2			.110	.030	-.242
3				-.138	-.041
4					.017
5					

Discussion of Results

In the following, prior provided results are being discussed with regard to both research objectives. Based on descriptive knowledge of audiences who attended the two biggest university popular music festivals held in 2019 in Germany, audience profiles are outlined in chapter 10.3.1. Available data regarding participants' motives and the results of the EFA will then be discussed in chapter 10.3.2 and discuss the motivational constructs of the participants of both events.

Audience Profile(s)

With respect to participants' assessments of the visited events, there are recognizable differences between the two surveys with regard to participants' general critique of the event but especially with regard to the sensed organization on site by participants. This is worth mentioning because both events take place annually about 3-4 weeks apart and, moreover, are planned and carried out by the same event agency. Exact underlying reasons for this cannot be explained based on the available data and further research is needed at this point.

As shown, findings of quantitative surveys provide complex descriptions of sponsorship culture with focus on the festival audience(s). Descriptive data regarding single motivators for festival attendance indicate great differences in significance between the items.

Furthermore, items—when staggered according to their relevance over both events—indicate an equal listing.

Ranked results of single motivators for festival attendance of each event suggest comparable similarities in relevance. Every single motivator is ranked equally over both events. However, this should not lead to a conclusion regarding a certain generalizability of student audience motivators for festival attendance, as this needs to be interpreted with caution and only be marked as a hint, as the scope of this study is too small to derive this kind of a statement from the data.

Socializing motives with values over 90 % (see table 21) are more important to the student audiences than music motives, this goes along with existing literature on similar studies such as Kulczynski et al.[47], Bowen and Daniels[48] as well as Crompton and McKray[49].

However, the importance of the line-up of both festivals can be described as very trivial in contrast to the 'liveness' of performed music as single motivator, as in Paderborn 20.8 % (Bielefeld: 12.8 %) assessed the line-up playing a neutral role as a motivating factor for them, and over 55 % (Bielefeld: 56.8 %) did not see the line up as a motivating factor for their event attendance. And this, despite the fact that line-ups of both events did not have to hide in recent years in terms of quality and reputation or in comparison with famous major German music festivals. Furthermore, as any other music festival, both events advertise more or less exclusively with their line-up. Whether social media postings, posters, or regular advertisements, they all put the line-up in the foreground and try to sell their tickets with it. The evaluation of the events' line-up as the third last point in both lists of single motivators can be seen as a major practical future implication for organizers as well as for future sponsors. Less focus and financial commitment to the line-up and an expenditure shift according to the motives discussed here, may improve the event's experience overall in the coming years. Nevertheless, the fact that music is being performed live, represents a major role besides the socializing motivators.

Escapism motives are located in the middle range here, this is only partially consistent with existing literature[50] of surveys who investigated audi-

---

47   Kulczynski, Baxter, and Young, "Measuring Motivations for Popular Music Concert Attendance," July 25, 2016.

48   Bowen and Daniels, "Does the Music Matter? Motivations for Attending a Music Festival."

49   Crompton and McKay, "Motives of Visitors Attending Festival Events."

50   Alicia Kulczynski, Stacey Baxter, and Tamara Young, "Measuring Motivations for Popular Music Concert Attendance," *Event Management* 20, no. 2 (July 25, 2016): 239–54, https://doi.org/10.3727/152599516X14643674421816.

ences who attended comparable events. As already mentioned, research on motives in the field of events is very complex and multilayered, as there are a large number of different kinds of events which influence the motivational constructs for attending them. However, this study lays a first foundation for the investigation of German student audiences and shows that escapism lies in the midfield with regard to significance of individual attendance motives.

Additionally, comparable studies implemented certain escapism concepts differently in relation to visitor's motives. In most studies, festival events were looked at through an (event) tourism lense[51]. Accordingly, there is of course an escapism aspect to be found and investigated as well, however, escapism in that sense is to be interpreted clearly in a different way than for this study.

The use of illegal drugs does not seem to be a motivation for visiting a university popular music festival in Paderborn or Bielefeld. Thus, future research may amend this implemented scale by leaving out item 29 ("consume drugs") as it is below a response rate of 10 %.

List of motivators was generated by literature and expert review as well as Study Two's focus group(s) results. Yet, it is possible that other motivators for popular music festival attendance exist that were not identified as motivators for other types of events in the literature and were not identified in the focus groups prior to development of this scale.

Descriptive data regarding the external value of the event attendance need to be interpreted with caution due to contradiction of the results which stand in contrast to related research[52][53], as there is no high level of agreement with the statements in the questionnaire across all items. Surprisingly, the results indicate that the majority of the audience(s) do not seem to comprehend the visit of the event as a status symbol, brag about it or see it as something to demarcate themselves from others. Especially contrary to expectations, results do not suggest participants to share their visit to the festival on social media. The reason for this rather contradictory result is still not clear at this point. Data regarding external value of visit would imply that sponsors should not necessarily pursue intensifying efforts in sponsorship activities incorporating this issue. It cannot be ruled out that the direct formulated wording used for

51   Graham MS Dann, "Tourist Motivation an Appraisal," *Annals of Tourism Research* 8, no. 2 (1981): 187–219.

52   Gannon, Taheri, and Olya, "Festival Quality, Felf-Connection, and Bragging."

53   Lee et al., "Instagram This! Sharing Photos on Instagram."

the items, was addressing these (sensitive) items too directly. Especially 'bragging about something' and demarcating oneself to others, might have created a negative bias in answering the Likert scales. Thus, further data collection in this specific subarea is required.

In the follow-up to the survey and evaluation of the results, it may be considered as somewhat unfortunate that the subarea dealing with sponsorship awareness in the questionnaires, was only explored by two items within this investigation, as the results appeared to reveal interesting new insights. As described in the instrumentation, participants were specifically asked about the brand or the brand appearance at the festival venue, that they would remember best. However, all the brands to be selected in the questionnaire have been existent in the years before, but were non-existent on either venue in 2019, whether as pure advertising nor as a sold product in any form.[54]

The results show clear differences between the two events, with an average of more than 66 % correct answers. In Bielefeld, this figure was even 73 % (Paderborn: 45.5 %) and thus almost three quarters of all respondents. If one also considers that the surveys were carried out in a three-week period after the event and therefore some answers were given up to 20 days after the actual visit, as well as the fact that a large proportion of visitors probably did not visit the festival completely sober, these are impressive figures. Figures, that lead to the assessment of the student audience of these events as attentive in relation to on venue sponsorship activities. Furthermore, this statement can be strengthened with the second item of this category. Here, the memory of a specific brand and the associated (branded) stage was queried. Again, after both events, about 60 % of the respondents were able to interpret the assignment correctly and remember it accordingly.

In response to participants' attitude towards sponsorship on university popular music festivals, broadly speaking, results suggest a well-suited notion and opinion of visitors regarding such activities at the festival venue. Findings clearly state a high understanding for the organizers' necessity to incorporate sponsorship to fund the respective events. Furthermore, results for item 36 ("too much advertising") suggest room for more possible sponsorship activities for both festivals. Data for item 38 ("question business practices of sponsoring brands") and item 39 ("not interested in which brands support

---

54   Nevertheless, participants had the choice for "answering" the question correctly by selecting the response saying: "None of the above"

the festival") are to be assessed positively from possible sponsors' and organizer's perspective. Since more than 40 % of participants stated to not being interested in who sponsored the festival and only a small part of those surveyed critically question sponsors' businesses, from a socio-political perspective, the statements made by those surveyed can be described as somewhat disconcerting, especially because audiences consist mainly of (well educated) students.

Data also show high acceptance for sponsorship if it helps lowering ticket prices, as strong rejection for higher ticket prices was stated in this context. As this study is the first step towards enhancing an understanding of sponsorship within the university popular music festival market, these findings represent a first glimpse in describing a predominantly distinctive comprehension and sort of sympathy for sponsorship within popular music festival audiences with high student share. Further research must investigate if this phenomenon is exclusive for student audiences of respective festivals and how this relates to other event/festival audiences.

More than half of all respondents in both audiences identify at least partially with their faculty as well as their university, while results of both events can be described as very similar. Linking these findings to the discussed interwovenness between cities, regions, and their universities, one might derive that young people's feelings of identification with their university may be transferable to the identification of respectable municipalities and cities. Future research with more focus on municipal or city marketing should incorporate these issues. Sponsors as well as organizers may implement these findings in designing future event and event-sponsorship experiences. This could mean, for instance, a change in certain wording structure within the communication and advertisement policy of both actants and/or when creating future graphic designs for festivals.

Motivational Constructs

The described process of factor analysis of Study Three resulted in different dimensional outputs for both events in the final analysis. Both samples lean towards a female bias as well as show a lower semester status for participants of the surveys than the average student's semester status of both universities. Twelve items loaded on four dimensions in Bielefeld whereas 13 items ultimately loaded on five dimensions in Paderborn. Both factor structures differ partly in their item composition. Although both festivals coexist in the same state, only 50 km apart from each other, this difference is to be underlined and could provide a tentative hint and consideration to investigate further whether motive constructs from other university festivals are equally distinctive from each other.

Bielefeld results show four items of a certain escapism aspect contained by first dimension with highest loadings, F1 (item 17: "everyday life escape", item 20: "flee from everyday boredom", item 19: "experience sth. special", item 18 "behave inappropriately"). Thus, the first dimension of Campus Festival Bielefeld's motivational construct is labeled *Escapism*. However, it needs to be restated, that this study has a distinct explorative character, thus, it can only be cautiously claimed that this outcome goes in line with other studies[55][56][57] in thematically related fields. What stands out, however, is the fact that the escapism dimension is the part of the motivational construct, that is most heavily loaded. On the contrary, as described in the previous chapter, when looking at items' relevance as single motivators for event attendance, this first factor is the one which has the highest factor loadings while containing two items with medium relevance (item 17: "everyday life escape", item 20: "flee from everyday boredom"), one item with medium-high relevance (item 19: "experience sth. special") as well as one item with low relevance (item 18 "behave inappropriately"). Following from this, it can be concluded that a certain escapism dimension within the motivational construct for visiting a university popular music festival (in Bielefeld) is existent, which has a moderately important relevance due to average factor loadings of about 46 % itself and thus constitutes a corresponding part within audiences' motivational construct.

Bielefeld's second factor, F2 is the most obvious and expectable dimension when researching motivational constructs for music festival attendance. Including "line-up" and "experience live music" it can clearly be labeled as the *Music* dimension of the motivational construct. As already described in detail in the previous chapter, this is the part of the construct, with which advertising for the event is almost exclusively concerned every year. From a motivational point of view, it is what the event, the music festival is obviously about at first glance. The fact that 'liveness' and the 'line-up-item' are loading on the

---

55   Crompton and McKay, "Motives of Visitors Attending Festival Events."
56   Manolika, Baltzis, and Tsigilis, "Measuring Motives for Cultural Consumption."
57   Abreu-Novais and Arcodia, "Music Festival Motivators for Attendance."

same factor has been expected here, as well as in other similar studies[58] and thus confirms the robustness of the method.

Linking this with described results from the previous chapter, where items' relevance as single motivators for event attendance is analyzed, this second factor is one which has high factor loadings while containing one item with high relevance (item 24: "experience music live") and one item with low relevance (item 25: "line-up"). Following from this, it can be concluded that an existing music dimension within motivational construct for Campus Festival Bielefeld 2019 attendance exists, whereby only the 'liveness' plays an important role for the audience while the line-up does not nearly as much. This is further underlined by the rejection (two negatively conjugated selects of the Likert scale) of the motivator 'line-up' of 56,8 % by Bielefeld participants (see appendix).

F3 is labeled *Social Partying*, containing dimensions of leisure activities such as "have fun" or "dance" with known companions ("spend time with friends") as well as meeting new ones ("meet new people"), while consuming alcohol ("drink alcohol"). The socializing aspect of motivational constructs for university popular music festival attendance in Bielefeld has been confirmed and suggests a high complexity of the factor due to five loading items. This extends results of past studies to similar research subjects.[59] Everything a visitor does or aims to do during the experience, can (but doesn't have to) be linked to an underlying social aspect somehow. This goes especially for item 26 ("have fun") item 27 ("dance") as well as item 28 ("drink alcohol"). Linking this with described results from the previous chapter, where items' relevance as single motivators for event attendance is analyzed, this third factor contains the top two items (item 21: "spend time with friends", item 26) with the highest relevance. Furthermore, item 27 and item 22 ("meet new people") represent medium to high relevance, item 22 ("meet new people") represents a lower relevance but still was named by 32 % of participants. Thus, socialization appears as the most common dimension here, and according to Abreu et. Al[60], in more than 20 thematically related studies as well.

Forth factor is a composition of consuming legal ("drink alcohol") as well as illegal drugs ("consume drugs") and a misbehaving dimension ("behave in-

---

58   Bowen and Daniels, "Does the Music Matter? Motivations for Attending a Music Festival."

59   Bowen and Daniels.

60   Abreu-Novais and Arcodia, "Music Festival Motivators for Attendance."

appropriately") labeling the factor *Burst*. This research is the first known that incorporates a motivational aspect of the use of illegal substances within motivational construct for university popular music attendance in Germany. The fact that the item loads on this fourth factor was expected. However, its significance must be relativized in view of the low level of agreement among the participants to this item as a reason for their visit, as it has been shown in the previous chapter. Visitors of popular music festivals consume illegal drugs, as anyone who has ever been to one knows and can observe 'on every corner'. Nevertheless, the consumption does not seem to play into the motivational constructs at Campus Festival Bielefeld in 2019 with 3,1 % consent and 93 % rejection.

Paderborn results show three items of an underlying university character contained by the first factor, F1, with substantial loadings. Thus, motivational construct's first dimension for Paderborn's AStA Sommerfestival 2019 attendance is labeled *Uni Life* dimension. As this is the first quantitative investigation dealing with the university campus as event venue in Germany, this presents a first move in describing and incorporating student motives for festival attendance which are influenced by the university venue itself. In contrast to the Campus Festival Bielefeld 2019, item 23 "partying on campus" was a motive for more than half of the participants when looked at as single motivator, while the same item is loading on the first dimension in line with item 22 ("meet new people"), which in this context means meeting new, other students from the same institution as well as item 19 ("experience sth. special"). It needs to be stated, that the campus in Paderborn has a very good reputation regarding its condition, it is generally considered to be very nice among students. This could be a reason for this first factor with strong item loadings. Furthermore, Paderborn also has a very long tradition with its event, the AStA Sommerfestival has existed for more than 20 years which may confirm this statement additionally.

Paderborn's second factor is loaded by two items of a sort of escapism aspect (item 17: "everyday life escape", item 20: "flee from everyday boredom"). Thus, second dimension of motivational construct is labeled *Escapism*. As mentioned above for Bielefeld results, this study has a distinct explorative character, thus, it can only be cautiously claimed that this outcome goes in line with other studies in thematically related fields[61][62][63]. In contrast to Bielefeld results, *Escape* dimension in Paderborn is only loaded by two items with medium high relevance. Following from this, it can be concluded that a certain escapism dimension within the motivational construct for visiting a university popular music festival (in Paderborn) is existent, which has a moderately important relevance due to average factor loadings of about 46 % (same as in Bielefeld) itself and thus constitutes a corresponding part within audiences' motivational construct.

As in Bielefeld, the third factor is labeled *Social Partying* dimension while containing less dimensions than in Bielefeld. Items describe leisure activities such as "have fun" or "dance" with known companions ("spend time with friends"). The motivational construct's socializing aspect for AStA Sommerfestival 2019 attendance in Paderborn has been confirmed but suggest not a high complexity as it does in Bielefeld.

Paderborn's fourth factor is the most obvious and expectable dimension when researching motivational constructs for music festival attendance. Including "line-up" and "experience live music" it can be clearly labeled "music dimension". As in Bielefeld the performances' "liveness" is a major driving single motivator, whereas the line-up" seem to play an even smaller role than in Bielefeld with only 23,9 % consent of Paderborn participants. Furthermore, it is noteworthy that the rejection (two negatively conjugated selects of the Likert scale) of the motivator "line-up" was 55,3 % in Paderborn (see appendix).

Fifth factor is a composition of consuming legal ("drink alcohol") as well as illegal drugs ("consume drugs") and a misbehaving dimension ("behave inappropriately") labeling the factor *Burst* as in Bielefeld. Whereas relevance for consuming illegal drugs is twice as high than in Bielefeld, it is still below 10 % and 86,7 % rejection.

61   Crompton and McKay, "Motives of Visitors Attending Festival Events."

62   Manolika, Baltzis, and Tsigilis, "Measuring Motives for Cultural Consumption."

63   Abreu-Novais and Arcodia, "Music Festival Motivators for Attendance."

Overall Discussion

This chapter serves to highlight and discuss the results of the individual preceding studies, which can be fitted into Siegfried Schmidt's multidimensional concept of culture. Accordingly, the results are abstracted one step further from individual studies' discussions. However, since a holistic view is now taken onto all acting stakeholder groups within sponsorship culture, the discussion is structured according to the three groups and sub-structured into Schmidt's reality model as well as practical culture program.

As described in the fourth theoretical perspective the thesis, reality models are to be understood as conceptual arrangements which individual experiences are made available to society. These arrangements make it easier for individuals (and society) to deal with 'their world'. Reality models can be defined as systematized collective knowledge of the members of a community, which co-orients and thus communalizes their interactions via reflexive mechanisms (=expectations in the area of knowledge, imputations in the area of intentions and motivations).[12] Models of reality emerge through the construction and systematization of essential distinctions. Such essential distinctions concern five basic dimensions:

- the behaviors towards nature and environment such as event-venue, office(s), meetings (real/unreal, effective/effective, helpful/dangerous, above/below, outside/inside, etc.),
- towards co-actants such as co-workers, business partners, other members of an event audience (student/non-student, male/female, powerful/powerless, etc.),

1   Schmidt, "Kultur als Programm—jenseits der Dichotomie von Realismus und Konstruktivismus."
2   Schmidt, "From Objects to Processes: A Proposal to Rewrite Radical Constructivism."

- forms of socialization (institutions, organizations), i.e., openings for action or restrictions on action that actants accept or endure in the interest of common problem solving,
- in terms of norms and values (good/evil, sacred/profane, acceptable/unacceptable, etc.)
- as well as with regard to the enactment of affects (happy/sad, loving/cruel, etc.).

As mentioned above, according to Schmidt:

"Such a reality model can only become effective if a practical program for its application, a culture program, emerges at the same time."[3]

These practical programs which he describes as culture programs balance and administer possible associations between basic semantic differentiations, their relevance, intuitive content, and their significance with regard to a socially binding aspect. They *render* the world view(s) and/or power structures in them of stakeholders in a socially effective way.

Culture, from this perspective, appears as a

"program of socially practiced or expected references to models of reality."[4]

Meaning, we react to the semantic categories and action-guiding orientations made available to us by society.

Sponsorship culture is the mechanism that allows these contingent selection performances to be carried out in an intersubjectively accessible way for actants as well as for the social systems of different stakeholder groups. Sponsorship cultural programs control which selections are realized, they relate the selection types, distinguish socially acceptable ones and sanction others. In this way, culture(s) within sponsorship creates individual and social identity and compensates for the double contingency that determines communication. In other words, with the help of their (sponsorship) cultural program, stakeholder groups invisibilize the contingency of their practices.

The structure and content of the overall discussion will show that all three stakeholder groups differ greatly in their individual rendering culture programs. It is in the nature of things that between the audience which acts according to hedonistic characteristics as the two groups of sponsors and the

---

3   Schmidt, 3.
4   Schmidt, *Geschichten & Diskurse.*

organizer who approach the matter with entrepreneurial intentions, the differences are particularly extensive. Thus, different motivations of organizer and the sponsors not only shape their individual culture program but also offer a certain potential for conflict, which was also revealed in the interviews as described in Study One.

Organizer Reality Model

The festivals' organizer represents one of three (group) components within sponsorship culture in the German university popular music festival market with explicit emphasis on the two biggest respective events in 2019 in Germany, the AStA Sommerfestival in Paderborn and the Campus Festival in Bielefeld. In accordance with Schmidt's multidimensional concept of culture, an organizer's Reality Model is filtered from qualitative interview study results. This Reality Model is, which according to Schmidt, significantly characterized by the underlying knowledge, that's embodied in the organizer's practices, behaviors, communications, and contexts internalized by the organizer's employees, and which were surveyed in the qualitative interview study of this dissertation.

However, knowledge as a perceived component of the organizer's reality model could not be filtered out and analyzed clearly enough within this investigation. Unlike the sponsors, who understand obtained knowledge as key value for future business development and archive, develop and reuse it accordingly, the organizer is more focused on short term monetary goals regarding knowledge. In the case of the organizer, it is further the case that a single person is usually responsible for managing a corresponding event such as a university music festival which also includes certain sponsorship engagements. Accordingly, the most knowledge regarding the event as well as sponsorship activities obtained over time 'remains' more or less with this person. A Systematic, (IT-supported) archiving and processing of this knowledge and data does not take place in this particular case, which was examined here.

The behavior between organizer and sponsors is largely characterized by mutual legal safeguarding, thereby trust plays a significant role in the prior interaction, especially when new partnerships are initiated. In particular, for organizers, seeking to build long-term relationships with sponsors is essential because only by building up trust, can the mentioned legal processes be reduced to a minimum and cooperation is seen much more feasible.

Findings on concrete practices also became clear in the qualitative study. The subcategories of practices which evolved from the downstream coding process of Study One: the decision-making culture, the communication culture, and the expression of *Fingerspitzengefühl* that is underlying within these culture(s), is decisively shaped by the experiences and values by the involved actants. Decision-making culture encompasses all practices and considerations up to the point where a decision is made for or against a sponsorship deal. In the case of the organizing actant(s), this decision-making culture is mainly characterized by the financial scope of a possible contract and the suitability of the sponsoring company and/or its brand(s) with the festival's reputational image.

The communication between organizer and potential sponsors takes place at eye level, in most cases, and generally one seniority level below executive management. Nevertheless, the final decision for or against a sponsorship engagement is (still) a matter for the CEO/boss of the organizing company. Communication within the organizer's company is mainly characterized by flat hierarchies. According to the interviewees in the study, this seems to be a common model throughout the industry. Great care is taken (also with regard to possible external appeal on potential future employees) to appear modern, young, casual and to allow all those involved within the company to participate in any processes and to contribute their expertise.

Fingerspitzengefühl is a consistently described basic requirement within the interaction with sponsors, especially because of the indeterminable 'real' value of sponsorship in general. In addition, possible negotiations about a sponsorship engagement can be better achieved for both parties in the mentioned long-term relationship, because in the long term, both parties have a certain feeling or tact for this same intangible matter. Subsequent and overriding purpose of the mentioned long-term relationships is to build, expand and maintain a pool of potential sponsors for future events. However, this point of interaction between sponsor and organizer may also offer a certain potential for conflict, which again may be diminished by actant's *Fingerspitzengefühl*. The interaction and operative togetherness of the three groups is the basis not only for the functioning of the event but also for the co-existence of three different sponsorship cultures.

Organizer Practical Culture Program

According to Schmidt, the organizer's reality model is furthermore strongly influenced by the organizer's own norms and assessments regarding the market for university popular music festivals and its audience representing a rendering practical culture program. The organizer's assessment regarding the market for university popular music festivals in Germany is characterized by the assumption that it will develop above average—compared to the German event industry—in the near future. This circumstance can be seen as a fundamentally superior characteristic in the sense of the adjusting practical cultural program as it is a fundamental perception of the actants' working environment. Furthermore, the described niche of the market in which university popular music festivals as events are still located according to the organizer, is seen as an opportunity to grow as a company and also see the sponsorship activities here develop accordingly. Additionally, the organizer seems to be partially aware of the underlying links between the (desired) image and external effect(s) of the festival on the city, it's region and the university. This knowledge already finds harmony within norms when it is about to entangle the event in combination with possible sponsors and to design this in such a way to set possible accents in relation to them. It is well understood that these interrelationships enormous potential in terms of public and legal approval and support for the festivals, which can have an indirect positive effect on sponsoring activities on the events.

Interviews also showed that the organizers are consciously and partly unconsciously aware of the inner-German municipality competition and the challenges, German universities face due to the demographic change. Organizer are taking this as an opportunity, to hit a nerve at other universities and cities in other medium-sized German cities and thus create other similar student events to grow as a company.

Following on from this, the organizers are very aware of the special vibe of the festival(s). What is meant by this, is the emerging atmosphere through the festival's special on-campus location and the fact, that the audience is attending, experiencing, and partying in a place where they usually study and behave seriously, at a place where they spend most of their daily life and where they, for a couple of hours can escape the same daily routine. The organizer is already trying to convey this feeling within its own marketing campaign for praising the festival but has also started to communicate these contexts with potential sponsors and plans to do so even more in the near future.

The cross-sectional personal beliefs of the organizer are characterized by assessing the individualization of the current structure of visitors to these festivals as a great challenge for designing better event experiences as well as within their sponsorship. The ungroupability of the current visitor structure of popular music festivals asks for constant determination to reform and maintain the events in a tough to handle way. Additionally, a vibrant sponsorship culture within the sponsoring or organizing company is seen as mandatory for long term success.

Sponsors Reality Model

The festivals' sponsors represent the second group (component) within sponsorship culture in the German university popular music festival market with explicit emphasis on the two biggest respective events in 2019 in Germany: the AStA Sommerfestival in Paderborn and the Campus Festival in Bielefeld. In accordance with Schmidt's multidimensional concept of culture, the sponsors' reality model is filtered from qualitative interview study results. This reality model is, according to Schmidt, significantly characterized by the underlying knowledge, that is embodied, in the sponsors' practices, behaviors, communications and contexts internalized by the sponsors' employees, and which were surveyed in the qualitative interview study (Study One) of this dissertation.

Knowledge is the sponsor's foundation for acting. Evaluating (new) obtained knowledge data within the company, archiving, and developing it organically is one of the top priorities of the actants interviewed. Being aware that future sponsorship activities will increase in their complexity due to the discussed demanding visitor structures and current individualization tendencies, gaining and refining knowledge is seen as a possibility to cope with this. According to the interviewees, this is especially the case for the submarket for university popular music festivals, as the audience share of younger people is above average. The intersection between knowledge and transforming it into (new) practices, is the point where knowledge is being transformed into a common basis for practices, interaction, and communication, i.e., as an operative fiction. On the one hand, this is consistent with Schmidt's theoretical explanations from his proposal to rewrite radical constructivism and on the other hand, it is the sweet spot that has been recognized in practical business life by the named actants to extract insight, expertise and actively develop it. The way this is being done and how professionally it is carried out, is very different, depending on the size of the sponsoring enterprise. In short: the bigger the company, the bigger the corresponding amount of effort and money is invested in implementing a knowledge management structure including IT support in a very well thought out manner. Above all, the use of KPI programs underlines this very clearly. The increasing sheer amount of data (knowledge) collected also shows that humans are dependent on the help of machines as soon as a certain data size is reached.

The most obvious component of the sponsor's reality model is how the basic process or practice of sponsorship is portioned. According to Study One, every sponsor, regardless of the size of his company and grade of professionalism divides the general practice of sponsorship into three sub-areas: preparation/initiation, implementation, follow-up. Within these three spheres, sponsors' practices are fundamentally shaped by the communication and decision-making culture embodied by sponsorship managers as well as by the corporate culture within the whole company. What is meant here, is the way a decision is made for or against a sponsorship and how communication occurs within this process. Particularly noteworthy is the existence of flat hierarchies within the sponsoring companies, as described by all interviewees. Furthermore, the sponsoring managers enjoy a high level of trust within their companies and how they design the process regarding the aforementioned processing of data, which in the end should help deciding a possible sponsorship engagement. In addition to processing knowledge, gained experience from past events or interactions with (non-)trusted actants plays a major role in the decision-making process. Since a sponsorship deal appears unprofitable at first glance from an objective business point of view, the person responsible for sponsorship within the organization needs to be particularly sensitive (*Fingerspitzengefühl*) within this decision-making process and what follows from, after a judgement by the sponsorship manager is made. However, flat hierarchies and built trust towards the employee still do not replace the fact that the ultimate decision for or against—in particular with regard to extensive—sponsoring commitments is usually made by the director/C.E.O. of the company. Therefore, it is a matter of possessing some kind of a 'sales talent' when presenting sponsorship options to the 'big boss'. The best and most prepared data do not necessarily lead to a decision for or against sponsoring, but the way the manager conveys it to the director/C.E.O. most certainly does. As one can see, *Fingerspitzengefühl* is the cross-sectional term that is evolving throughout the behaviorist part of the reality model on the sponsor's side. It is further required when it comes to assessing the extent to which trust can be built up in the initiation phase for new festival cooperation. It is that critical time frame, in which both parties must try to get things going, although a legal contractual framework has not yet been established. Additionally, sponsors need *Fingerspitzengefühl*, when it comes to fill a sponsorship commitment with visible and subconscious content and to develop and refine it, to find a suitable wording and to integrate it suitably into an (existing) imagine of the festival. Sponsorship managers need to have a feel for the latest topics, trends, and content which and what is 'hip and cool', and what is already outdated and may dangerously be misinterpreted by visitors. Therefore, these considerations require tact and sensitivity to reduce possible potential of conflict between the organizer and sponsors in dealing with the respective contractual partners and processes that are linked with the organization and implementation of the festival. Accordingly, *Fingerspitzengefühl* can again be assigned its property as a lubricant of the co-existing sponsorship cultures at this point.

The fast pace of change within the event industry is a challenge for sponsors when it comes to operationalizing the handover of sponsorship activities. Changing contacts during implementation requires flexibility, good intuition in communication and experience regarding the big picture of the entire process(es). However according to the Schmidtian concept of culture with its reality model, knowledge is embodied in actants, processes, and contexts, the fast-paced nature within these procedures is something that brings this concept to its limits, as according to Schmidt the embodying of knowledge is an organic rather steady and protracted process.

Sponsors Practical Culture Program

According to Schmidt, the sponsor's reality model is furthermore strongly influenced by the sponsor's own norms and assessments regarding the market for university popular music festivals and its audience representing a rendering practical culture program.

The adjusting characteristics of this practical culture program are first and foremost characterized by the fact that the sponsors want to reach their advertising and marketing goals. These goals, as already described, even outweigh the conjecturable 'bad investment' of a music festival's sponsorship. Furthermore, these goals are significantly linked to the aforementioned urge for long partnerships. Following up the development of these partnerships can be found in the data for every interviewed sponsor. All practices and actions are adapted in line with this drive, as sponsors understand that long-term and sustainable deals are generally seen to be in line with their employer's goals.

The organizer's assessment regarding the market for university popular music festivals in Germany is characterized by the belief that it is a growing and increasingly important market. Students and music are two themes that fit perfectly for the sponsors, because many students are to be characterized as festival affine. Thus, operating a popular music festival on a university campus, seems like a fitting conflation of things. Furthermore, sponsors are aware of involved city and university marketing processes and the associated basic vibe of such events that come with these underlying issues. Accordingly, sponsors let these relations and differentiations gush into their practical actions.

The assessment regarding student university identification can be understood as another adjusting characteristic within the sponsor's practical culture program. However, based on the data, which was fueled by expert discussions, it can be stated that sponsors are still in the process of finding an accurate narration and interpretation of this aspect. Altered primarily through an increasing individualization of today's Generation Y, it is not yet possible to make any generalizations (i.e., across the higher German education landscape) and further research is required to get a more profound understanding.

Sponsor's assessment regarding festival participant's motivation for event attendance as part of the rendering practical program is not only subconsciously influencing behavior within a sponsorship context. Expert interviews revealed that the issue of understanding attendance motivation, is being apprehended and accepted by the sponsors as an elementary adjusting element. Therefore, sponsorship managers actively deal with this topic, conduct research, and are well read with the latest studies on the subject. Sponsors are partly faced with a dichotomy, as the discrepancy between the awareness of artists and the actual motives for visiting seem to differ more and more. Accordingly, more focus is placed on socializing emotions and sponsoring engagements are designed further in the corresponding direction.

Audience Reality Modell

The audience represents the third component of sponsorship culture within the German university popular music festival market with explicit emphasis on the two biggest respective events in 2019 in Germany, the AStA Sommerfestival in Paderborn and the Campus Festival in Bielefeld. In accordance with Schmidt's multidimensional concept of culture, an audience's Reality Model is filtered from the quantitative surveys' data:

These reality models of the two events' audiences are significantly characterized by the underlying practices, behaviors, and norms of their event attendances in Paderborn and Bielefeld and which was investigated in the quantitative surveys.

Data suggest participants for both events as having an affinity for music festivals in general. Many of them visit the university festivals more than once during their student life at the two universities. For many, attending the university festivals (in June) is the kickoff for their personal upcoming festival season in the summer. Very few participants attended the events alone, most do so, in a group of friends. Data show that especially in Paderborn, participants enter the festival venue much later than they actually could. One reason for this seems to be the prior attendance of a private preparty. A fact that the sponsors are already well aware of and something they are already incorporating into sponsorship measures alongside the actual venue.

The results showed a positive attitude towards sponsorship of both festival audiences and thus, represents a certain positive norm within the audiences' reality model. Furthermore, the data show that the visitor groups at the festivals agree with the basic assumption that such an event is only made possible through the (financial) support of sponsorship. The underlying reason for this understanding cannot be definitively derived, based on the study's data but may be rooted from the already mentioned affinity towards music festivals in general and a related background regarding festival's management and/or financing.

This can be formulated as a (partial) result of this investigation, which could have high practical relevance for the future design of sponsorships for these events and future sponsorship research. Sponsors as well as organizers could build upon these statistics and future engagements could be more extensively designed or address the target group in a concrete and direct way without fearing to overstress the interaction. However, further research is needed to fathom the background for this positive attitude.

The results allow further characterization of participants' norms: all four items dealing with the external value of the event (item 30 "Differentiate from others by visit", item 31 "Brag with visit", item 32 "Visit as status symbol", item 33 "Share visit on social media") show explicit rejection by participants. This shows, at least for this study, a clear break with the assumptions made by the experts from Study One (qualitative interview study), as well as assumptions within the literature on this topic. Because of this clear break, no concrete statements are made here with regard to the practicability of these data, since in such a situation additional research is needed.

The results regarding sponsorship awareness are to be seen as an issue "located" across or between audience's reality and culture program in terms of Schmidt's concept, as it is influenced by many factors such as the regulating motives (described in the following culture program section) as well as other psychological effects resulting from the whole event experience(s). Additionally, it may be seen as general behavior or at least as a behavioral aspect of experiencing or sensing "things",—such as a brand—during the participation of the festival. The data thus allow a cautious (practical) assumption, that the visitor groups of the two festivals are quite attentive to the individual brands or sponsor appearances.

Audience Practical Culture Program

According to Schmidt's culture term, a (practical) cultural program emerges and exists in parallel and subliminally regulates the above-described behavior which is embedded in the actant's reality model. According to Schmidt, the co-existing practical program regulates possible relations and differentiates them socially effective.[5] Thus, above all, the single motivators as well as the (motivational) constructs for attending events play a major role within this regulating culture model and have significant influence on sponsors' engagements and the inclusive sponsorship culture. It has been shown that the reasons and dimensions for attending the two festivals are primarily rooted in socialization aspects with known companions. This circumstance combined with the fact that the festival's line up is not of great importance for many to purchase a ticket, which in turn goes hand in hand with the fact that participants come late to the actual event and meet up with friends at other parties

---

5   Schmidt, "From Objects to Processes: A Proposal to Rewrite Radical Constructivism."

beforehand. This is something that is obviously still misjudged by organizers and some sponsors at the moment; this became clear in the interviews, but also by the way in which the festivals are advertised.

Nevertheless, liveness is a reason for attending both events. The escapism motives in the midfield clearly show the urge for a temporary change (by the participants) in behavior, which is more accepted in the context of the event than in normal life.

Surprisingly, results regarding external value of the event attendance speak a very clear language, as there is no high level of agreement with the statements in the questionnaire across all items. This may indicate the majority of the audience(s) do not seem to comprehend the visit of the event as a status symbol, brag about it or see it as something to demarcate themselves from others. Extraordinarily contrary to prior expectations, results also do not suggest participants to share their visit to the festival on social media. These findings stand in contrast to audience research literature as well as findings from qualitative interview studies suggesting event attendance as status symbol[6], as something with which visitors may even brag about or differentiate themselves from others and/or friends and seeming to be heavily fueled by social media use and in particular by the app Instagram.

The reason for these rather contradictory results is still not clear at this point. Data regarding external value of visit would imply that sponsors should not necessarily pursue intensifying efforts in sponsorship activities incorporating this issue.

However, these results need to be interpreted with caution due to the contradiction of the results which stand in contrast to related research[7] in this area. It cannot be ruled out that the direct formulated wording used for the items, was addressing these (sensitive) items too directly. Especially "bragging about something" and demarcating oneself to others, might have created a negative bias in answering the Likert scales. Thus, further data collection in this specific subarea is required.

The relatively high identification (> 50 % across both events) by participants with their faculty or university can according to Schmidt, be classified as a kind of status or as their program-dependent assignments of meaning and attributions of value.

---

6   Gannon, Taheri, and Olya, "Festival Quality, Felf-Connection, and Bragging."

7   Gannon, Taheri, and Olya; Lee et al., "Instagram This! Sharing Photos on Instagram."

Thus, identification with the university or faculty is something that has not happened immediately. It constantly has been developed due to different influences and experiences as well as different situations the participants have had with their university or faculty. Accordingly, the relationship with the institutions renders and adjusts certain behavior, participants' discussions, and norms they have. However, to what extent these program-dependent assignments of meanings root in certain actions or decisions by participants cannot be answered with the data collected and should explicitly be investigated in future research.

As already described in Study Three, both audiences are fundamentally d'accord with the event's sponsorship(s) and comprehend the economic reasons for it. More than half of all participants at the institutions show a medium to high level of identification with their university. How and whether this identification can be used to benefit cities associated with the universities, for example, should be part of future research in this area. Another regulating factor, thought—according to Schmidt's practical program—and with regard to on-venue behavior during the event attendance, is the low budget of student participants, as it limits participants in their (economic) spending at the venue. This has been also assumed before the research by the author as well as by participants of the qualitative interview study; meaning that the student audience continues to be an "investment for the future" for sponsors.

Additional Chapter: COVID-19

The corona virus has posed a major challenge to the world on a daily basis since spring of 2020. On 11th March 2020, the World Health Organization (WHO) has declared the global spread of COVID-19 a pandemic.

This pandemic has hit the German culture and creative economy hard since then[1]. The 13 % slump in sales in 2020 was the biggest setback since monitoring the development of the culture and creative industries began in 2009. Overall, the losses of the culture and creative economy for 2020 account for more than 22.4 billion euros. The decline has pushed individual subsectors back to their pre-2003 sales levels. In 2021, the sectors continue to particularly suffer by the corona pandemic and will thus take longer than other sectors to emerge from the crisis. In the event-related subsectors in particular, business has come to a standstill. It is precisely these sectors that are dominated by small-scale structures and record the greatest losses.[2]

It is already becoming apparent that the post-corona phase will be accompanied by a variety of problems and challenges that will have a major impact on the economic recovery in general, but especially on re-start of the event industry. Due to the pandemic, external disruptions within the value chain are particularly worthy of mention. These include, for instance, long lead times and ongoing planning uncertainties, increased production costs, financial bottlenecks, and investment gaps as well as publication backlogs, a shortage of skilled workers exacerbated by the crisis, changed consumer behavior, and challenges in the professionalization of digital business models. Particularly during the second corona year 2021, one could sense that during

---

1   The date of completion of the original dissertation is the end of May 2021. This chapter has been updated in May 2022 due to ongoing pandemic process.

2   "German Economy Strongly Affected in 2020, the Year of the Corona Pandemic," 020 (Wiesbaden: DESTATIS, n.d.), https://www.destatis.de/EN/Press/2021/01/PE21_020_811 .html.

the summer months, a temporary easing of practical restrictions but also, above all, due to the withdrawal of government restrictions, an improvement within the industry only occurred in the short term. New COVID variations forced governments worldwide to re-restrict public as well as private gatherings, again re-increasing business pressure on the event industry. Despite generous state aid, this back and forth is exacerbating the upheavals already seen in the industry in 2020. This primarily affects the outflow of personnel from the sector and prevents a fundamental ability to plan business activities as well as investments.

This work explored sponsorship culture in the German university popular music festival market. A topic incorporating considerations as well as results that are linked to a large extent with aforementioned socio-economic dynamics and which occur in an event-submarket that has been most hit by the pandemic.

Social behavior has changed fundamentally in the past two years in its principles due to government measures containing the pandemic as well as public fear to get infected with the virus.

It needs to be mentioned at this point, that it is accordingly difficult to assess at this point, how social behavior will transform in the near future when the pandemic, will hopefully slow down. It seems obvious that a strong increase in cultural consumption can be expected with the withdrawal of the pandemic-related restrictions. However, whether the everyday behavior of society will settle down to the same level as before the crisis remains to be seen. Hence, results and discussions of this study should therefore be viewed in a correspondingly differentiated manner until clarity sets in. Nevertheless, carrying out surveys with similar intention as in this dissertation in a time of 'post corona' would certainly represent an interesting and compelling task.

References

Abreu-Novais, Margarida, and Charles Arcodia. "Music Festival Motivators for Attendance: Developing an Agenda for Research." *International Journal of Event Management Research* 8, no. 1 (2013): 34–48.

Ali-Knight, Jane, ed. *International Perspectives of Festivals and Events: Paradigms of Analysis*. Advances in Tourism Research Series. Amsterdam: Academic Press, Elsevier, 2009.

Allmanritter, Vera. "Multi-, Inter- und Transkulturalität (als Begriffe) in der empirischen Kulturbesucherforschung." In *Kulturelle Übersetzer*, edited by Christiane Dätsch, 339–54. transcript Verlag, 2018. https://doi.org/10.143 61/9783839434994-022.

Anderton, Chris. "Branding, Sponsorship and the Music Festival." In *The Pop Festival: History, Music, Media, Culture*, edited by George McKay, 199–212. New York: Bloomsbury Academic, 2015.

Anderton, Chris. "Music Festival Capitalism." In *The Oxford Handbook of Global Popular Music*, by Chris Anderton, edited by Simone Krüger Bridge. Oxford University Press, 2021. https://doi.org/10.1093/oxfordhb/9780190081379.0 13.4.

Anderton, Chris. *Music Festivals in the UK: Beyond the Carnivalesque*. Ashgate Popular and Folk Music Series. London; New York: Routledge, Taylor & Francis Group, 2019.

Arcodia, Charles, and Michelle Whitford. "Festival Attendance and the Development of Social Capital." *Journal of Convention and Event Tourism* 8 (January 2007). https://doi.org/10.1300/J452v08n02_01.

Arnold, Matthew, and Jane Garnett. *Culture and Anarchy*. Oxford World's Classics. Oxford; New York: Oxford University Press, 2006.

Barnes, Trevor J, Jamie Peck, and Eric Sheppard. *The Wiley-Blackwell Companion to Economic Geography*. Hoboken: Wiley-Blackwell [Imprint] John Wiley &

Sons, Incorporated, 2016. http://onlinelibrary.wiley.com/book/10.1002/97
81118384497.

Bathelt, Harald, and Johannes Glückler. *Wirtschaftsgeographie: ökonomische Beziehungen in räumlicher Perspektive; 22 Tabellen.* 3., vollst. überarb. und erw. Aufl. UTB Geowissenschaften, Soziologie, Wirtschaftswissenschaften, Politikwissenschaften 8217. Stuttgart: Ulmer, 2012.

Beer, Bettina, and Hans Fischer, eds. *Ethnologie: Einführung und Überblick.* 6.,
überarb. Aufl. Ethnologische Paperbacks. Berlin: Reimer, 2006.

Bellenger, Danny N., Kenneth L. Bernhardt, and Jac L. Goldstucker. *Qualitative
Research in Marketing.* Monographs Series—American Marketing Association; 3. Chicago: American Marketing Association, 1976.

Bellinghausen, Raimund. *Das Musikfestival: Wirtschaftliche und touristische Aspekte.* Hamburg: disserta Verlag, 2014.

Bennett, Andy, Jodie Taylor, and Ian Woodward. *The Festivalization of Culture.*
London; New York: Routledge, 2016. http://www.tandfebooks.com/isbn/9
781315558189.

"Bevölkerungs- und Haushaltsentwicklung im Bund und in den Ländern."
Demografischer Wandel in Deutschland. Wiesbaden: Statistisches Bundesamt, 2011. www.statistikportal.de.

Blankennagel, Jens. "Um gute Mitarbeiter zu bekommen, kann Tesla mit dem
guten Ruf Berlins werben," May 20, 2021. https://www.berliner-zeitung.
de/mensch-metropole/um-gute-mitarbeiter-zu-bekommen-kann-tesla-
mit-dem-guten-ruf-berlins-werben-li.159923.

Blaukopf, Kurt. *Musik im Wandel der Gesellschaft: Grundzüge der Musiksoziologie.*
2., erw. Aufl. Darmstadt: Wissenschaftl. Buchges, 1996.

Bleicher, Konrad. "Organisationskulturen und Führungsphilosophien im
Wettbewerb." *zfbf,* no. 35 (1983): 135–46.

Blümle, Gerold, ed. *Perspektiven einer kulturellen Ökonomik.* Kulturelle
Ökonomik, Bd. 1. Münster: Lit, 2004.

Böhme, Hartmut. "Stufen der Reflexion: Die Kulturwissenschaften in der Kultur." In *Handbuch der Kulturwissenschaften,* edited by Friedrich Jaeger and
Jürgen Straub, 1–15. Stuttgart: J.B. Metzler, 2011. https://doi.org/10.1007/
978-3-476-00627-1_1.

Böhme, Hartmut. "Vom Cultus zur Kultur(wissenschaft). Zur historischen Semantik des Kulturbegriffs." In *Kulturwissenschaft—Literaturwissenschaft. Positionen, Themen, Perspektiven,* 48–68. Wiesbaden: Glaser, Renate/Luserke,
Matthias, 1996.

Böhme, Hartmut, Peter Matussek, and Lothar Müller. *Orientierung Kulturwissenschaft: was sie kann, was sie will.* Orig.-Ausg., 3. Aufl. Rororo Rowohlts Enzyklopädie 55608. Reinbek bei Hamburg: Rowohlt-Taschenbuch-Verl., 2007.

Bourdieu, Pierre. *Forms of Capital.* General Sociology, Volume 3. Cambridge: Polity Press, 2021.

Bowen, Heather E., and Margaret J. Daniels. "Does the Music Matter? Motivations for Attending a Music Festival." *Event Management* 9, no. 3 (January 1, 2005): 155–64. https://doi.org/10.3727/152599505774791149.

Brabec de Mori, Bernd, and Martin Winter, eds. *Auditive Wissenskulturen.* Wiesbaden: Springer Fachmedien Wiesbaden, 2018. https://doi.org/10.1007/978-3-658-20143-2.

Breyer-Mayländer, Thomas, and Christopher Zerres, eds. *Stadtmarketing: Grundlagen, Analysen, Praxis.* Wiesbaden: Springer Fachmedien Wiesbaden, 2019. https://doi.org/10.1007/978-3-658-26254-9.

Bridger, Sam. *Festivals Britannia.* Documentary, 2010. https://www.imdb.com/title/tt2190265/.

Brinkmann, U. "'Shared values' oder 'shareholder value'?—Die Untauglichkeit der 'Unternehmenskultur' als Integrationstechnik." *soFid Industrie- und Betriebssoziologie*, no. 2 (2006): 11–34.

Brown, Steven Caldwell, and Don Knox. "Why Go to Pop Concerts? The Motivations behind Live Music Attendance." *Musicae Scientiae*, 2016, 1029864916650719.

Bruhn, Manfred. *Sponsoring.* Wiesbaden: Springer Fachmedien Wiesbaden, 2018. https://doi.org/10.1007/978-3-658-13313-9.

Bruhn, Manfred, and Rudolf Mehlinger. *Rechtliche Gestaltung des Sponsoring: Vertragsrecht, Steuerrecht, Medienrecht, Wettbewerbsrecht.* 2., Überarbeitete und aktualisierte Aufl. München: C.H. Beck, 1995.

Bundesinstitut für Bau-, Stadt- und Raumforschung im Bundesamt für Bauwesen und Raumordnung. "Beiträge zum Siedlungsflächenmonitoring im Bundesgebiet—Flächenverbrauch, Flächenpotenziale und Trends 2030." 07. Berlin, 2014.

Bundesverband der Veranstaltungswirtschaft. "Live Entertainment in Deutschland." Hamburg, 2017.

Bundesverband Musikindustrie e. V. "Musikwirtschaftsstudie 2020," 2020.

Bundesvereinigung City- und Stadtmarketing e.V., Heribert Meffert, Bernadette Spinnen, and Jürgen Block, eds. *Praxishandbuch City- und*

Stadtmarketing. Wiesbaden: Springer Fachmedien Wiesbaden, 2018. http s://doi.org/10.1007/978-3-658-19642-4.

Carson, David. *Qualitative Marketing Research*. London; Thousand Oaks, Calif.: SAGE, 2001.

Clark, J. F., and A. Clark. "The Changing Culture of a Factory." *Mental Health* 11 (1951): 39–40.

Comrey, Andrew Laurence, and Howard B. Lee. *A First Course in Factor Analysis*. 2nd ed. Hillsdale, N.J.: L. Erlbaum Associates, 1992.

Creswell, John W., and J. David Creswell. *Research Design: Qualitative, Quantitative, and Mixed Methods Approaches*. Fifth edition. Los Angeles: SAGE, 2018.

Crompton, John L., and Stacey L. McKay. "Motives of Visitors Attending Festival Events." *Annals of Tourism Research* 24, no. 2 (1997): 425–39.

CTS Eventim. "Geschäftsbericht 2018." Geschäftsbericht, 2019.

Dalio, Ray. *Principles*. New York: Simon & Schuster, 2017.

Dann, Graham MS. "Tourist Motivation an Appraisal." *Annals of Tourism Research* 8, no. 2 (1981): 187–219.

De Long, David W., and Liam Fahey. "Diagnosing Cultural Barriers to Knowledge Management." *Academy of Management Perspectives* 14, no. 4 (November 2000): 113–27. https://doi.org/10.5465/ame.2000.3979820.

Deal, Terrence E., and Allan A. Kennedy. *Corporate Cultures: The Rites and Rituals of Corporate Life*. Reissued. Cambridge: Perseus Publ, 2000.

Destatis. "Bevölkerung im Wandel—Annahmen und Ergebnisse der 14. koordinierten Bevölkerungsvorausberechnung." Wiesbaden, 2019.

Deutsches Institut für Wirtschaftsforschung. "Bevölkerungsentwicklung in Deutschland bis 2050: Nur leichter Rückgang der Einwohnerzahl?" Berlin, 2017.

Dill, Peter. *Unternehmenskultur: Grundlagen und Anknüpfungspunkte für ein Kulturmanagement*. Schriften zur Kommunikationsarbeit. Bonn: BDW-Service-u.-Verl.-Ges. Kommunikation, 1987.

Dobbins, Michael, and Tonia Bieber. "Bildungspolitik in den USA." In *Handbuch Politik USA*, edited by Christian Lammert, Markus B. Siewert, and Boris Vormann, 381–401. Wiesbaden: Springer Fachmedien Wiesbaden, 2016. https://doi.org/10.1007/978-3-658-02642-4_24.

Dollase, Rainer, Michael Rüsenberg, and Hans J. Stollenwerk. *Demoskopie im Konzertsaal*. Mainz; New York: Schott, 1986.

Drengner, Jan. *Imagewirkungen von Eventmarketing: Entwicklung eines ganzheitlichen Messansatzes*. 3., Aktualisierte Aufl. Gabler Edition Wissenschaft. Wiesbaden: Gabler, 2008.

Drengner, Jan, and Steffen Jahn. "Erlebniswelten im Sponsoring." *Marketing Review St. Gallen* 30, no. 2 (February 2013): 60–67. https://doi.org/10.1365/s11621-013-0212-3.

Drengner, Jan, and Julia Köhler. "Stand und Perspektiven der Eventforschung aus Sicht des Marketing." In *Events und Sport*, edited by Cornelia Zanger, 89–132. Wiesbaden: Springer Fachmedien Wiesbaden, 2013. https://doi.org/10.1007/978-3-658-03681-2_5.

Ebers, Mark. *Organisationskultur: Ein neues Forschungsprogramm?*, 1985. http://link.springer.com/openurl?genre=book&isbn=978-3-409-13105-6.

Emory, William, and Donald R. Cooper. *Business Research Methods*. 4th ed. Homewood, IL: Irwin, 1991.

"Erstsemester: Traditionelle Begrüßung im Stadion | pflichtlektüre." Accessed August 26, 2020. http://www.pflichtlektuere.com/18/10/2016/erstsemester-traditionelle-begruessung-im-stadion/.

Everitt, B. S. "Multivariate Analysis: The Need for Data, and Other Problems." *British Journal of Psychiatry* 126, no. 3 (March 1975): 237–40. https://doi.org/10.1192/bjp.126.3.237.

Fabrigar, Leandre R., and Duane Theodore Wegener. *Exploratory Factor Analysis*. Understanding Statistics. Oxford; New York: Oxford University Press, 2012.

Fauser, Markus. *Einführung in die Kulturwissenschaft*. 4., Durchges. und aktualisierte Aufl. Einführungen Germanistik. Darmstadt: Wiss. Buchges, 2008.

Fehring, Kirsten Marei. *Kultursponsoring—Bindeglied zwischen Kunst und Wirtschaft? eine interdisziplinäre und praxisorientierte Analyse*. 1. Aufl. Rombach Wissenschaften Reihe Cultura 3. Freiburg im Breisgau: Rombach, 1998.

Festivalalarm. "Alle Festivals Deutschland 2019," n.d. https://www.festival-alarm.com/festival/region/Deutschland/2019/DE.

Field, Andy P. *Discovering Statistics Using IBM SPSS Statistics: And Sex and Drugs and Rock "n" Roll*. 4th edition. Los Angeles: Sage, 2013.

Flath, Beate. "'Wert-e-schöpfung-en' des Orange Blossom Special Festival (OBS)." Beverungen, 2017. https://www.orangeblossomspecial.de/wp-content/uploads/2018/01/Festivals_in_rural-regions_OBS_Beate-Flath_proposal_VMBRDays_2017.pdf.

Flick, Uwe. *Qualitative Sozialforschung: Eine Einführung*. Originalausgabe, 8. Auflage. Rororo Rowohlts Enzyklopädie 55694. Reinbek bei Hamburg: Rowohlts Enzyklopädie im Rowohlt Taschenbuch Verlag, 2017.

Fox, Mark. "E-Commerce Business Models for the Music Industry." *Popular Music and Society* 27, no. 2 (March 2004): 201–20. https://doi.org/10.1080/03007760410001685831.

Franken, Rolf, and Andreas Gadatsch. *Integriertes Knowledge Management.* Wiesbaden: Vieweg+Teubner Verlag, 2002. https://doi.org/10.1007/978-3-663-05808-3.

Franzpötter, Reiner. *Organisationskultur: Begriffsverständnis und Analyse aus interpretativ-soziologischer Sicht.* 1. Aufl. Nomos Universitätsschriften, Bd. 4. Baden-Baden: Nomos, 1997.

Frevel, Bernhard, ed. *Herausforderung demografischer Wandel.* 1. Auflage. Perspektiven der Gesellschaft. Wiesbaden: VS Verlag für Sozialwissenschaften, 2004.

Friedrichs, Jürgen. "Ist die Besonderheit des Städtischen auch die Besonderheit der Stadtsoziologie?" In *Die Besonderheit des Städtischen,* edited by Heike Herrmann, Carsten Keller, Rainer Neef, and Renate Ruhne, 33–47. Wiesbaden: VS Verlag für Sozialwissenschaften, 2011. https://doi.org/10.1007/978-3-531-93338-2_2.

Frith, Simon, ed. *Popular Music.* Critical Concepts in Media and Cultural Studies. London; New York: Routledge, 2004.

Frith, Simon, ed. *The History of Live Music in Britain.* Ashgate Popular and Folk Music Series. London: Routledge, Taylor and Francis Group, 2019.

Funke, Joachim. "Allgemeine & Theoretische Psychologie." Heidelberg, 2003. h ttps://www.psychologie.uni-heidelberg.de/ae/allg/lehre/wct/index.htm.

Gancarz, Eva. "Events als Instrument des Stadtmarketing," April 2, 2019. htt ps://zukunftdeseinkaufens.de/stadtmarketing/.

Gannon, Martin, Babak Taheri, and Hossein Olya. "Festival Quality, Felf-Connection, and Bragging." *Annals of Tourism Research* 76 (May 2019): 239–52. https://doi.org/10.1016/j.annals.2019.04.014.

Gebhardt, Winfried, Ronald Hitzler, and Michaela Pfadenhauer, eds. *Events: Soziologie des Aussergewöhnlichen.* Erlebniswelten, Bd. 2. Opladen: Leske + Budrich, 2000.

Geisthövel, Alexa, and Bodo Mrozek, eds. *Popgeschichte Band 1: Konzepte und Methoden.* Bielefeld: transcript Verlag, 2014. https://doi.org/10.14361/transcript.9783839425282.

Gelder, Gemma, and Peter Robinson. "A Critical Comparative Study of Visitor Motivations for Attending Music Festivals: A Case Study of Glastonbury and V Festival." *Event Management* 13, no. 3 (November 1, 2009): 181–96. ht tps://doi.org/10.3727/152599509790029792.

Gensch, Gerhard, Eva Maria Stöckler, and Peter Tschmuck, eds. *Musikrezeption, Musikdistribution und Musikproduktion: der Wandel des Wertschöpfungsnetzwerks in der Musikwirtschaft*. 1. Aufl. Gabler Edition Wissenschaft. Wiesbaden: Gabler, 2008.

"German Economy Strongly Affected in 2020, the Year of the Corona Pandemic." 020. Wiesbaden: DESTATIS, n.d. https://www.destatis.de/EN/Press/2021/01/PE21_020_811.html.

Getz, Donald. "The Nature and Scope of Festival Studies," 2010.

Getz, Donald. "Event Tourism: Definition, Evolution, and Research." *Tourism Management* 29, no. 3 (June 2008): 403–28. https://doi.org/10.1016/j.tourman.2007.07.017.

Getz, Donald, and Stephen J. Page. *Event Studies: Theory, Research and Policy for Planned Events*. 4th ed. Fourth Edition. New York: Routledge, 2020. | Series: Events management series | "First edition published by Butterworth-Heinemann 2007. Third edition published by Routledge 2016"—T.p. verso.: Routledge, 2019. https://doi.org/10.4324/9780429023002.

Glaser, Barney G., and Anselm L. Strauss. *The Discovery of Grounded Theory: Strategies for Qualitative Research*. 4. paperback printing. New Brunswick: Aldine, 2009.

Gontard, Maximilian. *Unternehmenskultur und Organisationsklima: Eine empirische Untersuchung*. Profession 36. München: Hampp, 2002.

Gorsuch, Richard L. "Exploratory Factor Analysis." In *Handbook of Multivariate Experimental Psychology*, edited by John R. Nesselroade and Raymond B. Cattell, 231–58. Boston, MA: Springer US, 1988. https://doi.org/10.1007/978-1-4613-0893-5_6.

Grabow, Busso, Dietrich Henckel, and Beate Hollbach-Grömig. *Weiche Standortfaktoren*. Schriften des Deutschen Instituts für Urbanistik, Bd. 89. Stuttgart: W. Kohlhammer: Deutscher Gemeindeverlag, 1995.

Graumann, Carl F., and Carl Friedrich Graumann. *Motivation*. 6. Aufl., unveränd. Nachdr. d. 5. Aufl. Einführung in die Psychologie, hrsg. von C. F. Graumann; 1. Wiesbaden: Akad. Verl.-Ges. [u.a.], 1981.

Gross, Philip. *Growing Brands Through Sponsorship*. Wiesbaden: Springer Fachmedien Wiesbaden, 2015. https://doi.org/10.1007/978-3-658-07250-6.

Gwinner, Kevin P., Brian V. Larson, and Scott R. Swanson. "Image Transfer in Corporate Event Sponsorship: Assessing the Impact of Team Identification and Event-Sponsor Fit." 2009, International Journal of Management and Marketing Research, 2, no. 1 (2010): 1–15.

Habermas, Jürgen, and Jürgen Habermas. *Zur Kritik der funktionalistischen Vernunft.* 4., durchges. Aufl., 24,5.-27,5. Tsd. Theorie des kommunikativen Handelns, Jürgen Habermas ; Bd. 2. Frankfurt am Main: Suhrkamp, 1987.

Hafen, Roland. *Hedonismus Und Rockmusik: Eine Empirische Studie Zum Live-Erlebnis Jugendlicher.* Paderborn, 1992.

Hafner, Carmen. "Sozialsponsoring als Benefit für beide Seiten?," 2009. http s://doi.org/10.25365/THESIS.3751.

Hair, Joseph F., Robert P. Bush, and David J. Ortinau. *Marketing Research: In a Digital Information Environment.* 4th ed. Boston: McGraw-Hill Irwin, 2009.

Hamburger, Jeffrey. "Vergleich deutscher und amerikanischer Universitäten." *Die Zeit—Forschung und Lehre,* 2008. https://www.academics.de/ratgeber/ usa-deutschland-vergleich-wissenschaft-bildung.

Harris, R., L. Jago, J. Allen, and M. Huyskens. "Towards an Australian Event Research Agenda: First Steps." *Event Management* 6, no. 4 (April 1, 2000): 213–21. https://doi.org/10.3727/152599500108751372.

Healy, Marilyn, and Chad Perry. "Comprehensive Criteria to Judge Validity and Reliability of Qualitative Research within the Realism Paradigm." *Qualitative Market Research: An International Journal* 3, no. 3 (September 2000): 118–26. https://doi.org/10.1108/13522750010333861.

Heckhausen, Heinz. *Motivation und Handeln: mit 52 Tabellen.* 2., völlig überarb. u. erg. Aufl. Springer-Lehrbuch. Berlin: Springer, 1989.

Heckhausen, Jutta, and Heinz Heckhausen, eds. *Motivation und Handeln.* 5., überarbeitete und erweiterte Auflage. Springer-Lehrbuch. Berlin [Heidelberg]: Springer, 2018. https://doi.org/10.1007/978-3-662-53927-9.

Hede, Anne-Marie, Leo Jago, and Margaret Deery. "An Agenda for Special Event Research: Lessons from the Past and Directions for the Future." *Journal of Hospitality and Tourism Management* 10 (January 2003): 1–14.

Heinen, Edmund. "Entscheidungsorientierte Betriebswirtschaftslehre und Unternehmenskultur." *ZfB,* no. 55 (1985): 980–91.

Heinen, Edmund. "Unternehmenskultur als Gegenstand der Betriebswirtschaftslehre." In *Unternehmenskultur—Perspektiven für Wissenschaft und Praxis,* 2nd ed., 1–48. München: Heinen, E./Fank, M., 1997.

Heinrich, Detlef. "Musik-Sponsoring als Wettbewerbsinstrument." *der markt* 29, no. 2 (June 1, 1990): 59–61. https://doi.org/10.1007/BF03031807.

Hermanns, Arnold. "Charakterisierung und Arten des Sponsoring." In *Handbuch Marketing-Kommunikation,* edited by Ralph Berndt and Arnold Hermanns, 627–48. Wiesbaden: Gabler Verlag, 1993. https://doi.org/10.1007/ 978-3-322-82539-1_32.

Hermanns, Arnold. "Corporate Social Responsibility und Sponsoring im Fokus Sponsoring Trends 2010." München, 2011. https://www.vibss.de/fil eadmin/Medienablage/Marketing/Sponsoring/Studie_Sponsoring-Trend s-2010.pdf.

Hermanns, Arnold, and Florian Riedmüller, eds. "Entwicklung und Perspektiven des Sportsponsoring." In *Management-Handbuch Sport-Marketing*, 2., vollst. überarb. Aufl., 389–407. München: Vahlen, 2008.

Hessisches Statistisches Landesamt. "Verteilung Der Musikfestivals Und - Festspiele in Deutschland Im Jahr 2015 Nach Besuchergrößenklassen." Statistische Ämter des Bundes und der Länder, 2017.

Hinkin, Timothy R., J. Bruce Tracey, and Cathy A. Enz. "Scale Construction: Developing Reliable and Valid Measurement Instruments." *Journal of Hospitality & Tourism Research* 21, no. 1 (February 1997): 100–120. https://doi.or g/10.1177/109634809702100108.

Hitters, Erik, and Carsten Winter. "The Festivalization of Live Music: Introduction," 2020.

Hochstadt, Stefan, ed. *Stadtentwicklung mit Stadtmanagement?* 1. Aufl. Wiesbaden: Verlag für Sozialwissenschaften, 2005.

Hofstede, G., Bram Neuijen, Denise Daval Ohayv, and G. Sanders. "Measuring Organizational Cultures: A Qualitative and Quantitative Study across Twenty Cases." *Administrative Science Quarterly* 35 (1990): 286–316.

Hölscher, Michael. *Wirtschaftskulturen in der erweiterten EU: die Einstellungen der Bürgerinnen und Bürger im europäischen Vergleich.* 1. Aufl. Wiesbaden: VS Verlag für Sozialwissenschaften, 2006.

Holt, Fabian. *Everyone Loves Live Music: A Theory of Performance Institutions.* Big Issues in Music. Chicago: The University of Chicago Press, 2020.

Howkins, John. *The Creative Economy, or, How Some People Profit from Ideas, Some Don't, and the Effect on All of Us.* London: Allen Lane, 2001.

Hülskamp, Nicola. "Der IW-Demografieindikator—Wie gut ist Deutschland auf den demografischen Wandel vorbereitet?" *IW-Trends*, no. 3 (2008). htt ps://doi.org/10.2373/1864-810X.08-03-07.

IEG. "Fair And Festival Sponsorship Spending," 2017. https://www.sponsors hip.com/Latest-Thinking/Sponsorship-Infographics/Fair-And-Festival-S ponsorship-Spending-To-Tota--1-.aspx.

IEG. "Music Sponsorship 2018." Annual Report. IEG, 2019. https://www.spon sorship.com/Latest-Thinking/Sponsorship-Infographics/Music-Sponsor ship-2018--$1-61-Billion.aspx.

IFPI. "IFPI Digital Music Report 2015," January 2015.

IFPI. "Musikindustrie-Umsatz weltweit 2016 | Statistik." Statista, 2017. https://de.statista.com/statistik/daten/studie/182361/umfrage/weltweiter-umsatz-der-musikindustrie-seit-1997/.

Jacke, Christoph. *Einführung in populäre Musik und Medien*. 2. Aufl. Populäre Kultur und Medien 1. Berlin: LIT-Verlag, 2013.

Jacke, Christoph. *Medien(sub)kultur: Geschichten, Diskurse, Entwürfe*. Cultural studies, Bd. 9. Bielefeld: transcript Verlag, 2004.

Jacke, Christoph. "Pop." In *The Creativity Complex: A Companion to Contemporary Culture*, edited by Timon Beyes, 201–6. Cultures of Society, volume 36. Bielefeld: transcript Verlag, 2018.

Jaeger, Friedrich, and Burkhard Liebsch, eds. *Handbuch der Kulturwissenschaften: Grundlagen und Schlüsselbegriffe*. Stuttgart: J.B. Metzler, 2011. https://doi.org/10.1007/978-3-476-00468-0.

Jöckel, Sven, Nico Hesser, and Andreas Will, eds. *Trendsetter, Innovatoren, Studentenbudget? Eine Mehr-Methoden-Studie zu Werbung und Produktpräferenzen bei Studierenden*. Vol. 4. Menschen—Märkte—Medien—Management: Schriftenreihe. Ilmenau: Universitätsverlag Ilmenau, 2009. http://uri.gbv.de/document/gvk:ppn:621462640.

King, William R. "A Research Agenda for the Relationships between Culture and Knowledge Management." *Knowledge and Process Management* 14, no. 3 (July 2007): 226–36. https://doi.org/10.1002/kpm.281.

Koopmans, Folkert, ed. *Von Musikern, Machern & Mobiltoiletten: 40 Jahre Open Air Geschichte*. Orig.-Ausg., Aufl. 1. Hamburg: FKP SORPIO, Konzertproduktionen GmbH, 2007.

Kotter, John P. *Corporate Culture and Performance*. New York: Free Press, 2014. http://www.myilibrary.com?id=899109.

Krätke, Stefan. *Stadt/Einführung in aktuelle Problemfelder der Stadtökonomie und Wirtschaftsgeographie/von Stefan Krätke*. Wiesbaden: VS Verlag für Sozialwissenschaften, 1995.

Kuckartz, Udo. *Mixed Methods*. Wiesbaden: Springer Fachmedien Wiesbaden, 2014. https://doi.org/10.1007/978-3-531-93267-5.

Kulczynski, Alicia, Stacey Baxter, and Tamara Young. "Measuring Motivations for Popular Music Concert Attendance." *Event Management* 20, no. 2 (July 25, 2016): 239–54. https://doi.org/10.3727/152599516X14643674421816.

Kutschker, Michael, and Stefan Schmid. *Internationales Management: mit 100 Textboxen*. 7., überarb. und aktualisierte Aufl. München: Oldenbourg, 2011.

Lacher, Kathleen T. "Hedonic Consumption: Music As a Product." *ACR North American Advances* NA-16 (1989). https://www.acrwebsite.org/volumes/693 2/volumes/v16/NA-16.

Lamnek, Siegfried, and Claudia Krell. *Qualitative Sozialforschung: mit Online-Material.* 6., überarbeitete Auflage. Weinheim Basel: Beltz, 2016.

Lattmann, Charles. *Die Unternehmenskultur: Ihre Grundlagen und ihre Bedeutung für die Führung der Unternehmung.* Berlin, 1990. http://link.springer.com/o penurl?genre=book&isbn=978-3-7908-0465-2.

Lave, J. "Situating Learning in Communities of Practice." In *Perspectives on Socially Shared Cognition*, edited by Lauren Resnick, Levine B., M. John, Stephanie Teasley, and D, 63–82. American Psychological Association, 1991.

Lee, Chei Sian, Nur Alifah Binte Abu Bakar, Raudhah Binti Muhammad Dahri, and Sei-Ching Joanna Sin. "Instagram This! Sharing Photos on Instagram." In *Digital Libraries: Providing Quality Information*, edited by Robert B. Allen, Jane Hunter, and Marcia L. Zeng, 9469:132–41. Lecture Notes in Computer Science. Cham: Springer International Publishing, 2015. https://doi.org/10.1007/978-3-319-27974-9_13.

Liefner, Ingo, and Ludwig Schätzl. *Theorien der Wirtschaftsgeographie.* 10., [Neu bearb. und umfassend erw.] Aufl. UTB Wirtschaftswissenschaften, Geographie 782. Paderborn: Schöningh, 2012.

Lincoln, Yvonna S., and Egon G. Guba. *Naturalistic Inquiry.* Beverly Hills: Sage Publications, 1985.

Live Nation. "Annual Report 2016," 2017. https://investors.livenationentertain ment.com/sec-filings/annual-reports.

Luhmann, Niklas. *Die Wirtschaft der Gesellschaft.* 1. Aufl. [Nachdr.]. Theorie der Gesellschaft, Niklas Luhmann[...]. Frankfurt am Main: Suhrkamp, 2008.

Maier, Gunther, Franz Tödtling, and Gunther Maier. *Standorttheorie und Raumstruktur.* 5. Aufl. Regional- und Stadtökonomik, Gunther Maier; Franz Tödtling; 1. Wien: Springer, 2012.

Mair, Judith, and Jennifer Laing. "The Greening of Music Festivals: Motivations, Barriers and Outcomes. Applying the Mair and Jago Model." *Journal of Sustainable Tourism* 20, no. 5 (June 2012): 683–700. https://doi.org/10.10 80/09669582.2011.636819.

Manolika, Maria, Alexandros Baltzis, and Nikolaos Tsigilis. "Measuring Motives for Cultural Consumption: A Review of the Literature." *American Journal of Applied Psychology* 3, no. 1 (2015): 1–5.

Marshall, Lee, Dave Laing, and Simon Frith, eds. *Popular Music Matters: Essays in Honour of Simon Frith*. Ashgate Popular and Folk Music Series. Farnham, Surrey, UK, England; Burlington, VT, USA: Ashgate, 2014.

Maslow, A. H. "A Theory of Human Motivation." *Psychological Review* 50, no. 4 (1943): 370–96. https://doi.org/10.1037/h0054346.

Mason, Jennifer. *Qualitative Research*. London: SAGE, 2002.

Matenaar, Dieter. *Organisationskultur und organisatorische Gestaltung: die Gestaltungsrelevanz der Kultur des Organisationssystems der Unternehmung*. Betriebswirtschaftliche Forschungsergebnisse, Bd. 85. Berlin: Duncker & Humblot, 1983.

Mayer, Verena, Mark Schlick, and Martin Groeger. "Landschaft als weicher Standortfaktor." *Raumforschung und Raumordnung* 59, no. 2–3 (March 31, 2001): 131–41. https://doi.org/10.1007/BF03184348.

Mayring, Philipp. *Qualitative Inhaltsanalyse: Grundlagen und Techniken*. 11., aktualisierte und überarb. Aufl. Beltz Pädagogik. Weinheim: Beltz, 2010.

McDermott, Richard, and Carla O'Dell. "Overcoming Cultural Barriers to Sharing Knowledge." *Journal of Knowledge Management* 5, no. 1 (March 2001): 76–85. https://doi.org/10.1108/13673270110384428.

McFarland, Marilyn R., and Hiba B. Wehbe-Alamah. "Leininger's Theory of Culture Care Diversity and Universality: An Overview With a Historical Retrospective and a View Toward the Future." *Journal of Transcultural Nursing* 30, no. 6 (November 2019): 540–57. https://doi.org/10.1177/1043659619867134.

McKay, George. *Glastonbury: A Very English Fair*. London: V. Gollancz, 2000.

McKay, George, ed. *The Pop Festival: History, Music, Media, Culture*. New York: Bloomsbury Academic, 2015.

Meenaghan, John A. "Commercial Sponsorship." *European Journal of Marketing* 17, no. 7 (July 1983): 5–73. https://doi.org/10.1108/EUM0000000004825.

Mikl-Horke, Gertraude, Reinhard Pirker, and Andreas Resch. *Theorie der Firma: Interdisziplinär*. Wiesbaden: VS Verlag für Sozialwissenschaften, 2011. https://doi.org/10.1007/978-3-531-93257-6.

Moosbrugger, Helfried, Helfried Moosbrugger, and Augustin Kelava. *Testtheorie und Fragebogenkonstruktion*. 2., Aktualisierte und überarbeitete Auflage. Springer-Lehrbuch. Berlin: Springer Berlin, 2012.

Mrozek, Bodo, and Zentrum für zeithistorische Forschung Potsdam. "Popgeschichte." *Docupedia-Zeitgeschichte*, 2010. https://doi.org/10.14765/ZZF.DOK.2.321.V1.

Müller, Julia. *Projektteamübergreifender Wissensaustausch: Fehlervermeidung und organisationales Lernen durch interaktive Elemente einer Wissenskultur.* 1. Aufl. Gabler Research Strategisches Kompetenz-Management. Wiesbaden: Gabler, 2009.

Mvududu, Nyaradzo H., and Christopher A. Sink. "Factor Analysis in Counseling Research and Practice." *Counseling Outcome Research and Evaluation* 4, no. 2 (December 2013): 75–98. https://doi.org/10.1177/2150137813494766.

Newbold, Chris, Christopher Maughan, Jennie Jordan, and Franco Bianchini. *Focus on Festivals: Contemporary European Case Studies and Perspectives*, 2015.

North, Douglass C. *Institutions, Institutional Change, and Economic Performance.* The Political Economy of Institutions and Decisions. Cambridge; New York: Cambridge University Press, 1990.

Nufer, Gerd. *Wirkungen von Event-Marketing Theoretische Fundierung und empirische Analyse.* Berlin, 2002.

Nünning, Ansgar. "Vielfalt der Kulturbegriffe—Dossier Kulturelle Bildung." bpb.de, 2009. https://www.bpb.de/gesellschaft/bildung/kulturelle-bildung/59917/kulturbegriffe.

Nünning, Ansgar, and Vera Nünning, eds. *Einführung in die Kulturwissenschaften: theoretische Grundlagen—Ansätze—Perspektiven.* Stuttgart Weimar: Verlag J. B. Metzler, 2008.

Ochsenbauer, C, and B Klofat. "Überlegungen zur paradigmatischen Dimension der Unternehmenskulturdiskussion in der Betriebswirtschaftslehre." In *Unternehmenskultur—Perspektiven für Wissenschaft und Praxis*, 76–106. München: Heinen, E./Fank, M., 1997.

Ostfalia. "Sponsoring Trends 2016," 2017. https://de.statista.com/statistik/daten/studie/302340/umfrage/anteil-des-kommunikationsbudget-von-unternehmen/.

Otte, Gunnar. "Die Publikumsstrukturierung eines Open-Air-Festivals für elektronische Musik." In *Empirische Kultursoziologie*, edited by Jörg Rössel and Jochen Roose, 27–64. Wiesbaden: Springer Fachmedien Wiesbaden, 2015. http://link.springer.com/10.1007/978-3-658-08733-3_2.

Ouchi, William G. *Theory Z: How American Business Can Meet the Japanese Challenge.* Avon Business. New York: Avon Books, 1993.

Page, Stephen, and Joanne Connell, eds. *The Routledge Handbook of Events.* London; New York: Routledge, 2015.

Parsons, Talcott. *Structure and Process in Modern Societies.* Glencoe, Ill.: Free Press, 1960.

Pascale, Richard Tanner, and Anthony G. Athos. *The Art of Japanese Management: Applications for American Executives*. New York: Warner, 1982.

Kruger Media PR Agentur Berlin | Musik, Lifestyle, Entertainment. "Pasta e Basta: Telekom Campus Cooking serviert die Nudel in all ihren Facetten," May 13, 2019. https://www.kruger-media.de/2019/05/13/pasta-e-basta-tel ekom-campus-cooking-serviert-die-nudel-in-all-ihren-facetten/.

Pelz, Corinna, Annette Schmitt, and Markus Meis. "Knowledge Mapping as a Tool for Analyzing Focus Groups and Presenting Their Results in Market and Evaluation Research." *Forum: Qualitative Social Research* 5 (2004).

Peters, Thomas J., and Robert H. Waterman. *In Search of Excellence: Lessons from America's Best-Run Companies*. London: HarperCollinsBusiness, 1995.

Pilot Checkpoint. "SPONSORS: Sponsor Visions 2010." Hamburg, 2010.

Pine, B. Joseph, James H. Gilmore, and others. "Welcome to the Experience Economy." *Harvard Business Review* 76 (1998): 97–105.

Pondy, L.R and Mitroff, J.J. "Beyond Open System Models of Organization." *Research in Organizational Behavior* 1 (1979): 3–39.

Powell, Walter W., and Kaisa Snellman. "The Knowledge Economy." *Annual Review of Sociology* 30, no. 1 (August 2004): 199–220. https://doi.org/10.114 6/annurev.soc.29.010202.100037.

Prentice, Richard, and Vivien Andersen. "Festival as Creative Destination." *Annals of Tourism Research* 30, no. 1 (January 2003): 7–30. https://doi.org/10.1 016/S0160-7383(02)00034-8.

Pümpin, C. "Unternehmenskultur, Unternehmensstrategie und Unternehmenserfolg." *GDI Impuls*, 2, 1984, 19–30.

Quinn, Bernadette. "Arts Festivals and the City." *Urban Studies* 42 (May 2005): 927–43. https://doi.org/10.1080/00420980500107250.

Rao, Sally, and Chad Perry. "Convergent Interviewing to Build a Theory in Under-researched Areas: Principles and an Example Investigation of Internet Usage in Inter-firm Relationships." *Qualitative Market Research: An International Journal* 6, no. 4 (December 2003): 236–47. https://doi.org/10.1 108/13522750310495328.

Reckwitz, Andreas. "Die Kontingenzperspektive der ›Kultur‹. Kulturbegriffe, Kulturtheorien und das kulturwissenschaftliche Forschungsprogramm." In *Handbuch der Kulturwissenschaften: Grundlagen und Schlüsselbegriffe*, edited by Friedrich Jaeger and Burkhard Liebsch, 1–20. Stuttgart: J.B. Metzler, 2011. https://doi.org/10.1007/978-3-476-00468-0_1.

Reckwitz, Andreas. *Die Transformation der Kulturtheorien: zur Entwicklung eines Theorieprogramms*. 1. Aufl. Weilerswist: Velbrück Wissenschaft, 2000.

Reckwitz, Andreas. *Unscharfe Grenzen: Perspektiven der Kultursoziologie*. 2., unveränd. Aufl. Sozialtheorie. Bielefeld: transcript Verlag, 2010.

Richards, Greg, and Julie Wilson. "The Impact of Cultural Events on City Image: Rotterdam, Cultural Capital of Europe 2001." *Urban Studies* 41, no. 10 (September 2004): 1931–51. https://doi.org/10.1080/0042098042000256323.

Richter, Felix. "The Largest Music Festivals in the World." Statista, 2019. https://www.statista.com/chart/17757/total-attendance-of-music-festivals/.

Roland, Gérard. "Economics and Culture." In *Emerging Trends in the Social and Behavioral Sciences*, 1–18. New York, 2015. https://doi.org/10.1002/9781118900772.etrds0091.

Rosenberg, Florian von. *Lernen, Bildung und kulturelle Pluralität*. Wiesbaden: Springer Fachmedien Wiesbaden, 2016. https://doi.org/10.1007/978-3-658-06365-8.

Rowley, Jennifer, and Catrin Williams. "The Impact of Brand Sponsorship of Music Festivals." *Marketing Intelligence & Planning* 26, no. 7 (October 24, 2008): 781–92. https://doi.org/10.1108/02634500810916717.

Ruyter, Ko de, and Norbert Scholl. "Positioning Qualitative Market Research: Reflections from Theory and Practice." *Qualitative Market Research: An International Journal* 1, no. 1 (April 1998): 7–14. https://doi.org/10.1108/13522759810197550.

Sackmann, Sonja, and Bertelsmann Stiftung. *Erfolgsfaktor Unternehmenskultur: Mit kulturbewusstem Management Unternehmensziele erreichen und Identifikation schaffen—6 Best Practice-Beispiele*. Wiesbaden: Gabler Verlag, 2013.

Sandler, D.M., D. Shani, Bernard M. Baruch College School of Business, and Public Administration. *Olympic Sponsorship Vs. "Ambush" Marketing: Who Gets the Gold?* Working Papers Series. New York: School of Business and Public Administration, Bernard M. Baruch College of the City University of New York, 1988. https://books.google.de/books?id=tox5GwAACAAJ.

Schatzki, Theodore R. *Social Practices: A Wittgensteinian Approach to Human Activity and the Social*. Cambridge: Cambridge University Press, 1996. https://doi.org/10.1017/CBO9780511527470.

Schmidt, Siegfried J. "Eine Kultur der Kulturen," 2006. https://doi.org/10.25969/MEDIAREP/1773.

Schmidt, Siegfried J. "From Objects to Processes: A Proposal to Rewrite Radical Constructivism." *Constructivist Foundations* 7, no. 1 (2011): 1–9 & 37–47.

Schmidt, Siegfried J. *Geschichten & Diskurse: Abschied vom Konstruktivismus.* Originalausg. Rowohlts Enzyklopädie 55660. Reinbek: Rowohlt Taschenbuch Verlag, 2003.

Schmidt, Siegfried J. "Kultur als Programm—jenseits der Dichotomie von Realismus und Konstruktivismus." In *Handbuch der Kulturwissenschaften,* edited by Friedrich Jaeger and Jürgen Straub, 85–100. Stuttgart: J.B. Metzler, 2011. https://doi.org/10.1007/978-3-476-00627-1_6.

Schmidt, Siegfried J. *Kulturbeschreibung—Beschreibungskultur: Umrisse einer Prozess-orientierten Kulturtheorie.* 1. Auflage. Weilerswist: Velbrück Wissenschaft, 2014.

Schmidt, Siegfried J. *Unternehmenskultur: Die Grundlage für den wirtschaftlichen Erfolg von Unternehmen.* 6. Aufl. Weilerswist: Velbrück Wiss, 2014.

Schubert, Dirk. "Ausgleich oder Spaltung? | bpb." bpb.de, 2018. https://www.bpb.de/politik/innenpolitik/stadt-und-gesellschaft/216868/aufrechterhaltung-gleichwertiger-lebensverhaeltnisse.

Schulz, Marlen, Birgit Mack, and Ortwin Renn, eds. *Fokusgruppen in der empirischen Sozialwissenschaft.* Wiesbaden: VS Verlag für Sozialwissenschaften, 2012. https://doi.org/10.1007/978-3-531-19397-7.

Schulze, Gerhard. *Die Erlebnisgesellschaft: Kultursoziologie der Gegenwart.* 8. Aufl., Studienausgabe. Frankfurt am Main: Campus-Verl, 2000.

Siebert, Yvonne. *Einstellungs- und Verhaltenswirkungen im Event-Sponsoring.* Wiesbaden: Springer Fachmedien Wiesbaden, 2013. http://link.springer.com/10.1007/978-3-658-02938-8.

Sistenich, Frank. *Eventmarketing Ein innovatives Instrument zur Metakommunikation in Unternehmen.* Berlin, 1999. https://doi.org/10.1007/978-3-663-08486-0.

Smudits, Alfred. *Mediamorphosen des Kulturschaffens: Kunst und Kommunikationstechnologien im Wandel.* Musik und Gesellschaft 27. Wien: Braumüller, 2002.

Spieß, Steffen. *Marketing für Regionen: Anwendungsmöglichkeiten im Standortwettbewerb.* Berlin, 1998. http://link.springer.com/openurl?genre=book&isbn=978-3-8244-0395-0.

Statistisches Bundesamt. "Bevölkerungsvorausberechnung," n.d. https://service.destatis.de/bevoelkerungspyramide/.

Stehr, Nico. *Die Freiheit ist eine Tochter des Wissens.* Wiesbaden: Springer Fachmedien Wiesbaden, 2015. https://doi.org/10.1007/978-3-658-09516-1.

Stehr, Nico "Wissensgesellschaften." In *Handbuch der Kulturwissenschaften*, edited by Friedrich Jaeger and Burkhard Liebsch, 34–49. Stuttgart: J.B. Metzler, 2011. https://doi.org/10.1007/978-3-476-00468-0_3.

Stenbacka, Caroline. "Qualitative Research Requires Quality Concepts of Its Own." *Management Decision* 39, no. 7 (September 2001): 551–56. https://doi.org/10.1108/EUM0000000005801.

Studie des SVR-Forschungsbereichs 2015-2. "Zugangstor Hochschule Internationale Studierende als Fachkräfte von morgen gewinnen." Study. Berlin, 2016.

Temple, Julien. *Glastonbury*, 2006.

The Local de. "'Germany rocks': Elon Musk makes first visit to Berlin Tesla construction site," April 9, 2020. https://www.thelocal.de/20200904/german y-rocks-elon-musk-makes-first-visit-to-berlin-tesla-construction-site/.

Thiessen, Friedrich, ed. *Weiche Standortfaktoren: Erfolgsfaktoren regionaler Wirtschaftsentwicklung: interdisziplinäre Beiträge zur regionalen Wirtschaftsforschung*. Volkswirtschaftliche Schriften, Heft 541. Berlin: Duncker & Humblot, 2005.

Toffler, Alvin. *Future Shock*. Bantam Books. New York: Bantam Books, 1990.

Trice, Harrison Miller, and Janice M. Beyer. *The Cultures of Work Organizations*. Englewood Cliffs, N.J: Prentice Hall, 1993.

Tripodi John A. "Sponsorship—A Confirmed Weapon in the Promotional Armoury." *International Journal of Sports Marketing and Sponsorship* 3, no. 1 (January 1, 2001): 82–103. https://doi.org/10.1108/IJSMS-03-01-2001-B007.

Tschmuck, Peter. *Creativity and Innovation in the Music Industry*. Berlin: Springer Berlin Heidelberg, 2012. http://link.springer.com/10.1007/978-3-642-2843 0-4.

Tschmuck, Peter. *Ökonomie der Musikwirtschaft*. Musikwirtschafts- und Musikkulturforschung. Wiesbaden: Springer Fachmedien Wiesbaden, 2020. https://doi.org/10.1007/978-3-658-29295-9.

Tsiotsou *, Rodoula, and Dionysis Lalountas. "Applying Event Study Analysis to Assess the Impact of Marketing Communication Strategies: The Case of Sponsorship." *Applied Financial Economics Letters* 1, no. 4 (July 2005): 259–62. https://doi.org/10.1080/17446540500143764.

Tylor, Edward Burnett. *Primitive Culture: Researches into the Development of Mythology, Philosophy, Religion, Art, and Custom*. Repr. Cambridge Library Collection Anthropology. Cambridge: Cambridge Univ. Press, 2010.

UNICUM Media. "UNICUM—Kommunikation mit jungen, intelligenten Zielgruppen," 2020. https://unicum-media.com/.

Urban, Peter. *Rollende Worte, die Poesie des Rock: von d. Strassenballade zum Pop-Song: e. wissenschaftl. Analyse d. Pop-Song-Texte.* Orig.-Ausg. Frankfurt am Main: Fischer-Taschenbuch-Verlag, 1979.

Valck, de, Marijke. *Film Festivals: From European Geopolitics to Global Cinephilia.* Amsterdam: Amsterdam University Press, 2007. https://doi.org/10.5117/9 789053561928.

Walliser, Björn. "An International Review of Sponsorship Research: Extension and Update." *International Journal of Advertising* 22, no. 1 (January 2003): 5–40. https://doi.org/10.1080/02650487.2003.11072838.

Wefers, Ulrike. *Hochschulmarketing in Deutschland: Chancen und Herausforderungen.* Saarbrücken: VDM Verl. Dr. Müller, 2007.

Weihe, Kerstin. *Erlebens- und Einstellungswirkungen von Marketing-Events: eine Analyse unter Berücksichtigung der Besonderheiten des Event-Marketing und Event-Sponsoring.* 1. Aufl. Göttingen: Cuvillier, 2008.

Weiner, Bernard, Rainer Reisenzein, Wilfried Pranter, and Bernard Weiner. *Motivationspsychologie.* 3. Aufl., Unveränd. Nachdr. d. 3. Aufl. 1994. Weinheim: Beltz, Psychologie-Verl.-Union, 2009.

Wesselmann, Stefanie, and Bettina Hohn. *Public Marketing: Marketing-Management für den öffentlichen Sektor.* 4., Vollständig überarbeitete Auflage. Lehrbuch. Wiesbaden: Springer Gabler, 2017.

Wicke, Peter. "'Populäre Musik' Als Theoretisches Konzept." Humboldt-Universität zu Berlin, 1992. http://dx.doi.org/10.18452/20156.

Wienand, Edith, Joachim Westerbarkey, and Armin Scholl, eds. *Kommunikation über Kommunikation.* Wiesbaden: VS Verlag für Sozialwissenschaften, 2005. https://doi.org/10.1007/978-3-322-80821-9.

Wilke, Jürgen. "Die Digitalisierung und der Strukturwandel des Mediensystems." In *Medienwandel durch Digitalisierung und Krise: Eine vergleichende Analyse zwischen Russland und Deutschland,* edited by Mike Friedrichsen, Jens Wendland, and Galina Woronenkowa, 1st ed., 27–33. Baden-Baden: Nomos Verlagsgesellschaft mbH & Co. KG, 2010. https://doi.org/10.5771/ 9783845227085-27.

Wilks, Linda. "Social Capital in the Music Festival Experience." In *The Routledge Handbook of Events.* Routledge, 2008. https://doi.org/10.4324/97802038039 36.ch17.

Williams, Michael, and Glenn A J Bowdin. "Festival Evaluation: An Exploration of Seven UK Arts Festivals." *Managing Leisure* 12, no. 2–3 (July 2007): 187–203. https://doi.org/10.1080/13606710701339520.

Winter, Rainer. "Stuart Hall: Die Erfindung Der Cultural Studies." In *Kultur. Theorien Der Gegenwart*, edited by Stephan Moebius and Dirk Quadflieg, 381–93. Wiesbaden: VS Verlag für Sozialwissenschaften, 2006. https://do i.org/10.1007/978-3-531-90017-9_30.

Wölfer, Jürgen. *Die Rock- und Popmusik: Eine umfassende Darstellung ihrer Geschichte und Funktion*. Orig.-Ausg. Heyne-Bücher; Nr. 7108. München: Heyne, 1980.

Yong, An Gie, and Sean Pearce. "A Beginner's Guide to Factor Analysis: Focusing on Exploratory Factor Analysis." *Tutorials in Quantitative Methods for Psychology* 9, no. 2 (October 1, 2013): 79–94. https://doi.org/10.20982/tqm p.09.2.p079.

Zanger, Cornelia, and Wissenschaftliche Konferenz Eventforschung, eds. *Erfolg mit nachhaltigen Eventkonzepten: Tagungsband zur 2. Konferenz für Eventforschung an der TU Chemnitz*. 1. Aufl. Gabler Research Markenkommunikation und Beziehungsmarketing. Wiesbaden: Gabler, 2012.

Zollinger, Helmut. "Thesen und Trends im Sponsoring," 118–24. St. Gallen: Tomczak, T./Miiller, F./Miiller, R., 1995.

Cultural and Museum Management

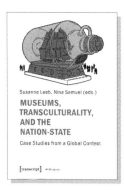

Susanne Leeb, Nina Samuel (eds.)
Museums, Transculturality, and the Nation-State
Case Studies from a Global Context

2022, 248 p., pb., col. ill.
38,00 € (DE), 978-3-8376-5514-8
E-Book:
PDF: 37,99 € (DE), ISBN 978-3-8394-5514-2

Constance DeVereaux, Steffen Höhne,
Martin Tröndle, Keith Nurse (eds.)
Journal of Cultural Management and Cultural Policy/Zeitschrift für Kulturmanagement und Kulturpolitik
Vol. 8, Issue 1: Arts Practices and Cultural Policies in Conditions of Disaster

2022, 230 p., pb., ill.
44,99 € (DE), 978-3-8376-5916-0
E-Book:
PDF: 44,99 € (DE), ISBN 978-3-8394-5916-4

Constance DeVereaux, Steffen Höhne,
Martin Tröndle, Anke Schad-Spindler, Tal Feder (eds.)
Journal of Cultural Management and Cultural Policy/Zeitschrift für Kulturmanagement und Kulturpolitik
Vol. 7, Issue 2: Transformation and Upheavals: The Effects of Crises and Conflicts on the Arts

2021, 236 p., pb., ill.
44,99 € (DE), 978-3-8376-5390-8
E-Book:
PDF: 44,99 € (DE), ISBN 978-3-8394-5390-2